CROSS-CULTURAL APPROACHES TO THEATRE
The Spanish-French Connection

by
Phyllis Zatlin

THE SCARECROW PRESS, INC.
METUCHEN, N.J., & LONDON
1994

British Library Cataloguing-in-Publication data available

Library of Congress Cataloging-in-Publication Data

Zatlin, Phyllis. 1938–
    Cross cultural approaches to theatre : the Spanish-French connection
/ by Phyllis Zatlin.
        p. cm.
    ISBN 0-8108-2729-8 (acid-free paper)
    1. Theater—France—History—20th century. 2. Theater—Spain—
History—20th century. 3. French drama—Spanish influences. 4.
Spanish drama—French influences. 5. French drama—20th cen-
tury—History and criticism. 6. Spanish drama—20th century—
History and criticism.   I. Title.
PN2635.Z38   1994
792′.0944′0904—dc20   94-493

TABLE OF CONTENTS

Chapter 8
   A Spanish-French Playwright: The Theatre of
   Carlos Semprun-Maura

Chapter 9
   Conclusion

Notes

Works Cited

Appendix A. Play Titles in Catalan

Appendix B. Play Titles in French

Appendix C. Play Titles in Spanish

Index

About the Author

PREFACE

Although there are a number of books that deal with intercultural relations between the Spanish and French stages in past centuries, very little work has been done on the most recent period, particularly from the perspective of theatre history. Although the significant contribution to the French theatre of Spanish-born playwright Fernando Arrabal is well known, little has been written about the participation of other Spaniards in the theatre world of France. These gaps in our knowledge of cross-cultural influences in contemporary European theatre inspired the present book. With the exception of the chapter on Spanish exile theatre in France, starting in the 1940s, the emphasis of my research has been on the past two decades, up to 1990.

In order to make the present study accessible to readers who do not know French, Spanish, and/or Catalan, I have provided English translations of quotations within the text. I have generally left play titles in the language of their performance: for example, a text written in Castilian Spanish and staged in France appears with its original title if performed in Spanish and with the French title if done in translation. Appendixes of play titles, by language, along with their English equivalents, are provided for the reader's clarification. In cases where I am aware of a published or staged English version, I have provided that title, even if it is not a transparent translation of the original. For a few plays that have received different titles in different translations, I have noted the first title under the later version. Excluded from the appendixes are play titles that would be the same, or virtually the same, in English as in the other language (such as titles that are proper names) and plays originally written in English, where that title has been provided in the body of the text.

My own interest in theatre and the Spanish-French connection dates from the late 1950s and my undergraduate years at Rollins College (Winter Park, Florida), where I completed majors in both languages, was encouraged to specialize in theatre by my French professor, Robert Morgenroth, and wrote a senior honors paper on comparative drama under the direction of my Spanish professor, Angela Paloma Campbell. While I never totally abandoned this dual interest, my affiliation with a Department of Spanish and Portuguese naturally shifted my scholarly research over the years away from French theatre. When, after a long hiatus, I decided to turn my attention again to France, I was pleased to receive encouragement from colleagues in both languages, at my own institution and elsewhere.

I wish to express my appreciation to Rutgers, The State University of New Jersey, for awarding me a Faculty Academic Study leave in 1987 that allowed me to spend time in both France and Spain, and to the Rutgers University Research Council for a grant in support of this project. I am also grateful to Hazel Cazorla, Felicia Hardison Londré, Martha O'Nan, and Peter Podol, who agreed to participate in a special session on cultural interchange and the contemporary Spanish and French stages at the Modern Language Association Convention in 1988; their expertise on Riaza, Lorca, Roblès, and Arrabal, respectively, greatly helped to focus my own thinking on the subject. I am also indebted to Leda Schiavo for her active encouragement of my work on Valle-Inclán in France.

Several chapters or portions of chapters of the present book have previously appeared as follows:

Chapter 2, in *Estreno* 16.2 (1990): 23–28;

Chapter 3, in *Bulletin of the Comediantes* 42.1 (1990): 23–33; and *Estudios en homenaje a Enrique Ruiz-Fornells*, ed. Juan Fernández Jiménez et al. (Erie, PA: ALDEEU, 1990), 694–700;

Chapter 6, in *Symposium* (HELDREF Publications, Washington, DC) 45.4 (1992): 303–315;

Chapter 7, in *Gestos* 7 (1989): 65–73; and
Chapter 8, in *Folio* 18 (1990): 38–49.
I wish to thank the editors of these publications for their early interest in my research and for their permission to reprint these sections.

In the process of my research I received the cooperation of many people: playwrights and others knowledgeable about theatre who agreed to be interviewed, librarians at several specialized theatre collections, personnel at theatre bookstores in Madrid and Paris and at the Sociedad General de Autores de España, and authors of prior studies who generously shared their data with me. I am grateful to all of them for their invaluable help. The list of their names is quite long, and I shall not repeat here those which appear in the text that follows. Additionally I would like to thank Julia García Verdugo and Joaquín Solanas at La Avispa theatre bookstore in Madrid; María Carmen Pérez de Arenaza and Odilo Gundía at the Juan March Foundation theatre library, also in Madrid; and Claude Chauvineau at the Gaston Baty library of the Sorbonne's Centre Censier in Paris, all of whom have repeatedly offered special assistance to facilitate my work.

My sincere appreciation to Martha Halsey and Diana Taylor for their helpful reactions to the book in progress, and to Nicolás del Río for his assistance in compiling the appendixes.

P.Z.

Chapter 1

INTRODUCTION

Much has been written in the twentieth century about intercultural relations between the French and Spanish stages of earlier periods, yet relatively little attention has been paid to the cultural exchange in contemporary theatre. Books and articles are readily available on Spanish sources for seventeenth-century French plays. Ernest Martinenche's *La Comedia espagnole en France de Hardy à Racine*, originally published in 1900 and reprinted in 1973, concluded that the works borrowed from Lope de Vega, Juan Ruiz de Alarcón, Pedro Calderón de la Barca, and others led the way for the modern French stage by revealing the eternal strategies of both tragedy and comedy. More recently, Alexandre Cioranescu has presented an exhaustive study of the subject with the suggestive title *Le Masque et le visage: Du baroque espagnol au classicisme français* (1983). Molière's debt to Spanish playwrights is well documented, as is his influence in turn on such Spanish authors as Ramón de la Cruz and Leandro Fernández de Moratín. The bibliographies of Lois Strong Gaudin (1930, reprinted 1973) and Francisco Lafarga Maduell (1980) cite a number of Spanish translations of Molière as well as studies of the French impact on the theatre of Spain in the eighteenth century.

Even as the Spanish stage assimilated models of French neoclassicism, authors in France turned again to their southern neighbor for inspiration. Edna C. Fredrick has observed that Beaumarchais, consistent with the suggestions of Alain-René Lesage and his *Théâtre espagnol* (1700), looked to Spanish plot construction as a way out of the static comedy that developed from Molière's emphasis on

1

character: hence the action-packed *Barber of Seville* (1775). The epitome of character subordinated to plot, however, was the theatre of Eugène Scribe, whose well-made plays found an eager audience in nineteenth-century Spain, including versions by Mariano José de Larra. The romantic period was characterized by crosscurrents between the two stages. In his 1922 *L'Espagne et le romantisme français*, Martinenche documents the impact of Spain and Spanish Golden Age theatre on both romantic drama and melodrama. Victor Hugo's most celebrated plays, *Hernani* and *Ruy Blas*, were only two of many works to reflect Spain as "exotic" and Spanish people as passionate. Conversely, John A. Thompson has shown the impact of Alexandre Dumas *père* on Spanish romantic drama; his 1938 book cites numerous Spanish translations and stagings of Dumas's plays.

Up through romanticism, there is an abundance of studies on cultural interchange between the two national theatres: thematic approaches—especially on the Don Juan figure—as well as influence and theatre history studies. For the twentieth century, however, especially the postwar period, one finds relatively little in-depth analysis of the interaction between the French and Spanish stages. There is no general overview of French theatre in contemporary Spain and only one book-length survey of Spanish theatre in France: Francisco Torres Monreal's 1974 dissertation covering the period 1935–1973. Even with respect to stagings of Golden Age drama over the years, for France there is no equivalent to Henry W. Sullivan's *Calderón in the German Lands and the Low Countries: His Reception and Influence, 1654–1980*. Nor are there any books dealing specifically with individual contemporary Spanish or French authors in terms of the impact their works have had on the neighboring stage.

This is not to say that cross-cultural influences have been totally ignored. There is a lengthy bibliography on the importance of Spanish themes in the works of several French-language playwrights. Notable among these are the heroic dramas of Henry de Montherlant (1896–1972). Maryse Bertrand de Muñoz identifies five of his plays, from *Les Bestiaires* in 1926 to *Le Cardinal d'Espagne* in 1960, as inspired by Spain (155). His treatment of the Inés de Castro theme, *La Reine morte* (1942), has frequently been compared to works by Iberian writers, ranging from the Golden Age Vélez de Guevara to the twentieth-century Alejandro Casona. Charles A. Carpenter's international bibliography *Modern Drama Scholarship and Criticism, 1966–1980* cites no fewer than fourteen monographs and articles that directly examine the Spanish influence on Montherlant's theatre.

Less studied but widely acknowledged is the importance of Spain in the work of Paul Claudel (1868–1955), who expressed a particular admiration for Calderón. His *Le Soulier de satin* (1924) has been compared to an *auto sacramental*; *Christophe Colomb* (1929) is but one of his plays to deal with Spain's exploration of the New World. Belgian dramatist Michel de Ghelderode (1898–1962) also wrote a Columbus play in 1929, and his *Don Juan ou les amants chimériques* centers on the Don Juan figure. The presence of Spain in Ghelderode's theatre has been frequently noted, leading Estrella de la Torre Giménez to remind us of the historical connections between Castile and Flanders during the reign of Charles I of Spain (Charles V of the Holy Roman Empire). She quotes a comment from Emmanuel Roblès that Ghelderode confessed his pride in having "a few drops of Spanish blood" (228). Roblès himself, born in 1914 in French Algeria, is of Spanish descent on both sides of his family. As various scholarly studies point out, Hispanic themes dominate his theatre.

The Spanish Civil War (1936–1939), sometimes labeled the last great "romantic" war, has been the subject of many literary works internationally. Bertrand de Muñoz has identified several French-language playwrights who wrote about it, although she observes that the stage, in France as elsewhere, was far less receptive than the novel to this subject (277). Her brief list includes, among others, Albert Camus (1913–1960), Armand Gatti (b. 1924), and Fernando Arrabal (b. 1932).

Camus, like Roblès, was born in French Algeria, and was of Spanish descent on his mother's side. He had a lifelong interest in Spanish culture and was instrumental in staging Spanish texts in French. His *Révolte aux Asturies* (1936) and

L'Etat de siège (1948) clearly reflect his sympathies for the Republican cause in the Civil War. Nevertheless, with the exception of an occasional article on his interest in Calderón, scholarly references to Camus and his Spanish connection are generally made only in passing. Gatti's polemical *La Passion du Général Franco par les émigrés eux-mêmes* attracted international attention in 1969 when the French government banned its performance at the subsidized Théâtre National Populaire because of political pressure from Spain. His later *La Colonne Durruti* (1972), directly inspired by the Spanish Civil War, has received less critical attention.

Outstanding among the authors mentioned by Bertrand de Muñoz is Fernando Arrabal. A native Spaniard, he has lived in France since the mid-1950s and is among the contemporary French-language playwrights to achieve the greatest international acclaim. He is likewise the best-known living Spanish dramatist of world theatre, and his name is undoubtedly the first to occur in any discussion of the Spanish presence on the contemporary French stage. Arrabal's work has given rise to an extensive critical bibliography, including repeated references to the impact on his life and work of the Civil War and Franco-era repression on the one hand and to the influence of French surrealism on the other. In recent studies, Peter Podol has focused more directly on the implications of Arrabal's bicultural experience, discussing Spain as a recurring theme in his theatre and also the influence of France on his dramaturgy.

While the Spanish inspiration identified on the twentieth-century French stage has stemmed either from the past (Golden Age drama or historical and legendary figures) or from political circumstances (the Civil War and its aftermath), contemporary French dramatists have been credited with a certain impact on individual Spanish authors. Although the references once again are generally made only in passing, critics have discovered ties to such diverse playwrights as Jean Giraudoux (1882–1944), Jean Anouilh (1910–1987), Jean-Paul Sartre (1905–1980), Eugène Ionesco (b. 1912), Samuel Beckett (1906–1989), and Jean Genet (1910–1986).

Giraudoux's demystification of history through the vehicle of anachronistic humor has found clear echoes in Spain. I suggested some of these thematic traces of Giraudoux in a brief note published in 1969 and later observed a related current in works of Antonio Gala (b. 1936), especially his *Anillos para una dama* (1973) with its debunking of the Cid-Jimena story ("El teatro de Antonio Gala" 57–58). Gala, who writes in a brilliant and highly creative language, may be compared to Giraudoux in stylistic terms as well. Anouilh's impact is also seen in the demythologizing of history, but perhaps more so in his metatheatrical, self-conscious bent. In *The Contemporary Spanish Theater, (1949–1972)*, Marion P. Holt highlighted the relationship of Anouilh and his illusion/reality themes with the comedies of Víctor Ruiz Iriarte (1912–1982), and singled out Giraudoux and Anouilh as two dominant foreign influences on some of the most commercially successful Spanish playwrights of the period (162).

Because of their social commitment and existentialist underpinnings, several plays by Alfonso Sastre (b. 1926) from the 1950s have been related to Jean-Paul Sartre (1905–1980), but the comparisons have proven controversial. Felix Ilárraz has carefully analyzed the philosophical bases of the two playwrights' works and refuted the notion of direct influence; he quotes Sastre as declaring that he had never even heard of Sartre when he wrote his earlier, experimental plays, which had also been compared to the French writer, with even less foundation (qtd. Ilárraz 13). Of special interest is Antonio Fernández Insuela's assessment of the possible relationship of foreign theatre to the so-called Realist Generation, which also emerged in the 1950s. In an effort to determine the opinions of the five authors associated with the group, Fernández Insuela reviewed their interviews and essays for the period 1956–1978. On balance, he found no reason to claim that the French were greatly admired by the Spanish realists (160). José Martín Recuerda (b. 1925) went so far as to find a negative influence of Camus and Sartre on writers like Sastre (qtd. Fernández Insuela 161). In contrast, José María Rodríguez Méndez (b. 1925) affirmed that the French existentialists had opened new horizons and had been instrumental in the formation of the realists, especially Sastre (qtd. Fernández Insuela 161).

Among the members of the Realist Generation, Fernández Insuela found frequent references, positive and negative, to the Theatre of the Absurd, as well as to the existentialists. Rodríguez Méndez asserted that younger Spanish authors, who were following the absurdist formulas, were victims of cultural colonization (qtd. Fernández Insuela 163), and other realists similarly urged Spanish writers to remain true to their own roots. Although Arrabal has often said that he had never heard of Beckett when he began writing the plays that linked him in the 1950s to the French absurdists, avant-garde playwrights in Spain in the 1960s and 1970s were indeed familiar with Beckett and Ionesco and reflected that influence in their work. Alberto Miralles rejects the antiabsurdist stance of the realists and affirms that he and other writers of the New Theatre deliberately looked beyond the Pyrenees for models in their desire to create a more universal stage (50). Hazel Cazorla, summing up the influences on the New Authors, correctly points out that they also assimiliated the theories of Antonin Artaud (1896–1949) and the example of Genet's theatre ("Avant-garde Spanish Playwrights" 184). Luis Riaza (b. 1925) in particular openly acknowledges the impact on his works of Genet's ritualistic and metatheatrical games (Personal interview 1987).

The impact of the absurdists and of the theatre of cruelty and ritual associated with Artaud and Genet goes beyond the thematic to affect performance texts and staging techniques. Nevertheless, as previously mentioned, there are as yet no general or in-depth studies of the reception or influence of these French authors on the contemporary Spanish stage. With respect to Spanish influence in France, the critical literature concentrates on thematic approaches, with particular emphasis on the works of Montherlant and Arrabal. For Arrabal, a native Spaniard, there are references to the possible influence of Ramón del Valle-Inclán (1866–1936); otherwise, the impact of Spanish authors in France is limited to the Golden Age. In essence, scholarly criticism to date seems to suggest that Spain provides French dramatists with subjects to write about, while France shows Spanish dramatists how to write for the contemporary stage.

Given both the paucity of studies on interrelationships between the Spanish and French stages in the twentieth century and the focus of existing critical references, it is not surprising that my initial research in the field yielded discouraging results. In 1986–87, I began by investigating the Spanish presence on the contemporary French stage: a theatre history approach that would include both Spanish plays staged in France and the participation in France of Spanish-born theatre professionals. At an international Brecht symposium in Toronto, I happened to meet the distinguished French theatre critic Bernard Dort. To my query about Spain's theatrical contribution in contemporary France, he immediately responded, "Il n'y a rien": There's nothing. As we continued to talk, I reminded him that Arrabal was a Spaniard, and so were such successful actors of the French stage as Maria Casarès and Josep Maria Flotats. Warming to my subject, I offered other Spanish names and mentioned Gatti's polemical *La Passion du Général Franco par les émigrés eux-mêmes*, conceived in Toulouse with the collaboration of the Spanish community there. Dort wished me luck but remained unconvinced: "Non, il n'y a rien."

Librarians at the several specialized theatre collections I visited in 1987 (Lincoln Center in New York, Juan March Foundation in Madrid, Theatre Institute in Barcelona, L'Arsénal Library and the Sorbonne's Gaston Baty Library in Paris) were gracious and cooperative but in essence gave me the same response as Bernard Dort. To their knowledge, except for the Torres Monreal dissertation which I was able to consult at the Juan March Foundation, there was nothing to establish a Spanish connection on the French stage. Nor, when I expanded my topic, was there any general study of the French presence on the Spanish stage. At the theatre bookstores in Madrid and Paris, the answer was the same. Had I identified for my research a nonexistent topic?

No, I had simply found a subject that had not yet been properly explored. If it remained invisible in scholarly publication, I would simply have to dig deeper in theatre annuals and rely more heavily on personal interviews. I have been fortunate indeed in the cooperative response of the playwrights, directors, and others knowledgeable about theatre whom I have consulted in the course of my research, including colleagues who agreed to participate in a special session at the 1988 Modern Language Association Convention that would open a dialogue on cultural interchange and the contemporary Spanish and French stages.

At Lincoln Center, I skimmed years of *L'Avant-Scène Théâtre* and began to uncover references to Spanish texts on the French stage and to Hispanic surnames among French theatre people. The columns of theatre critic André Camp were a rich source of information. Later, in May 1987, when I met Camp in Paris, I discovered not only that he had translated a number of Hispanic texts and had an extensive personal knowledge of my subject, but that he was instrumental in forming Ibéral, a new organization that would promote Hispanic theatre in France. Rather than studying a nonexistent topic, I had arrived at my research just as the status of Spanish culture in France was about to change radically.

The impetus for an increased cultural exchange between Spain and France has come from public as well as private agencies. With the entry of Spain into the European Community in January 1986, the governments of the two nations have actively fostered better communication in the arts. Suddenly, after years of relative obscurity, Spanish culture was in style in Paris. Beyond the surface level of painting exhibitions and film festivals, the link has been officially institutionalized. From 1988 to early 1991, the Spanish Ministry of Culture was headed by Jorge Semprun, a native Spaniard who had lived in France for a half century and achieved international recognition as a French novelist. Since 1989 the Théâtre de l'Europe in Paris has been under the direction of Lluís Pascual, a Spaniard who immediately announced his intention of promoting Hispanic theatre in France.

From an invisible topic without ready scholarly sources, my subject has expanded to one that I cannot pretend to exhaust in this brief study. Rather it is my intention to present an introduction to the interrelationship between the Spanish and French stages that may serve as the impetus for others' research on this aspect of cross-cultural theatre.

The first section of the book includes three approaches to theatre history studies: Spanish-language theatre in France, Spanish theatre on the French stage, and French theatre performed in Spain. The chapter on the Spanish-language stage in France logically begins with the arrival of the Civil War refugees in 1939; it traces the development from the amateur productions within the exile community at Toulouse to a later, more professional theatre there, the rise of a bilingual university theatre in Bordeaux, the contribution of Argentinian directors at the Théâtre des Nations in Paris, and the tours in France of Spanish companies, ranging from the politically motivated independent groups during the Franco regime to internationally acclaimed professional troupes. In the chapter on Spanish theatre performed in French, I have attempted to bring Torres Monreal's groundbreaking study up to date, with emphasis on the 1970s and 1980s. In the corresponding chapter related to French theatre on the Spanish stage, while I have referred to productions in the early postwar period, I have focused primarily on the quarter century from 1965 to 1990; to help identify patterns in the stagings of particular playwrights over time—that is, the rise and fall in their popularity—I computerized a data base drawn from twenty volumes of Francisco Alvaro's theatre annual.

The second section of the book provides a discussion of selected plays by four authors who are associated with cross-cultural currents in theatre. Perhaps not coincidentally, the texts chosen for analysis tend to be highly metatheatrical. If Sartrean existentialism or French-style absurdity may seem "foreign" to some Spaniards while Spanish passion and honor are "exotic" to the French, variations on metatheatricalism are equally at home on both sides of the Pyrenees. Referring to the popularity in Spain of Anouilh's Pirandellian techniques, Marion P. Holt has astutely observed that "the fascination for role-playing and the question of illusion versus reality are also part of a long

Spanish tradition that stems from Cervantes and Calderón" (51). That Spanish tradition has likewise been well received in France since the seventeenth century, when a Cervantine theatre within the theatre was mirrored by such plays as Pierre Corneille's *L'Illusion comique*. In *Métathéâtre et intertexte: Aspects du théâtre dans le théâtre,* Manfred Schmeling provides a historical overview that juxtaposes Spanish Golden Age writers and the French Molière. If an author born in Spain but educated in France writes metaplays, it is difficult to say whether he is revealing the influence of his native land, his adopted country, or a general current in world theatre. Moreover, the subjects of the chosen texts lend themselves particularly well to metatheatricalism and intertextuality.

Although Emmanuel Roblès is deeply immersed in French existentialism and generally follows classic French structures in writing his plays, his interest in Hispanic themes and characters is well known to critics of his work. Completely bicultural, he speaks Spanish fluently and has read widely in Spanish history and literature. I examine his Juana la Loca play, *Un Château en novembre,* in the context of a series of Spanish works dealing with the same historical figure. *L'Autre Don Juan,* an example of interlingual metatheatricality, is the work of Eduardo Manet, a Cuban-born writer of the French stage. Not content with simply translating Juan Ruiz de Alarcón, a Mexican-born writer of the Spanish Golden Age theatre, Manet creates an elaborate metadrama that incorporates Alarcón as a character and introduces lines from the original Spanish-language text. The dramatic strategy is not dissimilar to that used by Francisco Nieva in his *Sombra y quimera de Larra,* which places the author-character Larra into the action that frames a production of his *No más mostrador,* itself a reworking of a play by Scribe. The nineteenth-century Spanish writer was bitterly criticized for being a Francophile; like Larra, Nieva lived for many years in France. The final chapter is a more general study of the stage and radio plays of Carlos Semprun-Maura, younger brother of Spain's former cultural affairs minister. Born in Spain but educated primarily in France, Carlos Semprun is bilingual and bicultural. While he tends to deal with Hispanic themes more directly in his novels than in his theatre, his recent *Ma chanson la plus triste est espagnole* is a clear indication—in French—of his Spanish sensitivities.

Without doubt, there are essential cultural differences between France and Spain; Cioranescu has captured them well in his title, alluding to the baroque Spanish mask and the bare face of French neoclassicism. There are also many points of contact between the two cultures that have facilitated the travel of theatre and theatre people across the Pyrenees. Arrabal is by no means the only playwright of the contemporary stage to approach his works as a Spanish-French bilingual. As we shall see, there is a great deal to be said about the interrelationship of the contemporary Spanish and French stages.

Intercultural Relations Across the Pyrenees

Chapter 2

SPANISH-LANGUAGE THEATRE IN CONTEMPORARY FRANCE: FROM POLITICAL STATEMENT TO CULTURAL EXCHANGE

Since January 1986, when Spain entered the European Community, the Spanish government has made a concerted effort to have Spanish culture cross the Pyrenees. In the case of France, starting in the 1987–88 season, there were major art and film exhibits, literary roundtables, and theatrical performances in Paris. Spanish-language theatre has not, however, been totally absent from France in the postwar period. Indeed, although it has never been comparable to the more active and visible Hispanic stage in the United States, Spanish-language theatre in France has had a varied and interesting history, dating from the arrival of hundreds of thousands of political refugees at the fall of the Spanish Republic. Over a half century, that history has included (1) the politically motivated theatre of refugee groups in southern France, (2) the emergence of a high-quality community theatre in Toulouse, (3) the development of a university-based theatre in Bordeaux, (4) the promotion of tours in southern France by independent theatre groups from Spain during the last years of the Franco regime, (5) training of Spanish-speaking theatre professionals through the Théâtre des Nations in Paris, and (6) continuing involvement in theatre festivals and tours by mainstream professional troupes, culminating in Spanish participation in the Théâtre de l'Europe.

During the final months of the Spanish Civil War (1936–1939), more than 400,000 Spaniards fled to France; by the end of 1939, as a result of emigration to the Americas and deaths in concentration camps, their number had been reduced to a quarter million (Llorens 100). They settled primarily in the south, turning Toulouse into the "première ville espagnole de France" (Archet 14). Vicente Llorens observes that this Spanish population in France was largely working class; most professionals chose exile in Spanish America. The Spanish stage that took refuge in Buenos Aires was a professional one that included established dramatists and, because there was no language barrier, could reach the average playgoer (Domenech, Heming, Lewis). The Spanish stage that emerged in Toulouse may better be compared to that of the early Mexican immigrants in the United States: an ethnic theatre that served as a community center, that reinforced cultural values of the minority group, and that could be used to raise funds for political causes (Rosales).

In his doctoral dissertation on Spanish theatre in France (1939–1973), Francisco Torres Monreal deliberately set aside the question of Spanish-language stagings. Rather, his concern was with "penetration" and "integration." Clearly a theatre performed in a foreign language for a restricted audience can have little impact on the theatrical mainstream. Maria Casarès, who left Spain at the outbreak of the war when she was fourteen, for decades has been a leading actress of the French stage. But to achieve this, she had to be assimilated. In her autobiography she highlights the essential cultural difference that separated her native and adoptive countries: neighboring France, with its passion for reason, its bare intellectualism, its "madness" stemming from the "rejection of all madness," seemed more distant to her than Russia (239). It was with the Spanish exiles in Paris that she could recover her faith, her enthusiasm, even her righteous anger (240). Similarly the exile theatre in Toulouse gave to the emigrés the possibility of expressing their emotions while retaining their linguistic and cultural identity.

In 1945, when the exile theatre came into being, those emotions included a repudiation of Francoism and the hope of one day being able to return to a liberated Spain. Marlène

Archet notes that for the Spanish emigrés, culture and politics were inseparable (14). Theatrical productions served a dual ideological function: plays could be openly militant in their message and they could be used to raise funds for the Republican cause. Because of the need to sell tickets, however, the groups quickly learned to mix the didactic with the entertaining (Domergue and Laffranque 86). They repeatedly succeeded in filling the 400-seat Ciné Espoir (a favorite playhouse) and also in taking plays on tour through the other Spanish communities of southern France, from Perpignan and Montpellier to Bordeaux.

In Toulouse there emerged several different groups, representing not only speakers of both Catalan and Castilian, but also rival political factions: Socialists, Communists, Republicans, and Anarchists. During the almost-twenty-year period that the exile theatre flourished, there were often three to five troupes functioning simultaneously. Setting ideology aside, on occasion two or three of the groups would present collaborative stagings. The organizers of the various groups generally had had prior experience in amateur productions in Spain and therefore built on the Spanish theatre traditions of the 1930s (Archet 15). One of the early groups, that of Teodoro Monge, was in fact headed by a professional actor and director (Archet 23).

But of less importance than the theatrical quality of the productions, particularly in the early years, was the opportunity to raise money while maintaining a cultural and political heritage. Given the limited size of the potential audience, there was a constant demand for new productions. Performances might be given without adequate rehearsal time, and amateur actors could not be counted on to remember all their lines; in view of their common purpose, spectators were tolerant of mistakes (Archet and Serralta). Between 1945 and 1949, the group Iberia by itself raised more than a million francs for the antifascist cause (Archet 35).

During her painstaking research in Toulouse, Archet located and interviewed surviving members of several groups, collected playbills from people's attics, and, to the extent possible, compiled chronological listings of various repertories. The works she identifies are a curious blend, reflective of the cultural and political biases of the exiles, as well as the difficulty they had in securing Spanish-language texts in France.

Teodoro Monge, a theatre professional who moved his troupe to Montauban in 1948, began stagings in Toulouse in 1945 with modern classics of Spanish social drama: Joaquín Dicenta's *José Juan* and Angel Guimerà's *Tierra baja*, in the Castilian version by José Echegaray. The group Tomás Meabe reportedly staged major works of García Lorca during its twelve-year existence, starting in 1952 (Archet 91), but Lorca's works are absent from the detailed repertories cited by Archet for Iberia, Grupo Juvenil, Terra Lliure, Casal Català, and Llar de Germanor Catalana. Not surprisingly, the Catalan groups repeatedly turned their attention to Guimerà, Adrià Gual, and Santiago Russinyol, occasionally in bilingual Catalan-Castilian stagings but more generally solely in Catalan.

Atypically, Grupo Juvenil (1948–1962), a troupe closely linked to Iberia (1945–1963), included stagings of foreign authors in Spanish translation: Eugene O'Neill, Henrik Ibsen, and Albert Camus. It must be noted, however, that from the perspective of the Spanish exile in particular, Camus was not a French playwright per se. Born in Algeria of a Spanish mother, Camus strongly identified with the Spanish Republican cause and had ties to the Spanish community in France throughout his life. He maintained lifelong friendships with Maria Casarès and with Emmanuel Roblès, another French Algerian writer of Spanish descent. Camus and Roblès were instrumental in promoting the works of Lorca in French as an antifascist statement during the Spanish Civil War and the Nazi occupation of France. One of the Camus texts chosen by Grupo Juvenil in 1952 was *Le Malentendu*, a work of little impact in France that at least one French critic has found to be heavily influenced by the theatre of Lorca (A. Camp *L'Avant-Scène* 763: 51).

An analysis based on Archet's data for Iberia, the most important of the Toulouse troupes, reveals a steady alternation between the serious and the comic ("dramas sociales" and "juguetes cómicos"), between the established authors of early-twentieth-century Spain (Joaquín and Serafín Alvarez Quintero, Manuel Linares Rivas, and, to a lesser extent, Benito Pérez Galdós and Jacinto Benavente) and new writers from within the exile community, who spoke directly to their compatriots. The popularity of the Alvarez Quintero brothers—five titles, some of them enjoying revivals—could be rivaled only by that of the exiled Alejandro Casona. Starting with *Nuestra Natacha*, one of Iberia's first productions in 1945, Casona—represented by a half dozen titles—was a favorite with both Iberia and Grupo Juvenil. *Los árboles mueren de pie* reached spectators in Toulouse in 1951, only two years after its premiere in Buenos Aires and long before it became available to Madrid audiences. For Grupo Juvenil, Carlos Arniches was also a staple, but the groups in France initially did not have either access to or the desire to stage works by contemporary playwrights residing in Spain. One notable exception was a 1955 production by Iberia of Víctor Ruiz Iriarte's *El pobrecito embustero*; it is doubtful that the author was aware that his light satirical comedy, premiered in Madrid in 1953, had so readily crossed the Pyrenees (Víctor García Ruiz).

The repertory of Iberia and the other groups documented by Archet stands in marked contrast to the Spanish works being produced in France for French-speaking audiences during the same period of time. For the fifteen-year span beginning in 1945, Torres Monreal cites 85 productions in Paris and the provinces. Those productions included 37 of Golden Age authors (14 for Cervantes and 11 for Calderón), authors not staged at all in Toulouse. Lorca, with 35 productions in French, was also much more accessible in translation than in Spanish-language productions. Valle-Inclán and Alberti, neither of whose names appear in Archet's lists, were represented by 3 and 4 stagings in French, respectively. Two contemporary Spanish authors, Buero-Vallejo and Mihura, also reached the French stage in one production each but were as yet unknown to Spanish audiences in Toulouse. The one playwright with a certain overlap between the Spanish and French-language listings is Casona, who received 3 stagings in French during the

1945–1959 period. Perhaps the groups in Toulouse shied away from the Golden Age drama and at least some of these modern texts because of the difficulty they would pose to amateur actors.

The groups in Toulouse were also interested in new works that could not be expected to reach French playgoers. In 1947 the Servicio de Cultura y Propaganda of the Movimiento Libertario Español sponsored a contest to encourage the creation of texts that could address directly the experience of the exile community. The winner of that contest, *Que en España empieza a amanecer* by Ceferino R. Avecilla, became perhaps the most visible of the Spanish-language scripts to be written and staged in France, but it was not the first. In January 1946 Iberia had produced a "sainete cómico" by Morales Guzmán, titled *Un andaluz en Toulouse*, and followed in April with *¡Abajo las armas!*, by Emilio Gómez de Miguel and Eduardo Borrás. The prizewinning Avecilla text, subtitled a "drama de costumbres españolas," was premiered 18 July 1948 in a joint production by Iberia, Grupo Juvenil, and the Compañía Teodoro Monge. As is often the case with exile theatre, the texts produced in Toulouse have proved ephemeral. Indeed, as early as 1949 Felipe Alaiz, in a long article published on the first page of an Anarchist weekly, criticized both *¡Abajo las armas!* and *Que en España empieza a amanecer* for being facile propaganda pieces; he recommended a variety of other paths the local theatre groups might follow more fruitfully (qtd. in Archet 35–40).

By the late 1950s and early 1960s, the situation of the Spanish community in France was undergoing substantial change. There would be no early end to the Franco dictatorship, as the emigrés had originally hoped. The children of the political exiles were rapidly losing their Hispanic culture and becoming "ideologically illiterate" (Domergue and Laffranque 94). Moreover the Spanish community now included the so-called economic exiles (the waves of Spaniards who headed north seeking employment) and, with the independence of Algeria in 1962, the repatriated French Algerians, many of whom were of Spanish descent. The kind of plays that Alaiz deplored in 1949 no longer had an audience a decade later, and the Spanish-language theatre in Toulouse was ripe for a second phase. That phase, more refined and creative than the earlier one, found expression in a new group: the Amigos del Teatro Español (ATE), under the direction of José Martín Elizondo (Archet and Serralta).

Martín Elizondo (b. 1922) left Spain for France in the late 1940s, at the age of twenty-five. After working at a number of jobs in various cities, he studied in Paris and from there moved to Toulouse, where, in 1956, he assumed the direction of the Grenier, the city's regional theatre. It was with this professional background that he formed the ATE. Setting aside the ideological divisiveness of the earlier groups, the ATE's bylaws strictly prohibited any political or religious propaganda in its midst. They set forth broader goals: to bring Spanish culture to French and Hispanic audiences, and, through a bilingual orientation, to enhance communication between the two cultures. The new group quickly attracted the most professional of the actors from the various amateur companies (Archet and Serralta). According to Martín Elizondo, it also drew upon the support of French Hispanists and the university community in Toulouse. (Personal interview, May 1987).

The ATE began with a popular production of Zorrilla's nineteenth-century *Don Juan Tenorio* and then largely moved away from the classics. In choosing texts for the ATE, Martín Elizondo intentionally broke with the pattern of the amateur groups, which he has described as a mix of Arniches, Casona, and various second- and third-rate playwrights (Interview, Berenguer 55). Instead he identified major authors whose works were still prohibited in Franco Spain, while also seeking out new or lesser-known writers of quality throughout the Spanish-speaking world. During their 1959 and 1960 seasons, for example, ATE presented staged readings of Valle-Inclán's *Las galas del difunto*, Rafael Alberti's *La pájara pinta*, and Miguel Hernández's *El labrador de más aire*. The group also did *El vendaval* by José García Lora, a Spanish playwright exiled in England; and *Milagro* by Lauro Olmo, a Spanish author within Spain who was to achieve national acclaim with *La camisa* in 1962. Martín Elizondo takes pride in having provided the Spanish-language premieres of various texts, including Valle-Inclán's *Luces de bohemia* (Personal interview, May 1987).

While these performances of ATE were only readings, labeled "lectures-spectacles," the staging in January 1961 of Manuel Martínez Azaña's *La forja de los sueños* was a full-scale production (Archet 94–95). Azaña (b. 1935) is the great-nephew of Manuel Azaña, last president of the Spanish Republic during the Civil War years. In this, his first original play, Martínez Azaña gave poetic expression to his anguished assessment of Spain (Linsalata and Sedwick xiii). The play premiered in Madrid in May 1960, but not without prior problems with the censor. Following that production, the young author's situation in Spain became increasingly difficult and he sought refuge in France as a political exile (Interview). Thus began an association with Elizondo that altered both the focus of ATE and Azaña's involvement in theatre.

With Elizondo's encouragement, Azaña turned to directing, and in March 1961 staged Elizondo's *Durango*, a play based on the 1937 bombing of that Basque town. *Durango* met with considerable success, and ATE subsequently staged several of Elizondo's original plays. Azaña soon moved from Toulouse to Bordeaux, where he established a university theatre. Under Elizondo's guidance, ATE continued to stage three productions a year in Toulouse and to perform throughout southern France. The group eventually disappeared. Elizondo, who has written and directed plays in both Spanish and French, moved to Fontainebleau where he worked in French with an amateur group (Personal interview, October 1987). In 1989 he returned to Spain, establishing his residence in Madrid.

Azaña's theatre in Bordeaux is not the only example of university-based Spanish-language productions in France. Torres Monreal indicates that there have been sporadic activities in many French universities, but the concentrated efforts have come in Bordeaux, Toulouse, and at the Sorbonne (*El teatro español en Francia* 5). In Bordeaux Azaña created a kind of extracurricular laboratory theatre, with the enthusiastic support of his colleagues in Spanish studies, the university president, and, eventually, officials from the French Ministry of Education. Functioning as the theatre of the Instituto de Estudios Ibéricos e Iberoamericanos, the group came to be called TIEIT.

For sixteen seasons, before Azaña returned to Madrid in 1978, TIEIT staged a production a year. They worked successfully with such challenging texts as Valle's *La rosa de papel* and Alberti's *La pájara pinta*. The student-actors perfected their Spanish pronunciation in the university language laboratory, which was directed by Azaña's wife. Wishing to make the students aware of the subtle cultural differences between Spanish and French in such matters as gesture and movement, Azaña had them perform some plays in both languages, for example pairing Robert Marrast's French translation of *La rosa de papel* with Valle-Inclán's original text. But the productions, like similar Hispanic cultural activities in some American universities, also served as a recruitment device: a means of attracting to the university the children of Spanish laborers living in Bordeaux. Azaña estimates that he worked with 500 students over the years and notes with pleasure the example of an alumnus who teaches in Fumel, a community with a heavy concentration of Hispanics, and who has taken Spanish-language stagings out to the people there.

The students in Bordeaux were good enough to be invited to national and international theatre festivals, but, perhaps even more significantly, for a dozen years Azaña organized an annual Spanish cultural festival in Bordeaux. Consisting of art, music, film, and lectures, as well as theatre, the festival attracted a number of troupes from France and Spain. Azaña recalls in particular stagings of *Luces de bohemia* by the ATE, of Lorca's *La zapatera prodigiosa*, and of Olmo's *Condecoración* and *La camisa*. (It should be noted that *La camisa*, a play dealing with Spanish workers who are forced to go abroad because of poverty and unemployment, was staged numerous times to sympathetic Hispanic audiences in several European countries.)

Theatre troupes from Spain not only participated in the Bordeaux festival but were invited on tour throughout the refugee community in southern France. Many Spaniards in France considered independent groups, like La Cuadra de

Sevilla, Els Joglars, and Tábano, to be political activists who were helping to bring an end to the Franco era; for several years, starting in the late 1960s, the visiting troupes received a "fantastic" welcome in Toulouse, playing to enthusiastic full houses at the Ciné Espoir (later renamed the Théâtre du Taure) (Archet and Serralta). With little financial backing, the troupes often traveled "like gypsies" but in Toulouse could count on their ties with political and labor organizations (Gallego).

Andrés Gallego, a professor of Spanish at the university in Toulouse, cites the great success of such productions as La Cuadra de Sevilla's *Quejío*, *Herramientas*, and the more recent *Andalucía amarga*, and of Tábano's *Castañuela 70 and El retablo del flautista*. He observes that protest statements against repression and the dehumanizing impact of modern technology struck a responsive chord among the Spaniards in Toulouse. Gallego's memory of the reception in France to Tábano's stagings is confirmed by the now-defunct company's own records. In February 1971 *Castañuela 70* toured Dijon, Nice, Aix-en-Provence, Montpellier, Perpignan, Bordeaux, and Toulouse. In Bordeaux, hosted by TIEIT, it played three nights and in Toulouse filled 370 of the 400 seats in the house (Equipo Pipirijaina 53). In December of that same year, Tábano's production of Jordi Teixidor's *El retablo del flautista* also had a three-night run at the TIEIT in Bordeaux and in Toulouse played three nights for a total audience of 1130 (Equipo Pipirijaina 54).

Following Franco's death in 1975, Spanish-language theatre in France entered a period of change. The political reason for inviting the independent groups no longer existed. Both the ATE in Toulouse and the TIEIT in Bordeaux eventually ceased to exist. If the directors of those theatres, who had fostered Spanish culture in France for so many years, expected the theatre world of democratic Spain to give them a warm welcome, they were initially disappointed. Martín Elizondo did win a prize at the Sitges festival in 1979; and in 1981 Azaña directed Elizondo's *El otro Paulo y el minotauro* for two performances in Madrid. But, for the most part, neither of these two Spaniards found the doors open to him in his native land. In 1988, however,

Martín Elizondo's *Antígona entre muros* won the first international play-writing contest for the annual Mérida festival and, as a result of that staging, his situation in Spain has since improved. Back in Toulouse the Casa de España continues to sponsor a variety of cultural activities, including a series of semiprofessional theatre productions for the Spanish emigré community (Gallego). University-based productions, like the successful *La casa de Bernarda Alba* in 1983, attract a sizable audience, consisting perhaps of 50 percent Spanish refugees and their children, 40 percent students, and 10 percent French residents of the city (Archet and Serralta).

In at least one notable case, Spanish exile theatre in Toulouse did have a direct impact on the French stage. French director and playwright Armand Gatti became acquainted with the exiles and with Martín Elizondo's Amigos del Teatro Español, which was then raising funds for the striking miners in Asturias. It was in Elizondo's house, taping conversations with the exiles, that Gatti developed the first script for *La Passion du Général Franco par les émigrés eux-mêmes*, an overtly anti-Francoist political work that gained considerable notoriety when the French government prohibited its performance in any subsidized theatre (Elizondo, Personal interview, May 1987). It was already in rehearsal in 1969 at Jean Vilar's Théâtre National Populaire when a complaint from the Spanish embassy convinced President de Gaulle to ban the production rather than offend the Spanish government at a time of delicate economic negotiations. Not staged in France until after Franco's death, the play premiered in Germany, where Gatti was extremely touched by the spontaneous participation of migrant Spanish workers who came from miles around to attend performances in Kassel (Gatti).

Spanish-language theatre has also been a presence in radio productions emanating from France. For some twenty years these programs, aimed at Spain, Portugal, and Latin America by Radio Française, were directed by André Camp, noted theatre critic and translator of Hispanic drama. Camp involved a great number of Spanish-speaking professionals of the French theatre world and notes that productions of the Spanish classics from the university-based theatre at the Sorbonne have often been taped for future broadcast as well (Personal interview, May 1987).

The chief point of entry to the French stage for Spanish-language theatre, however, has come indirectly through the university of the Théâtre des Nations, located in Paris from 1961 to 1968. Martín Elizondo studied there, along with Jorge Lavelli, Jérome Savary, and the late Víctor García (Elizondo, Personal interview, May 1987). These three Argentinians came to be major directors of the French stage, but with continuing ties to their Hispanic roots. Even Savary, whose father was French and who lived in South America only a few years, developed affinities for Hispanic theatre because of his association with García (Knowles 526). For example, all three directed plays by Fernando Arrabal, who left Spain for France in the mid-1950s. Starting in the 1970s García and Lavelli, through their collaboration with the Spanish troupe of Nuria Espert, were instrumental in introducing Spanish-language productions of Lorca and Valle-Inclán to French audiences.

But García's contribution dates back to 1963 and his stagings of García Lorca and Valle-Inclán for the Spanish-language workshop of the Théâtre des Nations. García's first two productions in France were of Lorca's *El retablillo de don Cristóbal* and Valle's *La rosa de papel*. In a 1984 issue of Les Voies de la Création Théâtrale, dedicated to García's memory, Monique Monory recalls in glowing terms the creativity of those stagings: the visual impact of the Lorca play, with its tragic image surfacing in the final scene of the comedy (114), and the "transfigured and purified vision" of the dark forces underscoring the baroque theatre of Valle-Inclán (122). She reminds us that García's Valle-Inclán came on the heels of major productions in French of *Divinas palabras* and *Luces de bohemia*, directed by Roger Blin and Georges Wilson, respectively. *El retablillo de don Cristóbal* won for García first prize in a Théâtre des Nations contest, and both versions were staged numerous times in France and abroad to unanimous acclaim.

Torres Monreal, in analyzing the relative lack of Spanish plays in the French theatre repertory, has observed a tendency to import an entire production rather than translate and restage the text. He affirms that when a particular work in Spain has received favorable reviews in the foreign press, the whole troupe has been brought to France to give the work in Spanish. The examples he specifically notes are the independent groups like La Cuadra de Sevilla and the collaborative efforts of Víctor García and Nuria Espert (Diss. 1: 123).

In the tumultuous days of 1968 in Paris, following the student takeover of the Odéon theatre, the Théâtre des Nations moved to London. García did not follow. Instead, for the next several years, he worked in Brazil with Ruth Escobar and in Spain with Nuria Espert (Temkine 1: 35–36). García and Espert created three productions together in Spanish: Jean Genet's *Las criadas*, 1969; Lorca's *Yerma*, 1971; and Valle-Inclán's *Divinas palabras*, 1975. García took the plays on international tours, including stagings in France. It was *Las criadas*, winner of the grand prize at the Belgrade International Theatre Festival, that made Espert internationally famous (Londré 1985). When it played at the Théâtre de la Cité Universitaire in April 1970, Paris "discovered" Nuria Espert and "loved her" (Godard). García's famous version of *Yerma*—on a trampoline—toured the world for four years, reaching a major Parisian playhouse, the Théâtre de la Ville, in September 1973 (Temkine 2: 269). The third of the García-Espert collaborations, *Divinas palabras*, in fact reached Paris before Madrid or Barcelona. It ran in February and March 1976 at the Théâtre National de Chaillot but did not open at the Monumental in Madrid until the following January.

In an interview with Evelyne Ertel, Espert expressed a desire to provide a French-language tape of *Divinas palabras* for the benefit of spectators who did not understand Spanish. (Espert, who speaks fluent French herself, would have recorded her own role.) The project apparently was not realized, but Espert's performances have met with an enthusiastic response in France without benefit of translation. Subsequent to her collaboration with García, she worked with Jorge Lavelli on productions of Lorca's *Doña Rosita la soltera*, 1980, and Shakespeare's *The Tempest*, 1983. Lavelli

Lluís Homar and Walter Vidarte in *Tirano Banderas,* Lluís Pasqual's stage version of Valle-Inclán's novel. Created under the auspices of Spain's Quincentennial Commission, the touring Spanish-language production was staged in Paris in March 1992 with French subtitles. (Photo by Ros Ribas; courtesy of L'Odéon-Théâtre de l'Europe)

Leonor Manso in *Tirano Banderas,* adapted and directed by Lluís Pasqual. (Photo by Ros Ribas; courtesy of L'Odéon-Théâtre de l'Europe)

affirms that the Spanish production of the Lorca play, which toured throughout Europe for months, was appreciated by mainstream audiences. From his perspective, the acting company had no difficulty transcending the language barrier (Telephone interview).

Another major Spanish-language staging reached Paris during the inaugural season there of the Théâtre de l'Europe in 1984. Directed by Lluís Pasqual, Valle-Inclán's *Luces de bohemia* indeed was performed in France eight months before opening in October of that year at Spain's own national theatre, the María Guerrero in Madrid. The production of *Luces de bohemia* has met with acclaim wherever it was presented and has brought international recognition to Pasqual and the Centro Dramático Nacional (CDN). Contrary to Lavelli's opinion about *Doña Rosita la soltera,* however, André Camp felt that to appreciate fully the Spanish production of *Luces de bohemia* one would have to know Spanish—and Spanish history (*L'Avant-Scène* 749: 48.)

Through association with the Théâtre de l'Europe, the presence of Spanish-language theatre in France has now been formalized; the CDN production of Lorca's *El público* was also staged there in 1988. Pasqual's work was so admired that the following season Antoine Vitez, head of the Comédie Française, invited him to be a guest director. In October 1989, the French Minister of Culture Jack Lang appointed Pasqual to the directorship of the Théâtre de l'Europe at the Odéon National Theatre in Paris.

In recent years, Spanish troupes appearing in international theatre festivals in France are no longer independent groups, traveling "like gypsies," but rather recognized companies that are often the recipients of subsidies from the federal Ministry of Culture or from the various autonomous regional governments. Pasqual, for example, participated in the 1984 festival at Avignon with the national drama center's staging of Brecht's version of Marlowe's *Edward II*. To be sure, such a production, while given in Spanish, did nothing to make the works of contemporary Spanish playwrights better known to audiences in France. In the 1980s, the twentieth-century Spanish writers most accessible to spectators north of the Pyrenees, whether in French translation or Spanish originals, continued to be Lorca and Valle-Inclán.

Even if they have done little to promote contemporary Spanish playwrights, the traveling companies have established themselves as creative groups of the highest caliber. Els Comediants, one of Spain's outstanding troupes, has been invited on more than one occasion to present the opening or closing production at the festival in Avignon. El Tricicle, a mime troupe from Catalonia, was well received at the festival of Théâtre Franco-Espagnol at Bayonne in November 1984 and went on to participate in the international festival of mime at Arles in 1985. The positive reception they have received in France was evident in their being scheduled for the 1987–88 season at Paris's municipal Théâtre de la Ville. In reviewing the 1984 Bayonne festival, the first open to Spanish troupes, Camp concluded that the two Spanish groups were superior to the French ones and by themselves made his trip from Paris worthwhile (*L'Avant-Scène* 762). The second troupe receiving Camp's high praise was a Basque collective that staged *Oficio de tinieblas*, a baroque spectacle based on Camilo José Cela's novel of the same name.

The warm reception in France to Spanish troupes in the 1980s did not necessarily erase the cultural difference between the two countries that Maria Casarès felt so strongly in her youth. And not all Spaniards were sure they wanted to become a European Community country and thus be absorbed into Europe. The response to this situation by Albert Boadella and Els Joglars was *Virtuosos de Fontainebleau*, a trilingual (Catalan-Castilian-French) satire of the French and their stereotyped notions of Spanish reality. Not surprisingly, the spectacle did not travel widely in France, only to Bayonne (Pérez de Olaguer 34).

Els Joglars's wildly funny but controversial *Virtuosos de Fontainebleau* once again underscores the political potential of theatre. If Gatti's *La Passion du Général Franco par les émigrés eux-mêmes* was banned by de Gaulle because of pending trade agreements with Franco, the more recent work was precisely intended to raise questions about Spain's entry into the European Community. Spanish-language theatre in French from the 1940s to the present has often been overtly political: a didactic tool for the exile community, a means of raising funds for political causes, a support for those trying to bring an end to the Franco regime.

For the most part, however, since the advent of democracy the presence of Spanish-language theatre in France has served primarily to establish stronger cultural and economic ties between two neighboring nations. This cultural interchange reached new levels in 1992, with numerous activities marking the 500th anniversary of Columbus's first voyage of discovery. The Odéon–Théâtre de l'Europe, under the continuing direction of Lluís Pasqual, scheduled several Spanish-language productions, as well as French translations of a variety of Spanish and Latin American plays, in its special Hispanic Cycle. Among the works presented in Spanish were three major projects sponsored by Spain's Quincentennial commission: Pasqual's own adaptation of Valle-Inclán's novel of Latin American setting, *Tirano Banderas*; José Sanchis Sinisterra's *Lope de Aguirre, traidor*, a historical drama cast in the mold of Greek tragedy, directed by José Luis Gómez; and Els Joglars's collective improvisation, *Yo tengo un tío en América*, directed by Albert Boadella. The action of Els Joglars's satire takes place in an insane asylum, where the inmates create a schizophrenic metaphor for the Spanish conquest of America. Adopting a technique developed for opera, the performances were made more accessible to the French-speaking audience through the use of subtitles. Clearly Pasqual was cooperating fully so that 1992 might be the year of discovery for Spanish theatre in Paris.

Chapter 3

SPANISH THEATRE ON THE CONTEMPORARY FRENCH STAGE

Juan Solano is a frustrated Spanish playwright. Among his failures, he recalls that his one chance at being staged in Paris was thwarted when the theatre went bankrupt two days before the first rehearsal. He comforts himself with the knowledge that his situation is not unique: "Il n'y a pratiquement pas d'auteurs espagnols joués à Paris. Pratiquement pas. Si on y réfléchit cinq minutes, il y en a même pas du tout, ces derniers temps" (There are practically no Spanish authors staged in Paris. Practically none. If you think about it for five minutes, lately there is none at all) (*Ma chanson la plus triste est espagnole* 25). The character, created by Carlos Semprun-Maura in a radio drama aired by France-Culture in 1988, is fictitious, but the lament has a ring of authenticity. The noted French drama critic Bernard Dort, confronted unexpectedly with the question in October 1986, indeed could think of no Spanish presence at all on the contemporary French stage (Personal interview).

In 1974, when Francisco Torres Monreal was finishing his comprehensive study of Spanish theatre in France, 1935–1973, he contacted several Spanish dramatists on the subject. José María Rodríguez Méndez responded that, with the possible exception of the classics, Spanish theatre was not of interest across the Pyrenees: "Los franceses solo valoran lo suyo y aquello otro que pueda servir para consolidar lo suyo. Todo lo que les resulta extraño a su manera de pensar y vivir lo consideran sin valor" (The French only value their own culture and whatever else enhances their own. Anything that is different from their way of thinking or living they consider without value) (Letter rptd. in Diss. 2: 765). Thirteen years later, Antonio Buero-Vallejo offered a similar opinion, that France has almost always had an attitude of superiority toward Spanish culture (Personal interview).

It is precisely this stereotype of the French—or, more precisely, this reflection of an assumed French perception of a Spanish stereotype—that Albert Boadella and Els Joglars satirized in their trilingual (Catalan-Castilian-French) *Virtuosos de Fontainebleau*. Premiered in October 1985, on the eve of Spain's entry into the European Community, this wildly funny production stands in radical opposition to the official promotion of cultural exchange between Spain and France that has led to a wave of highly visible and well-attended expositions of Spanish art, film, and literature in Paris starting in 1987. By the fall of that year, the young director and actor Marc-Ange Sanz could affirm that Spain was commercially in vogue in Paris, noting, however, that many French were stunned to learn that Picasso's paintings had Spanish antecedents (Personal interview).

To be sure, through the 1980s there continued to be an imbalance in cultural trade across the Pyrenees. The newspaper announcement that Spaniard Lluís Pasqual had been invited to direct a play for the Comédie Française affirmed once again that the number of French theatrical companies invited to Spain exceeds the number of Spanish troupes touring in France (*El País* 1989). Likewise, successful plays from the Parisian stage have readily been translated for staging in Madrid while the reverse has not been true. In the 1950s and 1960s, the dominant foreign theatre in the French capital was British or American; in subsequent decades, the tide has swung to German-language theatre. In Dort's compilation of plays he reviewed in the period 1970–1978, not one Spanish text appears. But Dort, a specialist in Brecht and Brechtian theatre, has obviously made a personal selection. André Camp, on the other hand, has had a lifelong interest in Hispanic theatre, and the pages of *L'Avant-Scène Théâtre*, the influential biweekly journal with which he has been associated since its beginnings some forty years ago, do highlight a certain Spanish presence on the French stage. While it cannot be compared to the Anglo-American or Germanic impact, Spanish theatre has never really disappeared in France and, in the 1990s, promises to become increasingly visible.

Throughout most of the Franco era in Spain (1939–1975), as discussed in Chapter 2, there was, in fact, an active Spanish-language theatre in France, centered in Toulouse. But that Spanish emigré theatre, aimed as it was at a limited audience, could not be expected to achieve integration or even, in Torres Monreal's terms, "penetration." With respect to French-language theatre during the period of his analysis (1935–1973), Torres Monreal concluded that for the classic writers, one could speak of "a small number of integrated works" but not, truly, of integrated writers (*El teatro español en Francia* 3). Among twentieth-century Spanish authors, however, he found two who had been integrated into the French stage: Federico García Lorca and Fernando Arrabal. In the case of Arrabal, who has lived in France since the mid-1950s, Torres Monreal felt that by 1967 (Jorge Lavelli's staging of *L'Architecte et l'empereur d'Assyrie*) this playwright had been as fully accepted in French theatre as fellow Spaniards Luis Buñuel and Pablo Picasso had earlier been in the worlds of cinema and art (*El teatro español en Francia* 45).

Although some of Torres Monreal's assessments are still valid today, enough time has passed to make worthwhile a further examination of the Spanish presence on the French stage. To do so, several groups of authors will be considered: (1) the classics, especially Pedro Calderón de la Barca, (2) Lorca, (3) other twentieth-century playwrights of Lorca's generation or earlier, (4) Arrabal, (5) other Spanish playwrights living in France, and (6) other playwrights living in Spain. Of significance in this examination are the influence of the directors or theatres that have chosen to stage Spanish works and the role that Hispanics within the French theatre world have played in promoting Spanish culture.

The official French stage (that is, the heavily subsidized Parisian showcase) is, of course, the Comédie Française. To the extent that incorporation into their repertory means integration, four Spanish names have achieved that goal since 1973. García Lorca (*La casa de Bernarda Alba;* French trans., *La Maison de Bernarda*) was added in 1974, Fernando de Rojas (*La Célestine*) in 1975, and Arrabal (*La Tour de Babel*) in 1979, in time for the Comédie's 300th anniversary (Dux 216). But Jeanyves Guérin observes sardonically that it "was only in 1982 that the baroque Calderón entered the repertory of the . . . temple of classicism" (Guérin 26). This belated recognition of Calderón is part of a recent effort to internationalize the classical repertory of the Comédie Française, thus returning to a trend introduced years before, first by Charles Dullin and then by Jean Vilar with the Théâtre National Populaire (TNP).

Spanish classics have had their moments of popularity in France for reasons often extraneous to their merits, a phenomenon Torres Monreal has labeled "mediaciones externas." Jean-Louis Vaudoyer, the director of the Comédie Française from 1941 to the end of the Occupation, "decided that the playwrights of the Spanish Golden Age were right for the times: their plots were well removed from either France or Germany and they had already been successfully performed by German companies" (Bradby 1984: 20). Twenty years later, at the time of the Algerian war of independence, these same classical Spanish plays were deemed appropriate vehicles for making contemporary political statements. The production of Calderón's *L'Alcade de Zalaméa,* directed by Jean Vilar in 1961 at the festival of Avignon and the following year at the TNP in Paris, was interpreted as a commentary on the acquittal of three military officers who had tortured and killed an Algerian woman (Bradby 1984: 103). The subversive potential of Spanish Golden Age drama was not a new discovery, however. Jean-Louis Barrault had given an Artaudian staging to Cervantes's *Numance* in Paris in 1937 precisely for the purpose of calling attention to the Spanish Civil War.

At the TNP, Vilar's interest in Spanish theatre was multifaceted. He considered the classic works of such playwrights as Corneille, Sophocles, and Calderón to be "faithful mirrors" of the present (Vilar 93). In speaking of the dramatic language he wished to recreate, he cited the "magic, incantational" qualities of Aeschylus, Shakespeare, Racine, and Lorca (Vilar 36). Theatre, he said, was a man of the people, a woman of the people; that was the lesson to be learned from traditional Japanese theatre, Molière, the Elizabethans, Lope de Vega and Calderón (Vilar 94). Vilar's stance on Golden Age drama was shared by Roger Planchon, the other great director of "popular theatre" in the postwar period. The private Théâtre de la Comédie, which he directed in Lyon from 1950 to 1958, had "a unique splendor in France" (White 198). His programming, which is not mentioned in Torres Monreal's extensive list of productions in Paris and the provinces, included Calderón's *La vida es sueño* (*La Vie est un songe*) in 1952 and *L'Alcade de Zalaméa* in 1955.

The period following World War II in France was one of decentralization in the theatre: the creation in the provinces of national dramatic centers, cultural houses, and summer theatre festivals. Torres Monreal has observed that Spanish classics were highlighted in this movement and often preferred to French works, in part because they were "created for the people" and originally intended for outdoor performance. In the Festival de Languedoc-Montauban, in particular, Spanish classics outnumbered the French; the festival in 1958 was devoted to Tirso de Molina, in 1961 to Calderón de la Barca, and in 1962 to Lope de Vega (Diss. 1: 98).

While Montauban, a city that welcomed large numbers of Spanish emigrés, cannot be considered typical, Kenneth S. White's overview of the seven provincial dramatic centers in the period 1945–1965 mentions Spanish works for all but one of them. In the summer of 1961, the Grenier de Toulouse staged outdoors two "delightful comedies": Cervantes's *El retablo de maravillas* (*Le Rétable des merveilles*) and Lorca's *La zapatera prodigiosa* (*La Savetière prodigieuse*), subsequently taking the former of these to the Théâtre de France–Odéon in Paris (White 37–38). Directed by Jean Dasté, La Comédie de Saint-Etienne had earlier done the Cervantes and Lorca farces in 1946 and 1950, respectively. Their production of Calderón's *La Vie est un songe* in 1959, described as "imposing" (White 76), was one of their most successful. Of the fourteen plays White lists from the

1954–55 to 1958–59 seasons, it enjoyed the fourth-longest run—fifty-three performances—and ranked sixth in average number of spectators—599 (White 79).

The Centre Dramatique de l'Est in Strasbourg did Lorca's *La Maison de Bernarda* in 1949–50 and Calderón's *L'Alcade de Zalaméa* in 1954–55. White observes that Daniel Leveugle's staging of the Golden Age work made it known to a wide audience before Vilar and the TNP: "Ce tableau d'injustice et de persécution sociales produit une forte impression en province" (This portrait of social injustice and persecution made a strong impression in the provinces) (White 104). Calderón's *La Vie est un songe* was done in 1959–60 at La Comédie de l'Ouest in Renne and Cervantes's *Le Rétable des merveilles*, in open-air performance, in the summer of 1953 at La Comédie en Provence.

The Centre Dramatique du Nord was established in 1960 under the direction of the innovative and daring André Reybaz. He decided to inaugurate the playhouse at Tourcoing with the French première of Calderón's *Le Schisme d'Angleterre*. The unknown work drew an average of 439 spectators per performance, "an exceptional occurrence" for a new center (White 229). The critic for a regional newspaper praised the staging, the costumes, and the acting, calling the total production an "émerveillement" (marvel) (White 224). The Comédie de Bourges, the last of the centers discussed by White, was founded in 1962, under the direction of Gabriel Monnet. In 1964 the company did both Arrabal's *Pique-Nique en campagne* ("a virulent satire") and Calderón's *La Vie est un songe*. With the Golden Age play, Monnet was able to repeat the remarkable success of the earlier Comédie de Saint-Etienne production (White 249).

Torres Monreal includes most of the above provincial stagings in the appendix to his two-volume dissertation, but his list is arranged by years. White's discussion center by center gives a somewhat different view of the extent to which a playwright like Calderón had, in fact, been "integrated." In 1959 the Comédie en Provence surveyed its spectators, asking what authors they would like the troupe to perform of the French classics, contemporary French, and foreign playwrights. The response to this third question was, in descending order: Shakespeare, Lorca, Ibsen, Brecht, Chekhov, Goldoni, Strindberg, Steinbeck, and Calderón (White 188). The inclusion of Calderón in a list of integrated playwrights is reinforced by data on provincial stagings included in Mireille Willey's study of popular theatre. There are 3 Spaniards among 54 playwrights staged 5 or more times from the "beginning of decentralization" (the exact period is not identified): Lorca, 17; Calderón, 9; and Arrabal, 8.[1] While both Calderón and Arrabal place in the bottom half (the list is headed by Molière with 136 stagings, Shakespeare with 84, and Brecht with 48), the 9 productions of Calderón place him on a par with French playwrights Camus, Cocteau, and Gatti (Willey 195).

An increasing interest in Calderón is documented in Torres Monreal's own study. His appendix includes 85 French productions of Spanish plays between 1945 and 1959. Of these, 37 are authors of the Golden Age: Cervantes, 14; Calderón, 12; Lope de Vega, 6; Tirso de Molina, 4; and Guillén de Castro, 1 (Diss. 2: 697–719). For the next fourteen years, 1960–1973, he lists a comparable 35 productions of playwrights from the Golden Age or earlier but with a shifting emphasis: Calderón, 15; Cervantes, 9; Lope de Vega, 4; Tirso de Molina, 3; Fernando de Rojas, 2; Lope de Rueda, 1; and Gil Vicente, 1 (Diss. 2: 719–742). The interest in Calderón could only have been enhanced by Jerzy Grotowski's staging of *Le Prince constant* at the Théâtre des Nations in Paris in 1966. The Polish director's internationally acclaimed production was chosen, along with Víctor García's innovative staging of Arrabal's *Le Cimetière des voitures*, for the first volume of the series on stage productions, *Les Voies de la Création Théâtrale.*

The identification of Spanish authors, particularly those of the Golden Age, with "popular theatre" is underscored by dramatic texts chosen for publication. L'Arche Editeur in Paris developed a series of fifty plays, all foreign, in their "Répertoire pour un théâtre populaire." While the selection leans toward Strindberg (six titles) and Pirandello (five), it included seven Spanish works, starting with Cervantes's *Numance* as No. 2 in the collection. Cervantes is also represented by his short plays, the *Intermèdes;* there are two plays by Tirso and one each by Calderón, Lope, and the contemporary writer Rafael Alberti. Other Spanish texts, including works by Cervantes, Lorca, Valle-Inclán, and Alberti, were published in the TNP's own journal, *Théâtre Populaire.*

The French directors mentioned thus far who chose Spanish texts for their productions include some of the most influential in the postwar theatre (Barrault, Vilar, Planchon, Dasté). Others who have been instrumental in promoting Spanish playwrights have themselves had a "Spanish connection." In his recent book, *Stage Directors in Modern France,* David Whitton singles out the group of Latin Americans: García, Lavelli, and Savary. These three Argentinians have played key roles in the development of Arrabal's career, but García and Lavelli also staged major productions of other Spanish authors. In the specific case of Golden Age drama, Torres Monreal cites the considerable contribution of Albert Camus with his versions of Calderón's *La Dévotion à la croix* and Lope's *Le Chevalier d'Olmedo* for the Festival d'Art Dramatique at Angers in 1953 and 1957 (*El teatro español en Francia* 26–28). As noted in Chapter 2, Camus, not surprisingly for a French Algerian, was of Spanish descent on his mother's side; his interest in Spain is thus somewhat akin to that of the Argentinians.[2]

In his biography of Camus (1913–1960), Herbert R. Lottman highlights this Spanish side, quoting, among others, novelist and playwright Emmanuel Roblès (Camus's close friend and fellow French Algerian of Spanish descent). Roblès has frequently analyzed his own works and character in terms of their Spanish essence. He recognized in Camus as well a preoccupation with the "tragic sense of life" that Unamuno found in the heart of every Spaniard (qtd. Depierris 47). Camus's longtime involvement, professionally and personally, with Spanish-born actress Maria Casarès further underscored his interest in Spain: "She represented Camus's Spanish blood, later his concern not only for Spain's political plight but for its literature, its stage; she was his private way to remain in touch with the Mediterranean" (Lottman 317–318). Indeed Casarès collab-

Thierry Hancisse as Segismundo in Calderón's *La Vie est un songe.* The French-language production, directed by Spaniard José Luis Gómez, was staged in Paris 11 April-14 June 1992 as part of a series of Hispanic cultural activities scheduled in conjunction with the Quincentennial. (Photo by Ros Ribas; courtesy of L'Odéon-Théâtre de l'Europe)

orated with Camus in translating the Calderón and Lope texts. She also starred in *La Dévotion à la croix.* The outdoor production at Angers received national press attention and, in the opinion of a local critic, "the Calderón work was so perfectly performed it could never again be played on an ordinary theater stage" (Lottman 525). For the 1960s, Torres Monreal lists three productions of *La Dévotion à la croix*: Festival de Montauban, 1961; Centre Théâtrale du Limousin, 1966; and the Comédie des Alpes (Grenoble), 1969.

Over the centuries, Spanish theatre, particularly the drama of the Golden Age, has served as a source of inspiration to numerous French playwrights, with Pierre Corneille being a classic example. When Denis Llorca revived Corneille's *Le Cid* at the Théâtre de la Ville in Paris in 1972, he added an extra character to the cast: Guillén de Castro, the author of the original text. The production, by this and other changes to the seventeenth-century play, "provoked passionate and contradictory reactions" (Willey 93). Although Llorca explained that the character of Castro and his lines in old Castilian merely served as a musical, percussion interlude (qtd. Willey 94), it is tempting to conjecture that Llorca, whose own name hints at Catalonian origins, was making a point about the Spanish contribution to the French stage. Certainly Eduardo Manet, who in the same year wrote his *L'Autre Don Juan*, was quite direct in incorporating Don Juan Ruiz de Alarcón into a complex metaplay based on *Las paredes oyen*. Manet, who was born in Cuba of Spanish parents, was asked to prepare a French version of a Golden Age work for a summer festival (Avant-Propos to *L'Autre Don Juan* 7). He settled on the Mexican-born Alarcón, inspiration for Corneille's *Le Menteur*, but placed the playwright within the play to protest changes made to his work and even to insist that some scenes be left in Spanish.

In the 1980s at least two productions of Calderón were staged by Hispanic directors. In 1981 Víctor García (1934–1982), in one of his last productions, mounted a collage of seven *autos sacramentales* at the Théâtre National de Chaillot in Paris. Intended to be a "drame de tous les temps" (a drama for all times), instead it was a failure, due to staging problems and poor acoustics (A. Camp 693: 53). Far more successful was Raúl Ruiz's staging of the *La Vie est un songe*, which was well received at the Avignon festival in 1986. The Chilean director, who heads the Maison de la Culture in Le

Havre, did not choose the Calderón play that has become part of international repertory but rather the one-act *auto sacramental* of the same name. André Camp enthusiastically proclaimed that Ruiz "a su nous restituer cette oeuvre inspirée" (knew how to restore this inspired work to us) (795: 66).

The interest in the shorter allegorical works of Calderón is paralleled by continuing attention to Cervantes and his brief farces. As we have seen, *Le Retable des merveilles* has enjoyed considerable popularity over the years. In 1983 it was combined successfully with three other *intermèdes* (*entremeses*)—*La Sentinelle vigilante, Le Vieillard jaloux, La Caverne de Salamanque*—in a stage version of J. Jourdheuil and J. F. Peyret. Premiered in Lille in May, the Cervantes production was staged that summer in Avignon and then in the Festival d'Automne in Paris.

As part of Lluís Pasqual's 1992 Hispanic Cycle at the Odéon–Théâtre de l'Europe, already mentioned in the previous chapter, Parisian playgoers had a new opportunity to see Calderón's full-length *La Vie est un songe*. Running from 11 April to 31 May in the 1015-seat theatre, the production was directed by José Luis Gómez, one of Spain's best-known film and theatre actors. The French text, by Céline Zins, was based on the stage version written some dozen years earlier by Alvaro Custodio, José Sanchis Sinisterra, and Gómez. In 1981 Gómez had directed the work for Madrid's municipal Teatro Español, playing the lead role himself. For Spanish critics Gómez's Segismundo reminded them of Hamlet, and they found unexpected moments of comic relief. Of special note was the single, relatively bare stage set, with its innovative lighting effects that emphasized Calderon's astrology theme. Gómez's French staging, which played to enthusiastic full houses, retained elements from his earlier, nontraditional interpretation of the Golden Age masterpiece.

Pasqual, like Camus and Lorca before him, decided to give Lope de Vega equal prominence with Calderón. The work he chose to premiere at Avignon in 1992, as part of the festival's Hispanic emphasis for the Quincentennial, was *Le Chevalier d'Olmedo*. A new French translation, by the poet

Zéno Bianu, was described by the Odéon's press release as being more faithful than Camus's in rendering the variations in meter and tone that underscore changes in dramatic situation. Following the summer festival, Lope's cloak-and-sword comedy was to tour Barcelona and two French cities, Le Havre, and Clermont-Ferrand, before a November-December run in Paris. At least for the Odéon's public relations staff the Lorca myth has not died: their release carefully notes that *La Vie est un songe* and *Le Chevalier d'Olmedo* were the only two classic Spanish plays to be performed by Lorca's touring company, La Barraca.

If in the case of Calderón we may speak of the dramatist's integration into the French stage, with Fernando de Rojas we may speak of only one work: *La Celestina*, 1499. In his separate study of J. Gillibert's 1972 adaptation, Torres Monreal indicates that the first French-language staging of the pre-Golden Age masterpiece was that of Camus in Algeria in 1936 ("La Célestine" 765). In the manifesto for his Théâtre de l'Equipe, Camus indicated that, in seeking to express truth, simplicity, violence in feeling, and cruelty in action, the troupe would turn to such playwrights as Rojas, Calderón, and Cervantes (Lottman 166). Camus himself played Calixte in the production. Coincidentally, Casarès in her autobiography reveals that one of her first stage roles was also in *La Célestine;* in 1942, at the age of nineteen, she played one of the secondary roles (Casarès 186). Thirty years later, in the Gillibert production at the Festival de Châteauvallon, she headed the cast.

Torres Monreal describes Gillibert's modernization as a "mythical interpretation" of the work and reports that from Châteauvallon it went on tour throughout France, Belgium, and Switzerland, reaching hundreds of thousands of spectators ("La Célestine" 766). Critic Guy Dumur of *Le Nouvel Observateur* attributed much of the success of the liberating, frenetic, violent production to Casarès—"au triple galop"—and wondered if her being Spanish had helped (qtd. Torres Monreal, "La Célestine" 767). The Gillibert version skillfully blended "the magic of a sacred ritual" with a crude vision of a world in disorder (Torres Monreal, "La Célestine" 776).

Germaine Kerjean as Bernarda in Lorca's *La Maison de Bernarda*, 1945–46. Directed by Maurice Jacquemont at Studio des Champs Elysées, Paris. (Photo by Agence de Presse Bernand; courtesy of *L'Avant-Scène Théâtre*)

The version of *La Célestine* that reached the Comédie Française in 1975 was a new, controversial one by Pierre Laville. Directed by Marcel Maréchal with Denise Gence in the title role, the production aroused a violently mixed reaction among critics and spectators, some of whom complained in writing to the management that the play was "garbage" and "an embarrassment." *L'Avant-Scène Théâtre* responded by printing the text and dedicating part of an issue to "la bataille de *La Célestine*." Jean-Jacques Gautier, writing in *Le Figaro*, labeled the performance "disturbing, rather stupid, a bit scandalous, and revolting, indefensible" (*L'Avant-Scène* 566: 6). Pierre Dux, director of the Comédie

Domitilia Amaral and Genicia Athanasiou in García Lorca's *Yerma*, 1954, Théâtre de la Huchette. Directed by Guy Suarès. (Photo by Bernand; courtesy of *L'Avant-Scène Théâtre*)

Française, defended it as "a grand ceremony from the lower depths, an exaltation of life, of the senses, of pleasure, against morality and misery" (*L'Avant-Scène* 566: 7). The excerpts of criticism selected for publication after the text, however, were all favorable, highlighting its subversive,

Amour de Don Perlimplin, by García Lorca. Directed by Bernard Jenny at Théâtre Lutèce, Paris, 1957. (Photo by Bernand; courtesy of *L'Avant-Scène Théâtre*)

Laurent Terzieff and Jean-Marie Serreau in García Lorca's *Lorsque cinq ans seront passés.* Théâtre Recamier, Paris, 1958. Directed by Guy Suarès. (Photo by Bernand; courtesy of *L'Avant-Scène Théâtre*)

baroque aspects. For Dominique Jamet of *L'Aurore*, the production was "remarkable work" and the text, exceptionally beautiful. Gilbert Chateau of the *Nouvelle Revue Française* called it "one of the ten most important plays in 30 years of theatre" and found Gence's Célestine to be "shocking, tortured, infinitely touching" (*L'Avant-Scène* 566: 46). Philippe Tesson of *Le Canard Enchaîné* questioned if such a grand, baroque expression of love, liberty, and life was rejected by the snobbery of some spectators because it defied the rules of classic theatre and was "not truly French" (*L'Avant-Scène* 566: 45). Given the decibel level of the debate, it is indeed surprising that this Spanish play at least does not appear in Dort's book covering the 1970s.

Fernando Rojas's text was again revived in 1989 by the late Antoine Vitez, director of the Comédie Française. His production, using a new translation by Florence Delay, ran the full four and a half hours. Starring the celebrated actress Jeanne Moreau, Vitez's *La Célestine* was featured at the annual Avignon festival and scheduled for the Odéon National Theatre in Paris the following fall. In the meantime, its summer tour included Barcelona. In Spain, Moisés Pérez Coterillo considered Moreau's performance to be magnificent—brilliant and passionate enough to make the long evening in the theatre worthwhile. But, like the French critics he cites in his own review, Pérez Coterillo found Vitez's version defective. Yannis Kokkos's set design of labyrinthian stairways was too metaphysical, and the director had failed to integrate the parodic aspects of the Spanish work (Pérez Coterillo *El Público*: 70–71: 8–9). Vitez not only did not repeat the scandalous approach of Laville but was accused by French critics of being too conservative. Writing for *Le Figaro*, Pierre Marcabru found this *Célestine* lacking in liberty: "Mephistopheles has stayed home. Vitez closed the door on him" (qtd. Pérez Coterillo *El Público* 70–71: 9). The revival, apart from Moreau's portrayal of the title character, was not successful, but Vitez's recognition of *La Celestina* as one of the masterworks of the world stage nevertheless represents a significant moment in the history of Spanish theatre in France.

Surprising as it is that Dort overlooked *La Célestine*, it would be even more difficult for anyone to ignore Federico García Lorca (1898–1936) in a discussion of the postwar French stage. His popularity for two decades starting in 1945, when *La Maison de Bernarda* (Jean-Marie Créach's translation of *La casa de Bernarda Alba*) was the biggest hit of the Paris theatrical season, led Torres Monreal to speak of "the Lorca myth in France," a myth based in part on a misinformed version of the poet and playwright's tragic death. But Torres Monreal also concluded that the myth was fading and that Lorca was being staged less and less in France—by the 1970s, hardly at all. His own listing of productions in Paris and the provinces includes thirty-two for Lorca in the period 1945–1959 and only eighteen from 1960 to 1973. Felicia Hardison Londré, in her analysis of the fifty-year production history of Lorca in France—from *Noces de sang* (*Bodas de sangre*) in 1938 to *Le Public* and *La Savetière prodigieuse* (*El público* and *La zapatera prodigiosa*) in 1988—similarly concludes that French interest in Lorca reached its peak in the 1960s. On the Paris stage, where four Lorca plays ran simultaneously in 1963–64, that is doubtless true. But for the provinces, at least on the surface, both of these conclusions are at odds with data provided by the Sociedad General de Autores de España (SGAE).

Based on information from the SGAE, the late Francisco Alvaro regularly published in his theatre annual, *El espectador y la crítica*, a list by country of Spanish plays staged abroad. The list, of course, could include only productions for which performance rights had been requested, and Alvaro never indicated if there had been multiple requests for the same play or where the play had been performed. The SGAE records do not reveal whether any particular production was to be done in the original Spanish or in translation. Accordingly, stagings in French are intermingled with Spanish-language productions at international summer festivals, in university-based theatres, or elsewhere. The data in *El espectador y la crítica* therefore provide only a general sense rather than an accurate picture of a particular playwright's impact in another country. The pattern with Lorca, however, is quite clear: year after year his works continue to be staged north of the Pyrenees.

For 1973, the last year of his study, Torres Monreal lists only one Lorca production in France (one inspired by *El poeta en Nueva York*). By contrast, Alvaro cites seven Lorca plays that year: *Bodas de sangre, El retablillo de don Cristóbal, La casa de Bernarda Alba, La zapatera prodigiosa, Los títeres de Cachiporra, Mariana Pineda,* and *Yerma.* For the period 1973–1985, Alvaro lists stagings of ten different texts, the others being *Así que pasen cinco años, Doña Rosita la soltera,* and *El maleficio de la mariposa.* The frequency of performance of these plays naturally varies. At the top are *La zapatera prodigiosa,* listed by Alvaro for twelve of the thirteen years,

A puppet staging of García Lorca's *Le Petit retable de Don Cristobal,*
Alliance Française, 1960. Les Marionnettes d'Alain Recoing. (Photo by
Bernand; courtesy of *L'Avant-Scène Théâtre*)

and *La casa de Bernarda Alba,* cited for eleven years. At the
bottom is *El maleficio de la mariposa,* listed only three times,
starting in 1981. The range of citations for the other seven
plays is from nine to five years.

As mentioned above, Alvaro's lists do not take into
account multiple productions during a given year. Supple-
mentary information provided by SGAE indicates that
some of Lorca's plays may enjoy amazing popularity in
France. For example, in 1983 there were productions of
Bodas de sangre in no fewer than seven cities. The staging in

Revival of *Le Petit retable de Don Cristobal*, by García Lorca. Théâtre de Plaisance, 1968. Directed by Jean Collomb. (Photo by Bernand; courtesy of *L'Avant-Scène Théâtre*)

April 1981 of *El maleficio de la mariposa*, Lorca's first play, was followed by a second in May of that year and four more stagings in 1982 (January, April, and two in December). While it is possible that the same troupe took the play on tour (the cities where *El maleficio de la mariposa* was performed were Ollioules, Montpellier, Toulouse, Pau, Nîmes, and Béziers, all in the south), the repeated stagings certainly suggest that the play was far better received in France in the 1980s than it had been in Madrid in 1920.

Although one cannot discount the possibility that at least some of the many Lorca productions found in SGAE records were Spanish-language ones, all of these Lorca texts are readily available in French translation. Indeed the January 1987 catalog of the Librairie Théâtrale in Paris lists his complete theatre in four volumes (fifteen titles), along with several separate play editions. The theatre bookstore's own series, "Collection Éducation et Théâtre," includes *Le Petit rétable de Don Cristobal*, translated by André Camp; *Don Perlimplin*, translated by Jean Camp (André's father); and *La Savetière prodigieuse*, translated by Mathilde Pomès. Additionally, the 1970 special Lorca issue of *L'Avant-Scène Théâtre*—which contains *La Maison de Bernarda Alba*, newly translated by André Belamich, along with *Le Petit retable de Don Cristobal* and a wealth of information on Lorca and French stagings of his plays—is still in print.

Nor are all Spanish-language productions in France necessarily without impact on the French stage. Víctor García—along with Jorge Lavelli and Patrice Chéreau, one of the three major directors to emerge through theatre competitions in the 1960s—initially gained recognition for his stagings at the Spanish-language workshop of the Université du Théâtre des Nations in Paris. As mentioned in Chapter 2, his first two productions in France were of Lorca's *El retablillo de don Cristóbal* and Valle-Inclán's *La rosa de papel*. In a 1984 issue of *Les Voies de la Création Théâtrale*, dedicated to García's memory, Monique Monory recalls in glowing terms the creativity of those stagings: the visual impact of the Lorca play, with its tragic image surfacing in the final scene of the comedy (Monory 114), and the "transfigured and purified vision" of the dark forces underscoring the baroque theatre of Valle-Inclán (Monory 122).

A decade later, the García-Nuria Espert version of *Yerma*—on a trampoline—caused a sensation at the Théâtre de la Ville. The Lorca tragedy had been previously staged in Paris to much acclaim in 1948 and 1954, and, less successfully, in 1964. According to Odette Aslan, it was García, with his "prodigious vision of the plastic aspects of the theatre," who restored to *Yerma* its status as masterpiece (Aslan 1977: 29). Raymonde Temkine, who also labels it a masterpiece, first discovered the García-Espert production in Barcelona and recalls seeing it again with joy in Paris, when it arrived there during its four-year international tour

(Temkine 1: 42). In 1980 Jorge Lavelli collaborated with Espert in creating a Chekhovian staging of Lorca's *Doña Rosita la soltera*. Following a long run in Madrid, the play made an extensive tour throughout Europe, always in the original Spanish; according to Lavelli, the language of the text was no barrier to reaching a wide audience (Telephone interview). The importance of Lluís Pasqual's staging of *El público* at the Théâtre de l'Europe in 1988 is also quite clear: it was awarded the French Critics' prize for the best foreign-language production of the year, and Pasqual was subsequently named to the directorship of the prestigious theatre.

Londré believes that the popularity of Lorca's theatre in France is unquestionable although the approach to take in producing his works for a French audience has been the subject of considerable debate. She defines the opposing tendencies as stylized abstraction and *espagnolade*. The former approach has generally received the approval of the critics while the latter, emphasizing a "tourist-bureau vision of Spain," has often been more successful at the box office (Londré 1988). García and Lavelli, Hispanics themselves, have avoided the gratuitous addition of flamenco dancers and Andalusian folklore to their stagings of Spanish texts. In this regard, the parodic intent of Manet's metaplay based on Alarcón's *Las paredes oyen* is of interest. The Hispanic playwright-within-the-play protests loudly when the French director inserts a bullfight scene in his comedy. (Manet's version of the Golden Age text is discussed in Chapter 6.)

In her analysis of the three Lorca productions in Paris early in 1988, Londré points out that director Jacques Nichet found an appropriate balance between the use of Spanish guitars for choral effect and a "spare, earthen, ochre and brown setting" in staging *La Savetière prodigieuse,* and that both Jorge Lavelli's French version and Lluís Pasqual's Spanish version of *El público* avoided the extremes of either *espagnolade* or facile abstraction. A divided critical response to the Lavelli production notwithstanding, Londré finds in these three stagings a positive sign "that French theatre has begun at last to explore a greater range of possibilities in interpreting Lorca" (Londré 1988).

La zapatera prodigiosa, Lorca's "violent farce in two acts" has had a prodigious performance record in France, starting in 1951. Marie Laffranque asserts that *La Savetière* is practically always on stage (Laffranque 21). Nichet's production, 5–23 January 1988 at Paris's municipal Théâtre de la Ville, was a revival of his successful staging in 1986 at the Théâtre des Treize Vents (Centre Dramatique National Languedoc Roussillon). Critic Danielle Dumas's reaction in her column for *L'Avant-Scène Théâtre* to the Paris performance was typical: "A ne manquer sous aucun prétexte" (Don't miss no matter what). Nichet had chosen the Lorca text for his inaugural production as artistic director at Treize Vents, affirming that the French theatre should look to Spain and its Mediterranean cultural heritage, not just to the United States, England, and Germany: "What good is it to play Shakespeare if we forget Cervantes, Lope de Vega, Calderón?" (qtd. Londré 1988).

Nichet had previously directed the Aquarium, a theatre first connected to the Ecole Normale Supérieure in Paris and then housed, like the Théâtre du Soleil, at the Cartoucherie de Vincennes. When he assumed the direction of the Aquarium in 1965, he developed an interest in technical experimentation and modern adaptations of the classics (J. G. Miller 116). Among his early choices of texts was Lorca's *Amour de Don Perlimplin.* When the journal *Théâtre à Toulouse et ailleurs . . .* in its second year of existence decided to change its format and initiate a series devoted to particular playwrights, the first writer highlighted was Lorca. Nichet was a guest editor for the 1986 issue, which coincided with the fiftieth anniversary of Lorca's death.

Jorge Lavelli, too, chose a Lorca text for his January 1988 inaugural production as director of the new Théâtre National de la Colline. The choice was, in many ways, a daring one. *El público* is a complex, surrealistic, metatheatrical defense of nontraditional theatre and homosexual love. The author considered it unstageable, and his incomplete manuscript was not published until forty years after his death. In assessing the mixed critical response to Lavelli's production, the Spanish critic Moisés Pérez Coterillo is doubtless correct that for French spectators, accustomed to a theatre that has become progressively more conservative, Lorca's *Le Public* must have seemed like a throwback to the wild 1960s (Pérez Coterillo, *El Público* 52: 5). Three months later, however, Pasqual's Spanish production (premiered at the Piccolo in Milan in 1986 and then performed at the Centro Dramático Nacional in Madrid) was received enthusiastically. André Camp, who preferred Pasqual's version to Lavelli's, anticipated the Critics' Prize by declaring it to be the best play done in a foreign language at the Théâtre de l'Europe in Paris that season (A. Camp, *L'Avant-Scène Théâtre* 834: 46).

These three productions of Lorca in 1988, two of them simultaneously in major theatres, belie Torres Monreal's concern fifteen years earlier that Lorca was disappearing from the French stage. He is still staged frequently in France, and, moreover, the texts chosen range from his most popular to ones Lorca himself thought could never be done: *El público, Así que pasen cinco años*, and *Comedia sin título*. Even this last work, which does not appear in Alvaro's list, was successfully "exhumed" by director Antoine Bourseiller at the small auditorium of the Théâtre Montparnasse in the 1979–80 season. In praising the production, Camp observes that actor Denis Llorca (previously mentioned here for his controversial staging of *Le Cid*) bore a striking physical resemblance to Lorca himself (*L'Avant-Scène Théâtre* 663: 42). Not only does the memory of Lorca's image remain alive in France, but Pasqual chose this same unstageable play to inaugurate his first season at the helm of the Théâtre de l'Europe. The revival of *Comedia sin título* in the fall of 1990 was of a new translation, by Claude Demarigny.

The theatre of Ramón de Valle-Inclán, considered by some to be Spain's greatest modern playwright, has not yet achieved anything resembling Lorca's acceptance in France, although that potential has been there for decades and may soon be realized through the efforts of Lavelli and Pasqual. To be sure, Valle's theatrical fortunes were not great even in Spain during his lifetime and for a quarter century after his death. His most innovative plays, the expressionistic *esperpentos* (grotesque tragicomedies), were thought to be unperformable, and his biting satire of official Spain and traditional "morality" put him at odds with government censors. *Los cuernos de don Friolera,* ostensibly an insult to the honor of military men, was not allowed on the Spanish stage in an unexpurgated version until after Franco's death. The French production of Robert Marrast's translation, *Les Cornes de Don Sapristi* (in Bordeaux in February 1955, followed by a Paris staging that May), came several years earlier than the Spanish production in 1959 of a censored, and hence hornless, *Don Friolera. Divinas palabras* was not revived in postwar Spain until 1961; in Paris it was done at the Théâtre des Mathurins to great acclaim in 1946. (That production, starring Germaine Montero—a French actress closely identified with performances of Lorca—shifted the ambience from Galicia to Andalusia, thus exploiting a certain *espagnolade*.) Similarly *Lumières de Bohême* was seen in Paris in 1963, eight years before *Luces de bohemia* reached Madrid audiences.

Although Valle-Inclán has not yet enjoyed the popularity of Lorca in France, 1963 was his year, too, in Paris. In March, within the space of ten days, two of his key works opened at major playhouses. Directed by Roger Blin (1907–1984), one of France's foremost directors of avant-garde theatre, *Divines paroles* was staged at the Odéon with a stellar cast: Jean-Louis Barrault as Septimo Miaou, Catherine Sauvage as Mari-Gaila, and Blin himself as Pedro Gailo. Eschewing *espagnolade,* Blin visited Galicia, discovering affinities between that region and France's Bretagne. Vilar's Théâtre National Populaire featured *Lumières de Bohême,* directed by Georges Wilson, who also played the lead role of Max Etoile. Critic Emile Copfermann describes the latter as an "atrocious yet funny picture of a cruel society, of brillant but starving human beings" (Copfermann 183). Supportive, as always, of Hispanic theatre, *L'Avant-Scène Théâtre* printed playwright Jeannine Worms's translation of *Lumières de Bohême* and dedicated an issue to the two productions. Of the five "plays of the month" chosen for photo reviews in a spring 1963 issue of *Paris Théâtre*, three were Spanish: Lorca's *Noces de sang*, starring Germaine Montero as the mother, and the two Valle-Inclán plays.

If there is one adjective used to characterize the Hispanic presence on the French stage, it is "baroque." Calderón is so labeled, with historical accuracy, but so are contemporary directors, like García and Lavelli, and modern authors, like Arrabal and Valle-Inclán. "Baroque" as a term is a double-edged sword whether it applies to the performance text or the dramatic text, for while it encompasses what some theatre professionals in France have creatively sought in their stagings, it also stands poles apart from the conventions of French classicism. Guérin includes Lavelli (along with Chéreau, Daniel Mesguich, and Ariane Mnouchkine) as one of four "star directors" but deplores their baroque stage for its "expense, waste, display, ostentation, and excess" (Guérin 31). Blin chose to direct Manet's *Les Nonnes* and *Lady Strass* precisely because the Cuban playwright reflected an extravagant, irrational baroque tendency that Blin found to be Hispanic, not French; but for critic Béatrix Andrade, that same tendency lay beyond European good taste (qtd. in *L'Avant-Scène Théâtre* 613: 31). The essential dichotomy is not far removed from what Casarès pinpointed in her autobiography as her initial sense of alienation in France, a country so geographically close to her native Spain and yet so different, so strange. It was through her friendship with Camus that she finally perceived the secret of the French soul: "the madness of this country consists precisely in rejecting all madness" (Casarès 239). The Hispanic baroque lays bare the excesses, the contradictory forces, the melding of the tragic and the grotesque in the same human condition that French classicism attempts to approach through reason and proper form.

Quite appropriately, the title for Jean Camp's contribution to the 1963 *L'Avant-Scène* issue on Valle-Inclán identifies the Spanish author as the "prince of a sumptuous, baroque art" (J. Camp 8). And therein lies the dilemma. The baroque art of Valle-Inclán includes both the stage directions, which require a cinematic mise-en-scène far removed from the single stage set of the well-made bourgeois drama,

Revival of Valle-Inclán's *Divines paroles* at Bayonne Festival, 1989. Directed and adapted by Jean Marie Broucaret. (Photo by Pierre Jean Soler; courtesy of *L'Avant-Scène Théâtre*)

and the dialogue, written in a rich language that defies easy translation. Lavelli, who is known for the "sumptuous, baroque art" of his stagings, notes that the real challenge with Calderón and Lorca, as well as with Valle-Inclán, comes in recreating the language of the dramatic texts (Lavelli, *Primer Acto* 184: 68). Of the two 1963 productions of Valle in Paris, *Lumières de Bohême* was well received, but *Divines paroles* was a failure. Although Marrast had distinguished himself with versions of other Spanish plays, his translation of *Divines paroles* was a major cause of that failure. Torres Monreal wonders why a new translation had been done at all, given that Maurice Coindreau's text for the same play had proven so successful in the 1940s (Diss. 2: 520).

The problem with Blin's *Divines paroles* may also be related to his desire to place the text in the author's native Galicia. In his review of reception to Valle-Inclán's theatre in France and Belgium, Rodolphe Stembert cites Jacques

Lemarchand's comparison of the 1946 and 1963 productions. Lemarchand, critic for *Le Figaro littéraire*, recalled with approval the "blinding sun" and "overwhelming heat" of Marcel Herrand's earlier staging, elements he considered in keeping with the violent action and Galician setting; in contrast, he was unmoved by the twilight and shadow and the "Norwegian" appearance of André Acquart's set (qtd. Stembert 272–273). Blin, of course, was striving for a Celtic atmosphere: the mists of Galicia that give rise to the superstitions that underscore Valle-Inclán's vision of his native region. Doubtless Lemarchand was not alone in erroneously believing that all of Spain is bathed in Andalusian sunlight.

Even a brilliant translation cannot compensate for differences in taste. French avant-garde playwright Arthur Adamov (1908–1970) affirmed that he was generally not moved by the poetic yet violent language that for him characterized most of the great modern Spanish dramatists, although he conceded that Valle-Inclán's language was truer and less literary than Lorca's (Adamov 57). On the other hand, he remembered being stunned by the 1946 production of *Divines paroles* because he found there a theatre of cruelty and ritual, associated in France with Artaud, that he sought in his own works (Adamov 56). That kind of theatre, however, even if it has exponents in France, can run counter to French "good taste." Renée Saurel, in her favorable reaction to both 1963 *esperpentos*, recounts that many Parisian spectators were offended by what they perceived to be violent, repugnant monstrosities, well within the deforming aesthetics of a Goya, a Buñuel or a Picasso, but diametrically opposed to the French love of moderation (Saurel 95).

Considering the difficulty of translating Valle-Inclán's creative language, it is not surprising that a substantial part of the dramatist's visibility in France has come through Spanish-language productions. There are at least four of these worth noting. Víctor García's *La rosa de papel*, staged in the Spanish-language workshop of the Université du Théâtre des Nations, came just a year after Roger Blin and Georges Wilson brought Valle-Inclán's *Divines paroles* and

Lumières de Bohême to the attention of Parisian playgoers. At the invitation of Jean-Marie Serreau, García participated in "Estival 64" with Lorca's *El retablillo de don Cristóbal* and the Valle text, both of which achieve a dehumanized vision of life by building upon puppet theatre. *La rosa de papel*, part of Valle-Inclán's *Retablo de la avaricia, la lujuria y la muerte*, along with Beckett's *Comédie*, was the summer festival's offering that most impressed spectators and critics alike. According to Monory, part of that success came from García's ability to transfigure and hence "purify" the obscure forces unleashed by a baroque theatre (Monory 122). The García production of the Lorca and Valle plays toured Europe and participated in various international festivals through 1969.

It was also in 1964, when García created his *La rosa de papel*, that the Mexican troupe, Compañía de Teatro Universitario de México, brought a decidedly baroque staging of *Divinas palabras* to the festival at Nancy and won first prize in that international competition. Ricardo Domenech, in his enthusiastic review from the festival, reported that the language barrier had been so obliterated that the spectators gave the production a standing ovation. The total spectacle (actors, set, lighting, etc.) was "exuberant," creating a wrenching vision of Valle-Inclán's Galicia (Domenech 1986: 106).

Divinas palabras again played to French audiences in February and March 1976, when the Víctor García-Nuria Espert version ran at the Théâtre National de Chaillot in Paris—even before their tour reached Madrid or Barcelona. The last of their three collaborative efforts, which began with Jean Genet's *Las criadas* (*Les Bonnes*) in 1969 and Lorca's *Yerma* in 1971, it was awaited with eager anticipation. Writing in *Le Monde,* Colette Godard affirmed that Paris had discovered Espert in 1970 and loved her, and that García-Espert were known for their "brilliant successes." This version of *Divinas palabras* has become as closely identified with its use of suggestive organ pipes and trumpets as *Yerma* was with the trampoline. It toured for some two years throughout Europe and North America and received enthusiastic responses virtually everywhere except Madrid.

Stembert, who personally thought that García's visual effects regrettably overshadowed Valle's dramatic text, notes that several Parisian critics compared the staging to a carefully choreographed ballet or opera (Stembert 274).

The fourth major Spanish-language production of Valle-Inclán in France came in 1984, with the opening season of the Théâtre de l'Europe in Paris. Lluís Pasqual's long association with Georgio Strehler of the Piccolo in Milan has facilitated Spanish involvement in European theatre. He and the Centro Dramático Nacional, which he directed in Madrid, were invited to coproduce Valle's *Luces de bohemia* with the Théâtre de l'Europe. The highly acclaimed production opened in Paris eight months before it reached the Madrid stage in October and was featured in the second issue of *Théâtre en Europe,* a journal published in Paris in conjunction with the Théâtre de l'Europe. Although André Camp thought the episodic *Luces de bohemia* would be hard to follow if one did not know Spanish and Spanish history (*L'Avant-Scène Théâtre* 749: 48), there can be little doubt that Pasqual's staging was viewed favorably in the theatrical world. Pasqual subsequently received repeated invitations to stage works in France, and his national María Guerrero Theatre in Madrid was named a participating center in the Théâtre de l'Europe.

Francisco Alvaro's listings of Spanish plays staged abroad do not reveal large numbers of productions in France of Valle-Inclán as they do for Lorca or Casona. There are only nine entries for the thirteen-year period 1973–1985, and two of those are García's *Divinas palabras,* 1976, and Pasqual's *Luces de bohemia,* 1984. There is a reported 1983 production of *Divinas palabras* and a 1979 one of *Flor de santidad,* an early novel, published in 1904, that apparently was specially adapted for that production. The remaining five stagings are of two short plays—*Farsa infantil de la cabeza del dragón,* 1977 and 1979, and *Ligazón,* 1973, 1976, and 1977. The former text, from Valle's *Tablado de marionetas,* is readily available in French translation; it is listed both in a separate edition (*Farce enfantine de la tête du dragon*) and as part of a collection (*Treteau de marionnettes*) in the Libraire Théâtrale catalog. The latter text, like *La rosa de papel,*

Maria Casarès and Isabel Karajan, *Comédies barbares,* by Valle-Inclán. Directed by Jorge Lavelli, 1991. (Photo by Lot; courtesy of Théâtre National de la Colline)

Luc-Antoine Diguero in *Comédies barbares,* by Valle-Inclán, at Avignon, 1991. Directed by Jorge Lavelli. (Photo by Brigitte Enguerand; courtesy of Théâtre National de la Colline)

belongs to Valle's *Retablo de la avaricia, la lujuria y la muerte;* titled *Lien de sang* in French, it was published in *L'Avant-Scène Théâtre* 122. The appeal to amateur or university theatre groups of these one-act plays, like that of the shorter works of Lorca, would be understandable.

Some forty years ago, Jean Camp and Jean Cassou collaborated on a version of Valle-Inclán's *Comedias bárbaras,* creating a synthesis around the character of Juan Manuel Montenegro. Camp affirmed that it had been the unfulfilled dream of Gaston Baty (1885–1952) to stage that work (J. Camp, *L'Avant-Scène Théâtre* 292: 8). Upon assuming the direction of the Théâtre National de la Colline, Jorge Lavelli was widely quoted as having a similar dream of bringing Valle-Inclán's epic trilogy (*Cara de plata, Aguila de blasón,* and *Romance de lobos*) to the French stage. Pasqual, in turn, announced that the key work of his second season at the Théâtre de l'Europe in 1991–92 would be a dramatization of Valle-Inclán's novel *Tirano Banderas* (*El País* 19 March 1990: 18).

By July 1991, Lavelli had already made good his promise. His staging of Valle-Inclán's *Comédies barbares,* translated to French by the Spanish-born playwright Armando Llamas, opened at the annual Avignon festival and was scheduled for an extended run in Paris from 20 October 1991 to 19 January 1992. In his promotional literature, Lavelli described Valle-Inclán's grotesque vision of the decaying feudal order in nineteenth-century Galicia as a reflection of human destiny, on a par with the works of Shakespeare. Included in the cast was Maria Casarès, who, back in 1964 in Buenos Aires, had played in *Divinas palabras*, under Lavelli's direction. At the Colline, Lavelli offered the spectators two options: seeing the trilogy in its full six and a half hours or divided in two parts, presented on consecutive evenings. Given the prestige of the director and his theatre, there can be no question that this landmark production will make contemporary French audiences aware of Spain's great playwright of the twentieth century.

It should be noted that Lavelli's affinity for Spanish texts is a natural one. Alfredo Rodríguez Arias, a fellow Argentinian

Valle-Inclán's *Comédies barbares,* at Avignon festival, 1991. Directed by Jorge Lavelli. (Photo by Marc Enguerand; courtesy of Théâtre National de la Colline)

who directs the national dramatic center in Aubervilliers, has expressed the issue quite clearly: "What is certain is that there is a tradition of very strong cultural ties between Argentina and Latin Europe. After all, I have Spanish blood in my veins" (qtd. Méreuze *El Público* 30: 51). Arias himself, after twenty years of voluntary exile in Paris, working in French, felt the need to recover his native Spanish and explore the different sensibilities evoked by the two languages. He was pleased to accept an invitation to direct the 1988 inaugural production for the regional dramatic center of Valencia, and chose Valle-Inclán's *La marquesa Rosalinda*. His staging was featured as the cover story for *El Público* and prompted a monograph on Latin American directors in Europe for the *Cuadernos El Público* series. *El Público* editor Pérez Coterillo labeled Arias's version of *La marquesa Rosalinda* an extraordinary spectacle of rare perfection that revealed the text's blinding beauty (Pérez Coterillo *El Público* 54: 4). Arias's participation in Valencia was facilitated by the French Ministry of Foreign Affairs, which has been fostering personal cultural exchanges between France and Spain. Pérez Coterillo observed that Arias's French connection made him a particularly appropriate director of Valle-Inclán's transitional text that, while suggesting the grotesque *esperpentos* that were to come, was inspired by eighteenth-century models, notably Marivaux.[3]

In his analysis of why certain Spanish playwrights reached the French stage in the postwar period, Torres Monreal conjectures that the image of the author was often a significant factor. The myth of Lorca was based on his status as martyr. Exiled authors, like Alejandro Casona (pseudonym of Alejandro Rodríguez Alvarez, 1903–1965) and Rafael Alberti (b. 1902), therefore appealed to impresarios who saw in them the progressive forces opposing the Franco regime. For Torres Monreal, this factor would explain the "incomprehensible penetration" of Casona in the French theatre. But in Casona's case, the exile myth did not coincide with the ideological content of his works. Thus when he returned to Spain from Argentina in the early 1960s, "the myth fell from the pedestal and no one in France paid any more attention to him" (Torres Monreal, *El teatro español en Francia* 8–9). The lists of productions in his dissertation would support Torres Monreal's assertion, but data from the SGAE tell a very different story.

The first Casona play done in France was *Notre Natache* (*Nuestra Natacha*) in 1944 at the Théâtre La Bruyère in Paris. *La Dame de l'aube* (*La dama del alba*) followed in 1948 at the Théâtre Gaîté–Montparnasse; it is worth noting that this was a text written in exile and premiered in Buenos Aires only four years before. In 1952 *La Barque sans pêcheur* (*La barca sin pescador*) was staged in Monte Carlo. All three of these versions were by Jean Camp, whose translations of Lorca texts were also being staged during the same period. Torres Monreal cites an amateur revival of *La Barque sans pêcheur* in the mid-1950s and a staging of *Inès de Portugal*, translated by André Camp, at the Festival de Bellac in 1964. After that, according to his data, Casona was heard from no more. On the other hand, Francisco Alvaro's annual lists of Spanish plays in foreign countries indicate that Casona is regularly staged in Latin America and throughout Europe and, in fact, has become part of international repertory. Under "France" for the thirteen-year period 1973–1985, Alvaro had seventy-two entries for Lorca and fifty-three for Casona. He cited productions in twelve of those years for *La barca sin pescador* and in eleven for *La fablilla del secreto bien guardado*, putting them at an equal frequency of performance with Lorca's *La zapatera prodigiosa* and *La casa de Bernarda Alba*. In all, Alvaro noted productions in France for eleven different plays by Casona. The others with entries for six or more years include *La dama del alba*, *La molinera de Arcos*, and *El mancebo que casó con mujer brava*.

As previously noted, SGAE data do not indicate if a play was done in Spanish or in translation. French translations, however, are readily available for all five of these frequently performed titles; they are among six Casona texts in the 1987 Librairie Théâtrale catalog. Of the ten Spanish plays available in the Librairie Théâtrale's own "Collection Education et Théâtre," five are by Casona, in translations by Jean or André Camp. Translations for two additional Casona texts were published in *L'Avant-Scène Théâtre;* even though those particular issues are now out of print, the translations could be tracked down by anyone seriously interested in them. The full-length works cited most frequently by Alvaro—*La barca sin pescador* and *La dama del alba*—present idealistic solutions to eternal moral problems and introduce supernatural, folkloric figures (the devil and death) that surely transcend the Pyrenees. Casona's excellent short farces, based on classic literary works, can be compared in their popularity with the *entremeses* of Cervantes or Lorca's short puppet plays.

Again, as with Lorca productions, Alvaro's lists do not give a complete picture of Casona in France. While Alvaro cites the short farce *Cornudo, apaleado y contento* for only three years (1973, 1977, 1978), SGAE data show two productions for 1982 and one each in 1984 and 1985. (The French translation, *Cocu, battu, content*, appeared in No. 75 of *L'Avant-Scène Théâtre*.) For the most popular of the short farces, *La fablilla del secreto bien guardado* (*La Fable du secret bien gardé*), SGAE is aware of no fewer than six stagings in 1982, five in 1983, and four in 1984. It is true that Casona is not being produced in Paris and only rarely appears in major theatre centers (*La barca sin pescador* at Nancy in 1983, for example), but Torres Monreal was incorrect in assuming that Casona had been forgotten in France.

André Camp provides a clarification of Casona's popularity in France (Personal interview 1989). The two major works, *La dama del alba* and *La barca sin pescador* were made into films in France and have been shown on television. Casona's plays were translated while he still lived in exile in Argentina, and until his return to Spain in the 1960s, his royalties, and hence data on performances, were handled by the French authors' society rather than the SGAE. There are several thousand amateur theatre companies belonging to the French federation. Plays published in *L'Avant-Scène Théâtre* and in the Librairie Théâtrale series are readily accessible to them and represent a principal source of texts. As a result, Casona's plays are indeed performed regularly.

Torres Monreal was also in error in believing that Alberti had disappeared from the French stage, although he was clearly not wrong in asserting that the "Alberti myth," launched in parallel to the "Lorca myth," simply did not gel: "The distance from exile to death was immense. The comparisons with Lorca did not help Alberti" (Torres Monreal, *El teatro español en Francia* 47). *El adefesio* (Fr. trans., *Le Repoussoir*, by Robert Marrast) premiered in France, under the direction of André Reybaz, at the 1956 festival in Arras. Following a long tour, it reached Paris, where it received a mixed critical reaction. Torres Monreal attributes its lack of commercial success to a staging that did not exploit the *espagnolade* then in vogue with Lorca (Diss. 2: 539). *Le Trèfle fleuri* (*El trébol florido*, also translated by Marrast), was done by experimental groups in 1958, 1960, and 1964, but evoked some hostile critical responses (Torres Monreal, *El teatro español en Francia* 48).

In his overview of twentieth-century theatre, Paul-Louis Mignon shares Torres Monreal's belief that Alberti and Casona were initially promoted in France for ideological reasons, but he gives a glowing description of Alberti's poetic theatre with its powerful images and disquieting, fantastic beauty (Mignon 1986: 283). His enthusiasm suggests why experimental directors in France have turned again to Alberti texts. Furthermore, his texts are readily available: the recent Librairie Théâtrale catalog includes the L'Arche edition of *Le Repoussoir* and two volumes of his theatre, including six other plays.

Noche de guerra en el museo del Prado, published in 1956 in Buenos Aires, reached the French stage in 1974, in a translation by Alice Gascar. Subtitled an "etching," this play in one act and a prologue draws its characters from paintings in the Prado. The paintings-come-to-life determine to fight off the French invaders in the war of 1808, but the allusions to 1936 are readily apparent. The performance text, filled with intertextual references to art and history, is a highly visual one that lends itself to a nonillusionary, Brechtian staging. Indeed Brecht himself was aware of the manuscript and expressed interest in it shortly before his death. According to Alberti, Pierre Debauche, who had directed *Le Trèfle fleuri* at the Thèâtre Daniel Sorano in Vincennes in 1964, had also planned to stage *Noche de guerra en el museo del Prado;* seeing in the text a protest against any reactionary movement, he had thought to use it as a commentary on the events of May 1968 in Paris

(Bernat 67). Instead it was an actor from Debauche's earlier Alberti production, Pierre Constant, who ultimately directed the French premiere at the Centre Dramatique de la Courneuve. In October 1974 the Courneuve production reached the Théâtre de la Cité Internationale in Paris. Writing in *Travail Théâtral*, Richard Monod did not consider the Courneuve version of Alberti's text to be didactic in a Brechtian sense but found reason to compare the innovative staging to *1793* at the Théâtre du Soleil.

Sylvie Caillaud was aware of the 1974 production when she decided to direct *Nuit de guerre au musée du Prado* during the 1986–87 season of the Théâtre du Nain Jaune, Centre Dramatique d'Issoudun. The text attracted her because of its use of paintings by Goya as an expression of a resistance movement; she knew of no other work with a comparable incorporation of art into theatre (Personal interview). The play opened in the regional theatre in November, and, following a provincial tour, ran 28 April–30 May at the Cité Internationale in Paris. With its fragmented structure and lack of traditional plot and characters, it is definitely not the usual fare of realistic, bourgeois theatre. But Caillaud, through an effective use of slides and the extension of the playing area into the whole auditorium, achieved her goal of creating a total ambience that immersed the audience in the action without requiring previous knowledge of either Spanish art or Spanish history.

A revival of *Le Repoussoir*, in its new version, also reached the French stage in the 1980s. Alberti had revised *El adefesio* for its Spanish premiere in 1976. The cast for the Madrid staging, which came thirty-two years after its original production in Argentina, was headed by Maria Casarès. (For Casarès, who had voluntarily refused to go to Spain while Franco was alive, this was a homecoming after forty years in France. Alberti, as a member of the Communist party, had been officially exiled throughout the Franco years.) The Spanish-Argentine-French connection of this particular text surely did not escape the attention of the Compagnie Persona that staged *Le Repoussoir* 2 May–11 June 1984 at the Théâtre Daniel Sorano in Vincennes. Of the three organizers of the troupe, two (Antonio Arena and Graciela

Cerasi) were born in Argentina and one (Françoise Pertat), in France. The Compagnie Persona announced that it was created precisely for the purpose of developing a cultural interchange between France and Spanish-speaking countries and was to involve the collaboration of French and Hispanic theatre professionals. André Camp confirms that the Théâtre Daniel Sorano for an extended period did produce a series of lesser-known Spanish classic plays and contemporary Latin American works by such authors as Mario Vargas Llosa (Personal interview 1987).

Simultaneous in Paris with the Caillaud staging of Alberti's *Nuit de guerre au musée du Prado* was Marc-Ange Sanz's production of *Wien 38* by Max Aub at the experimental Espace Marais, 24 April–24 May 1987. Aub (1903–1972), like Alberti and Casona, was a Spanish Civil War exile. However, there was no "Aub myth" in the postwar French stage, although André Camp, who knew him personally, had translated some of his work. The son of a French mother and Austrian father, Aub lived in Spain from early childhood and, in his later years, identified himself as a Spanish writer and Mexican citizen. Like Casona, he did return to Spain, but none of his theatre was staged there until after his death. While part of *Los muertos* was performed in French in Quebec in June 1962, the main introduction of Aub to the French-language stage must be attributed to Sanz and his Caprices-Compagnie.

Born in France of Spanish parents, Sanz has maintained a strong interest in his cultural heritage. He discovered a book about Aub while visiting Spain and chose him as the subject of his master's thesis in theatre at the University of Nanterre (Personal interview). Caprices-Compagnie, established in 1983, had previously done Lorca's *Amour de Don Perlimplin* and two other Aub texts: *Le Soupçonneux magnifique*, in 1984, and *Mathilde ou Les morts*, in 1985. *Wien 38* is Sanz's version of a monologue Aub wrote in Paris in 1939. It premiered at the Avignon "Off" festival in the summer of 1986, where it was favorably reviewed by French and Austrian critics. As performed by Anne Legrand, *Wien 38* is a compelling portrait of a lonely, aging widow who has lost everything: her family, her possessions, and her dignity.

She talks to an absent husband, executed at Dachau for being a Jew, and laments the loss of her son, a diplomat killed by the Communists in Barcelona at the outbreak of the Spanish Civil War. The continued relevancy of Aub's text in 1986–87 was underscored by the Waldheim affair in Austria and the Klaus Barbie trial in Lyon, which revived memories of the Holocaust and the atrocities of war. In the fall of 1987, Sanz included in his future plans a French version of Aub's last text, dealing with the Six-Day War.

The recent productions of Alberti and Aub, however imaginative and effective, have not reached the mainstream Parisian stage as Valle-Inclán and Lorca have done. If Lorca stands alone in his generation as a Spanish playwright integrated into the French theatre, Arrabal (b. 1932) unquestionably holds that distinction for the authors born in the 1920s and 1930s. Indeed, since the 1960s his international fame has made him simultaneously the best-known French and Spanish playwright of the contemporary period.

That fame was initially achieved through a series of landmark stagings: *Pique-nique en campagne*, directed by Jean-Marie Serreau at the Théâtre Lutèce in 1959; *Le Cimetière des voitures*, a collage of short plays created by Víctor García for the Dijon festival in 1966; *L'Architecte et l'empereur d'Assyrie*, directed by Jorge Lavelli at the Montparnasse in 1967. Arrabal, who has lived in Paris since the mid-1950s, typically writes his plays in Spanish and then translates them to French with the help of his wife, Luce Moreau. His avant-garde theatre reflects a unique blend of Spanish and French influences: of Cervantes, Quevedo, Goya, Valle-Inclán, and his own experiences in the repressive climate of Franco's Spain on the one hand, and of Breton's surrealism and Artaud's violent theatre of cruelty and ritual on the other. Odette Aslan, in her study of *Le Cimetière des voitures*, has described Arrabal as "an author of 'black masses,' halfway between Sade and Teresa of Avila" (Aslan 1970: 314). His earliest plays, with their strong autobiographical element, and a number of his later texts, written after he was imprisoned briefly in Spain in

1967, are filled with intertextual references to Spanish history and culture.

Arrabal is a prolific writer, of novels and essays as well as drama. By 1987 the collection of his theatre, published by Christian Bourgois, had extended to seventeen volumes including fifty-two titles. Not all of these have yet appeared in Spanish editions, but since Franco's death, Arrabal has become actively involved in the literary and theatrical life of his native land. Among his recent projects is a trilingual (French-Spanish-English) troupe with the potential for productions both across the Pyrenees and across the Atlantic.

The text with which Arrabal entered the repertory of the Comédie Française in 1979–80, *La Tour de Babel*, had its world premiere in 1976 in Belgium, under Arrabal's own direction. The original Spanish version, titled *Oye, patria, mi aflicción*, had been rejected by the censor in 1975 but ultimately opened in Madrid in May 1978. In many ways, it is one of the most "Spanish" of Arrabal's works. The oneiric, sometimes violent, sometimes comic, action of the sixteen scenes takes place in an isolated, termite-infested castle that, in its obvious decadence, stands as a metaphor for Spain. Most of the characters have dual identities, with one of their roles heavily steeped in Hispanic history: Santa Teresa, the Cid, Goya, Zapata, Che Guevara, etc. The actors form tableaux or speak lines rich in intertextuality. For example, the invasion of the castle by a group of beggars recalls Buñuel's *Viridiana*. When the Marquis de Cerralbo identifies himself as "Don Miguel de Cervantes, catholique, laid et sentimental," his choice of adjectives (Catholic, ugly, and sentimental) repeats the description of Valle-Inclán's character, the Marqués de Bradomín. Jacques Toja, director of the Comédie Française, declared during that institution's 300th anniversary year that he wanted the theatre to be open to new works, not just traditional repertory. With *La Tour de Babel*, he obviously put that concept into practice. Lavelli, who directed the production, affirms that it met with great success. He sees no reason that deeply "Spanish" works, like those of Arrabal or Lorca, cannot cross the Pyrenees and be appreciated in other countries (Telephone interview).

Not all of Arrabal's works, however, reveal so clearly his Hispanic roots. Such is the case of *Bréviaire d'amour d'un haltérophile*, which played 15 September–18 October 1987 in the small auditorium of the Théâtre National de l'Odéon. Imaginatively staged under the direction of Saskia Cohen-Tanugi, the murder-mystery farce revolves around an assassin (attractive young woman or transvestite trainer?) who specializes in killing weightlifters. Although *La Traversée de l'Empire* is subtitled *La Guerre des galaxies avec Puerto Rico dans les tranchées*, the text of this science-fiction fantasy blends elements from a variety of time periods and cultures, ranging from medieval to contemporary and from European to Japanese. Coproduced by Spain's Ministerio de la Cultura and directed by Arrabal, *La Traversée de l'Empire* opened in March 1988 in the small auditorium of the Théâtre National de la Colline. (It is interesting to note that of the six plays programmed by Lavelli for his inaugural season, three were by Hispanic authors: the text by Arrabal, *Le Public* by Lorca, and *Une Visite inopportune* by the late Copi, a fellow Argentinian who had also been fully integrated into the French stage.)

Although Arrabal is by far the best-known Spanish playwright of the French stage, he is not the only Spaniard living in France to have become involved in theatre. The great painter Pablo Picasso (1881–1973) collaborated as a set designer on fifteen productions between 1917 and 1962 and also wrote two short surrealistic plays. In 1972 *L'Avant-Scène Théâtre* dedicated its 500th issue to Picasso the dramatist, and published the texts: *Le Désire attrapé par la queue* and *Les quatres petites filles*. The first of these was written in 1941 but not staged until 1967; the other, written in 1947, had its world premiere at the Open Space Theatre in London in 1971.

Le Désire attrapé par la queue did receive a public reading as early as 1944, under the direction of Albert Camus; the actors included Simone de Beauvoir (La Cousine de la Tarte), Jean-Paul Sartre (Le Bout Rond), and Raymond Queneau (L'Oignon). The premiere, almost a quarter of a century later, was scheduled for the fourth Festival de la Libre Expression at Saint-Tropez, but, as it turned out, freedom of expression did not extend to the allegedly pornographic performance. When the mayor of Saint-Tropez prohibited the play, directors Jean-Jacques Lebel and Allan Zion moved their production to neighboring Gassin. Not surprisingly, Picasso's play received international press coverage both before and after the staging. Describing the work as a scenic poem, featuring automatic writing and primitive frenzy, Lebel considered *Le Désire attrapé par la queue* to be an ingenious suggestion of what total theatre might be. The response of critics and spectators was favorable; there was no moral outrage but rather appreciative laughter for a hilarious farce. Nevertheless, the review in *Le Monde* labeled it "Le souffle de la luxure, de la mort, du délire" (The breath of lechery, death, and delirium), terms that readily call to mind the grotesque *esperpentos* of Valle-Inclán (qtd. *L'Avant-Scène Théâtre* 500: 22).

The Spanish presence in the French theatre of the twentieth century involves several generations and a variety of different circumstances, ranging from artists who went to France voluntarily, to political refugees, to the French-born children of Spanish exiles. Picasso, drawn to the art world of Paris, first visited France in 1898. Arrabal, a half century later, left Spain because of the repressive Franco regime and a conservative response to his avant-garde theatre. The actress Maria Casarès (b. 1922) and the author Carlos Semprun-Maura (b. 1926) crossed the Pyrenees with their families in 1936 at the outbreak of the Spanish Civil War and received much of their education in France.

A novelist and essayist, as well as a playwright, Semprun-Maura has written more frequently for radio than for the stage. Nevertheless, his interest in theatre spans several decades, and his plays, while few in number, have been successfully staged by important directors and have been well received by the critics. (His work is discussed more fully in Chapter 8.) Two of his early short works were produced by Jean-Marie and Dominique Serreau, and *L'Avant-Scène Théâtre* published *Sur une plage de l'ouest*, 1959, and *La Salle d'attente*, 1967. Antirealistic, allegorical pieces that relate to surrealism and the Theatre of the Absurd, these one-act texts anticipate Semprun-Maura's first major stage play, *L'Homme couché*. Directed by Laurent Terzieff, who also played the lead role, *L'Homme couché* ran 9 January–9 February 1971 at Le Lucernaire in the Montparnasse section of Paris. The text was subsequently featured in *L'Avant-Scène Théâtre* 474, along with excerpts from reviews, all favorable.

Semprun-Maura's most successful play to date is *Le Bleu de l'eau-de-vie*, which premiered at the Petit Odéon under Jacques Toja's policy of opening the Comédie Française theatres to new works. The director for the 17 November–18 December 1981 production was Roger Blin. The two-actor cast for this psychological tour de force consisted of Maxence Mailfort and Patrick Chesnais. This text, too, was published by *L'Avant-Scène Théâtre*, in number 703, and the selection of accompanying criticism heaped praise upon the actors and went so far as to call the text a masterpiece. The play was revived the following year at the Petit-Montparnasse theatre for a run of several months and was also presented at the Avignon "Off" festival. In November 1990 it was again revived in Paris, this time as an "off" event associated with Ibéral's festival of Hispanic theatre.

Semprun-Maura's stage plays are closely tied in structure and theme to conventions of the contemporary French theatre. To find his Spanish roots, one must look beyond them to his other writings. In the case of José Martín Elizondo (b. 1922) and Agustín Gómez-Arcos (b. 1939), too, their theatre staged in French is not their most significant contribution to cultural interchange between their native and adoptive lands.[4]

Martín Elizondo moved to France in 1947 and, as mentioned in Chapter 2, for many years directed Amigos del Teatro Español, the Spanish theatre group in Toulouse. It was there that he began writing, and ATE began performing his Spanish-language texts in the 1960s. Some of his works have also been translated to French and produced, at times with the support of the city cultural center. His plays performed in Toulouse in French include *Pour la Grèce*, 1970; *La Cène du quatrième monde*, 1975–76; *Les Illuminations*, 1976–77; *Images d'une mise à mort*, 1977–78; *Dalilah et Dalilah*, written in 1979 and staged in 1983. After moving to Fontainebleau in the mid-1980s, he organized an amateur theatre group in that city. In March 1988, they staged his *Sigismond (ou l'ascension des trois petits cochons)* in the Zoo-Théâtre; the translation was by Madeleine Poujol, Martín Elizondo's wife. In 1989, he returned to Spain and established his residence in Madrid.

Martín Elizondo is a proponent of a popular theatre, but one of an expressionistic, experimental bent far removed from realism/naturalism. As a painter himself, he is also committed to creating a visual staging in which art and text merge. He recognizes Valle-Inclán as the key influence on him and the Amigos del Teatro Español. While Spanish history and culture are never far from him, not all of his French-language plays reflect them directly. *Dalilah et Dalilah*, for example, is a delirious yet comic scenic game in which Dalilah and her double, confronted by their problematic situation as women, debate whether to kill Sanson. As the title implies, however, Elizondo's 1988 work draws inspiration from Segismundo, the protagonist of Calderón's *La vida es sueño*. The author describes the text as a play-within-a-play that through its juxtaposition of humor and delirium draws the spectator into a dramatic world where it becomes impossible to distinguish between reality and dream (Personal interview 1988).

Winner of two important theatre prizes in Spain—the Sitges festival in 1979 and Mérida in 1988—Martín Elizondo has nevertheless not been integrated into the Spanish stage. When asked by Angel Berenguer in 1980 how he saw himself within the Spanish theatre and within the French theatre, he responded that he did not see himself at all. His marginal status on both national stages is similar to the situation of Gómez-Arcos, who moved to France in July 1968 and eventually switched from theatre to narrative with considerable success. Since 1974 he has been writing directly in French and now considers himself a French novelist of Spanish nationality.

Gómez-Arcos's move to France came several years after the Madrid staging of his *Diálogos de la herejía* was greeted with controversy. In Spain his involvement in theatre had included both his original works and his translations of

French plays, notably Jean Giraudoux's *La Folle de Chaillot* and *Intermezzo*. In France, he turned initially to cafe-theatre. Starting in February 1969, two of his short plays ran for seventy-one performances at the Café-Théâtre de l'Odéon. Translated to French by Rachel Salik, who also appeared in the cast, they were directed by the author. Raymond Gérome, in a preface to the *L'Avant-Scène Théâtre* edition of one of them, *Pré-Papa*, confesses a general disillusionment with cafe-theatre and says he thought he had no desire or need to go to the performance. But, he declares, in this case he was wrong. He was delighted by the two plays and determined that Gómez-Arcos—ferocious, idealistic, and irreverent—was a true dramatist as well as an excellent director (Gérome 37). Torres Monreal does not include Gómez-Arcos in his list of 1969 plays but does note a revival of *Et si l'on aboyait?* and *Pré-Papa* at the same cafe-theatre in 1972–73, under the direction of A. Duque.

In *Pré-Papa*, Gómez-Arcos combines comic fantasy with biting satire. The title refers to a pregnant man who, abandoned by his indignant wife and condemned by the fanatically pious Adèle, is urged by the Professor to give birth to his motherless child in space and thus start a new race that will be taught the opposite of all that he has seen on earth. In the dramatic world, what he has seen is already incongruous enough. The "ill" husband and his wife have been waiting in a doctor's office where Adèle is kneeling in confession and the Professor is giving a lofty speech. No doubt as further deliberate sex-role reversals—for the time when the play was written—the solicitous Nurse is a man and the Professor is a woman.

Gómez-Arcos's other published play in French, the one-act *Interview de Mrs Morte Smith par ses fantômes*, is more corrosive in its satire and more grotesque in tone. Written in 1972 and translated by Rachel Salik, it was published in 1985 in a bilingual edition. Over the years it has been staged in Toulouse and Brussels, as well as Paris, where it was part of the 1986–87 season at the Théâtre Marie Stuart. The Spanish original finally reached Madrid, with a February 1991 opening at the Sala Olimpia of the Centro de Nuevas Tendencias Escénicas, the government-subsidized stage for

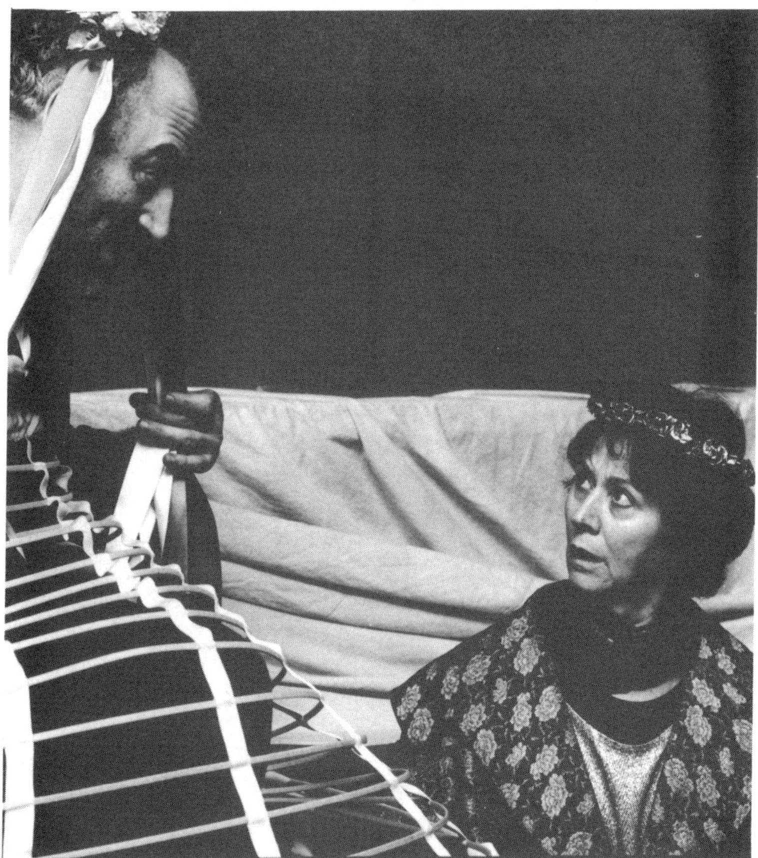

Agustín Gómez-Arcos's *Interview de Mrs. Muerta Smith por sus fantasmas* was staged in France long before it reached the stage in his native country. Manuel de Blas and Julieta Serrano in the 1991 Madrid production. Directed by Carme Portaceli at the Sala Olimpia. (Photo by Juan P. Clemente; courtesy of the Centro Nacional de Nuevas Tendencias Escénicas)

innovative new works, and it ran for seventeen performances. The play is set in a space capsule where the deceased Mrs Morte Smith and the dog trainer Double Nick are being preserved through freezing. They are accompanied by the faithful human-size dog Boby. The ghosts evoked by the dead woman are sexual and sacrilegious, an apparent reaction to a repressive Catholicism. Although the author recognizes the influence of Valle-Inclán on his theatre, he affirms that his character comes from Utah both because "Utah" sounds funny to the French ear and because she is American in her religious fanaticism and her decadent materialism (Personal interview). However, the level of sexual transgression in the play is one much more readily identified with the ghosts of Arrabal or other Hispanics, who are visibly rebelling against the moral rigidity of their Catholic upbringing, than with American Catholics (outside Utah, to be sure). While the "Spanish reading" of this text is perhaps a subtle one, in his later novels Gómez-Arcos has turned overtly to Spain for his themes.

In the younger generation of theatre professionals in France, there are doubtless many who, like Marc-Ange Sanz, come from Spanish families. One case in point is that of film director Pierre-Jean de San Bartolomé, whose first play, *Almira*, opened at the Espace Pierre Cardin in October 1977. The title refers to a little city on the border that has become symbolic of utopia: the point of contact between two countries and two cultures. The time is the present, following Franco's death. In an interview for *L'Avant-Scène Théâtre*, the author clarifies that his father is Spanish, that is, the child born in France to Spanish emigré parents (San Bartolomé 37). As a second-generation Frenchman, San Bartolomé obviously still feels ties to the land of his paternal grandparents.

But what about the dramatists who stayed in Spain? Have their fortunes on the French stage been as dismal as Semprun-Maura's character in *Ma chanson la plus triste est espagnole* would have us believe? Torres Monreal found little to be optimistic about in his study through 1973: a modest, but passing interest in Antonio Buero-Vallejo (b. 1916), Miguel Mihura (1905–1977), Alfonso Sastre (b. 1926), and Lauro Olmo (b. 1922)—but not even one integrated work from among them. The situation did not change much in the ensuing fifteen years. Nor do the SGAE data in *El espectador y la crítica* offer glimpses of significant "penetration" of any contemporary Spanish author residing in Spain. Buero-Vallejo, who personally fought on the losing

Republican side in the Civil War, is not alone in attributing this state of affairs to a prejudicial attitude toward writers who produced their creative work under Franco-era censorship—whether they supported the dictatorship or not (Personal interview).

Buero-Vallejo is considered by many to be the foremost Spanish dramatist living in Spain. His works, representing an impressive career spanning four decades, have been widely staged in Latin America, the Scandinavian countries, and Eastern Europe. In recent years he has also been produced by professional theatres in Baltimore, Philadelphia, and New York City. His *El sueño de la razón* (1970), an expressionistic tragedy that immerses the spectator in the paintings and inner world of the aging and deaf Goya, has been acclaimed in various countries. Yet the only production of note of any Buero text in neighboring France—of which the playwright himself is aware—was a short run of *En la ardiente oscuridad* (1950; French trans., *L'Ardente obscurité* by Odile Chavert) at the Nouveau Théâtre de Poche in Paris in November 1957. Jean Camp also translated the one-act *Palabras en la arena* and published it in a 1958 issue of *L'Avant-Scène Théâtre* under the title *Ecrit sur le sable*. Aside from these two early plays, Torres Monreal reported that Francine Caron at the University of Rennes had talked of translating *El tragaluz* (1967), but, that for all practical purposes, Buero-Vallejo was unknown in France (Diss. 1: 117–118).

The one Buero text that is staged in France with some regularity is *Palabras en la arena*: Francisco Alvaro lists it for 1973, 1974, 1977, 1978, and 1982. Once again it is reasonable to assume that these productions were, indeed, in French, given the availability of the Camp translation in *L'Avant-Scène Théâtre* 183. Alvaro also cites a 1976 performance of *Historia de una escalera* (1949), Buero's first play to be staged, and a 1982 production of *El tragaluz*. In all likelihood the latter two stagings were Spanish-language productions at festivals. In spite of the dearth of production history in France, Buero is not quite so unknown there as Torres Monreal believed, or at least not among theatre people interested in the Hispanic stage. In discussing the universality of Lorca or Arthur Miller, Jorge Lavelli observes that Buero's *En la ardiente oscuridad* is known "everywhere" (Telephone interview). Emmanuel Roblès similarly believes that Buero's theatre is known by many in French theatre circles even though he is not staged, probably for financial reasons: production costs are high and foreign theatre is always somewhat risky in France (Personal interview). For his own part, Roblès, whose original theatre emphasizes Hispanic history and the tragic mode, Buero's plays have a particular attraction; when he saw *El soñador para un pueblo* (1958) in Spain, he thought then that he would like to translate it.

André Camp agrees that the primary reason a Spanish author of Buero's stature has not reached French audiences is economic. Indeed, by 1987, he and several other theatre professionals in Paris had formed an association, Ibéral, for the sole purpose of promoting Hispanic theatre in France. Through their efforts, Buero's *Ecrit sur le sable* was included in a Saturday series of "théâtre à une voix" in March and April 1989. The one-actor readings of short plays by Spanish and Latin American authors were given at the Théâtre Essaïon, a small playhouse in Paris that is under the direction of José Valverde, the son of Spanish émigrés.

Success in the theatre anywhere is elusive, and Torres Monreal offers several suggestions as to why the initial stagings of Buero, Mihura, or Sastre did not lead to "integration." Paris has so many theatres that it is difficult for a new play of an unknown author to attract audience and critical attention without considerable advance publicity or, preferably, a previous production in an important provincial center (Diss. 1: 123). And then, beyond the question of how good the play is or how well it is staged, lie the external circumstances. In a 1974 letter to Torres Monreal, Sastre points out that his *Ana Kleiber* in Paris in 1961 had the misfortune of coinciding with the Algerian crisis (rptd. Diss. 2: 763–764): a classic case of bad timing. Moreover, these stagings in the late 1950s and early 1960s are simultaneous with Lorca's great popularity, specifically in productions that touted an *espagnolade* not appropriate to the more contemporary works.

Mihura's most famous play, the absurdist *Tres sombreros de copa*, was written in 1932 but not staged in Spain until 1952. It reached Paris in January 1959 at the Théâtre Alliance Française. The translation, *Trois chapeaux claque* by Hélène Duc and J. Estrada, was subsequently published in *L'Avant-Scène Théâtre* 191. Although the production was highly praised by some, and the play was recognized by Eugène Ionesco as a significant contribution to the Theatre of the Absurd, it was attacked by prestigious critics. The following year Mihura's detective story parody *Carlota*, translated by Emmanuel Roblès, met with failure at the Théâtre Edouard VII. As Torres Monreal observes, in the comedies of Mihura the Paris audience found a theatre far removed from the stereotypical notion of Spanish drama: "blood, tragedy, passion and honor" (Diss. 2: 573). And they rejected it.

This is not to say, however, that Mihura has disappeared from theatre in France. Alvaro cites productions of *Tres sombreros de copa* in 1973, 1974, and 1976, and even one of *Carlota* in 1984. He also lists stagings in 1973 and 1984 for *Ninette y un señor de Murcia* (1964), a light comedy with a story line that spans the Pyrenees. The gentleman from Murcia, eschewing the restraints of marriage, goes to France in search of romantic adventure "French style"—only to fall prey to Ninette, the daughter of Spanish emigrés. The text would have a natural appeal for Spanish language audiences in France. Also included in Alvaro's lists are performances in 1977 of *La decente* and in 1978 of *A media luz los tres*, two of Mihura's minor works that were revived in Spain in 1977.

The situation of Sastre in France is in some respects quite different from that of Buero or Mihura. Buero, in spite of having been imprisoned at the end of the Civil War, of criticizing Franco's Spain through the vehicle of metaphorical or historical tragedy, and of being in constant conflict with the censor, did succeed in having works staged in major Madrid playhouses at a fairly steady rate. For someone like Gómez-Arcos, who felt himself completely shut out, Buero in fact was "an official playwright" (Personal interview). Mihura, who left behind the more innovative aspects of his absurdist theatre to write popular farces, had no trouble having his later works produced. Sastre, on the other hand, was persona non grata, and could readily become the basis of another myth. Moreover, like Alberti, he was promoted in France for ideological reasons: a leftist intellectual in battle with a Fascist regime.

Torres Monreal quotes an article in *Combat* that identified Sastre as the Spanish Arthur Miller whose works had been prohibited in Spain seven times (Torres Monreal, *El teatro español en Francia* 49). The two Sastre plays staged in Paris in the early 1960s were *Ana Kleiber*, at the Théâtre Hebertot in 1961, and *Escuadra hacia la muerte* (translated by Marrast as *Escouade vers la mort*) at the Cité Universitaire Internationale the following year. Although these dramas, particularly the latter, fall into Sastre's existentialist period and could be related to the politically committed theatre of a Sartre or a Camus, they were generally not well received by the critics or the public. Torres Monreal thus believed that Sastre, too, had disappeared from the French stage.

But one volume of a projected five-volume collection of Sastre's works was published in France and remains in print. It includes three historical dramas in a more or less Brechtian mode: *Guillaume Tell a le regard triste, M.S.V. ou le sang et la cendre,* and *Chroniques romaines*. The first of these is known to theatre professionals working in Europe because of a performance at a festival in Belgium some years ago; Francisco Alvaro cites a staging in France in 1980. For *Chroniques romaines,* Alvaro notes productions yearly for the 1979–1982 period. Numancia (a city under siege whose inhabitants committed collective suicide rather than surrender to the Romans), the subject of *Chroniques romaines,* is one already familiar to the French through repeated stagings of Cervantes's famous play on the same subject. This one Sastre text at least appears to have achieved a level of "penetration."

Lauro Olmo's *La camisa,* 1962, has been staged in Spanish repeatedly in France and other European countries to audiences of Spanish workers. The first postwar play in Spain to deal realistically with the problems of poverty, *La camisa* takes place in a shantytown and shows a family torn by the need of one of them to emigrate in order to find work. *La Chemise*, the French translation by Francine Caron, reached the Comédie de Saint-Etienne, under the direction of Pierre Vial, in 1970. Consistent with Torres Monreal's commentary, a staging in a major provincial center could attract attention in Paris. The review of Xavier Marula in *Le Monde* reports a warm reception by the spectators in Saint-Etienne and describes the play's success as being well deserved. He praises Olmo's combative spirit, his use of a clear, popular language, and his insight into his characters. He also suggests that *La Chemise* should serve as a consciousness-raising vehicle for the French who have become the hosts for visiting workers from Spain and elsewhere (Marula). Alvaro cites subsequent productions in France in 1973 and 1976, and the playwright is aware of a 1975 revival in French at the Nouveau Gymnase in Liège, Belgium, under the direction of André Gille (Personal interview).

In bringing Torres Monreal's analysis of Spanish theatre in France up to date, by far the most disturbing factor for some fifteen years was the lack of new names on the list of playwrights who have crossed the Pyrenees. Alvaro's data, for the period ending with 1985, include no names of dramatists who became known in Spain after Olmo, with the signficant exception of directors of companies, like Albert Boadella and Els Joglars or Salvador Tavora and Cuadra de Sevilla, that toured France in original-language productions. One minor breakthrough, after *El espectador y la crítica* ceased publication, has been that of Luis Riaza (b. 1925). An avant-garde playwright who writes baroque, metatheatrical games of cruelty in the vein of Jean Genet, Riaza did not achieve a major production in Spain until his *Retrato de dama con perrito* was done by the Centro Dramático Nacional in 1979. It was that same text which he submitted to La Théâtrale, a group in France that selects promising plays and circulates synopses to French theatre groups. Generally the texts chosen are by French authors, but quite exceptionally they included Riaza's play. It was subsequently staged in February 1986 by the Compagnie Martin Cendre in Lille. The translator, Françoise Lehmann, had plans to do other Riaza texts for possible publication, and there was some hope that his *Revolución del trapo*, dealing with the French Revolution, would likewise be translated and staged (Personal interviews). Another encouraging note was the translation by Maria-Luisa Marco Ferrín of José María Rodríguez Méndez's *Flor de Otoño* as a thesis at the University of Toulouse–Le Mirail; in conjunction with the completion of the French version, in late January 1992, the university staged the Spanish original and invited the author to attend the last of the four performances.

As the decade of the 1980s drew to a close, the group Ibéral in Paris offered great promise for a renewed interest in Hispanic theatre in France. Headed by Claude Demarigny, a French diplomat and playwright who lived for many years in South America, and André Camp, the critic and translator, Ibéral has received support from private and public sources in France, Spain, and Latin America. The founding members include the actress Maria Casarès, who was named honorary president, playwrights Martín Elizondo and Semprun-Maura, and the directors Jorge Lavelli and José Valverde, as well as distinguished writers, scholars, translators, and others connected with the culture and communication worlds. The organization proposed to select significant Hispanic texts, arrange for their translation, and promote their publication and staging. To see that Hispanic plays reach French audiences, they would create a special data base for Théâtrothèque to list translations of Ibero-American works. They determined to sponsor Hispanic theatre festivals in Paris along with visits to France of Hispanic playwrights.

Ibéral's first major endeavor came to fruition in the spring of 1989. The Saturday series of readings, which began on 4 March with Buero's *Ecrit sur le sable*, continued with works by two Argentinian writers, and then concluded on 1 April with *Le Poison du théâtre*, by the Catalan playwright Rodolf Sirera (b. 1948), and *Je meurs donc j'existe*, by Jorge Díaz (b. 1930), an internationally acclaimed Chilean-born author who has resided in Madrid since the 1960s. In mid-March, there was a week of Spanish playwrights, also at the Essaïon, featuring a production of *Putain de ta mère!* (*La madre que te parió*, translated by Camp and Demarigny) by José Luis Alegre Cudos (b. 1951), a staged reading of *L'Appel*

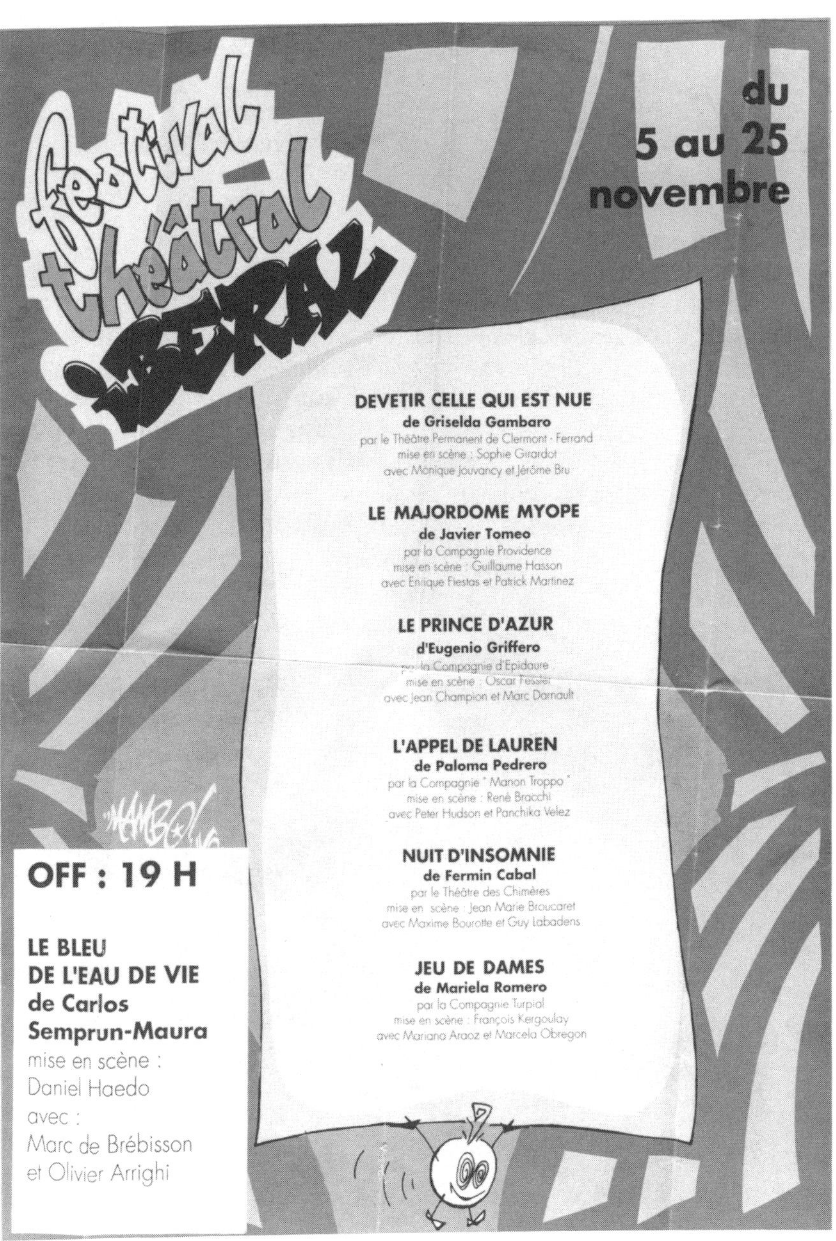

Poster announcing Ibéral's November 1990 theatre festival in Paris.

de Lauren (*La llamada de Lauren*, translated by Camp), by Paloma Pedrero (b. 1957), and a reading by Valverde of Jaime Salom's *Le coq volait bas* (*El corto vuelo del gallo*, translated by Camp and Demarigny). The week's activities included roundtables in which the authors participated and the publication in *L'Avant-Scène Théâtre* 846 of the Alegre Cudos and Pedrero texts.

For Pedrero and Salom (b. 1925), Ibéral has opened the door to widespread interest from the French theatrical world. *L'Appel de Lauren* was scheduled for performance in Nice in April 1990 and, staged by the Compagnie Manon Troppo, reached Paris for a week's run at the Théâtre Nesle during Ibéral's 5–25 November Hispanic theatre festival. Pedrero's two-actor play deals with a moment of crisis in a young marriage when the husband reveals to his wife and himself his transvestism; the Lauren Bacall costume he dons

Paloma Pedrero's *L'Appel de Lauren* by the Compagnie Manon Troppo, Festival Ibéral, Paris, 1990. (Photo courtesy of *L'Avant Scène Théâtre*)

Fermin Cabal's *Nuit d'insomnie,* Festival Ibéral, 1990. Directed Jean Marie Broucaret. (Photos courtesy of *L'Avant-Scène Théâtre*)

for carnival fits him more comfortably than the masculine role imposed upon him by society. The 1985 Madrid premiere created controversy among establishment male critics, but the play has traveled well: to Portugal, Brazil, Argentina, and the United States—for a professional staged reading in Houston—as well as to France. In February 1990, Salom's *Le coq volait bas*, an expressionistic treatment of Franco's family, with emphasis on the Generalísimo's libertarian father, was broadcast by France-Culture, in its important series of radio plays. Salom was represented in the 1990 festival by a staged reading of his *Una hora sin televisión*; writing in *El Público*, French critic Irène Sadowska-Guillon predicted that the two-actor play, which also deals with a marital crisis, would reach the Parisian stage the following season ("I Festival Iberal" 145). Other works by Salom that have attracted attention in France are his poetic metaplay, *El baúl de disfraces*, under consideration in Toulouse, and *Una hoguera al amanecer*, a historical tableau based on the life and passion of Bartolomé de las Casas, Apostle to the Indians during the Spanish conquest of the Americas. Through Ibéral's efforts the latter text was given a reading at a July 1992 festival in Grenoble, in connection with the Quincentennial.

Ibéral's November 1990 festival presented three other Spanish authors to Parisian audiences. Also running for one week each at the Théâtre de Nesle were *Nuit d'insomnie* (*Vade Retro!*, translated by Demarigny and Camp), by Fermín Cabal (b. 1948) and *Le Majordome myope*, based on the novel by Javier Tomeo (b. 1932) in the French version of Dominique Labarrière. *¡Ay, Carmela!*, by José Sanchis Sinisterra (b. 1940), was given a one-actor reading; Sadowska-Guillon also predicted a 1991 staging for this two-actor metaplay set during the Spanish Civil War ("I Festival Iberal" 145). Carlos Saura's highly acclaimed movie based on Sanchis Sinisterra's text has already given *¡Ay, Carmela!* international visibility.

It is perhaps not by coincidence that several of the plays promoted by Ibéral require only two actors, for the small cast removes the economic restraints that have kept many Spanish dramas—notably Buero-Vallejo's major works—

off the boards. Cabal's *Vade Retro!* presents a night of often comic confrontation between two priests, the younger of whom has decided to leave the Church to seek his fortune. The Paris staging appropriately was by the Théâtre des Chimères from Bayonne (Basses-Pyrénées), under the direction of Jean-Marie Broucaret; as Sadowska-Guillon points out, the Bayonne group had just hosted its tenth annual French-Spanish theatre festival, which has made a significant contribution to cultural interchange between the two countries ("Bayona" 144). Broucaret's commitment to Spanish theatre is also reflected in stagings by the Théâtre des Chimères of Lorca's *La casa de Bernarda Alba* in 1984 and of Valle-Inclán's *Divinas palabras* in 1989. Prior to reaching Paris, *Nuit d'insomnie* was performed at the October Bayonne festival; it also toured in the French provinces in the fall and was scheduled for Portugal in January 1991. The text was chosen for publication in *L'Avant-Scène Théâtre* 878, the issue coinciding with Ibéral's November 1990 activities.

Javier Tomeo is a novelist who initially reached the stage by accident. Jacques Nichet, director of Treize Vents, the national drama center of Languedoc Roussillon in Montpellier, read a review of the French translation of the novel *Amado monstruo* that praised its dramatic dialogue and structure; intrigued, he prepared a stage version, in collaboration with Jean Jacques Préau, and invited a skeptical Tomeo to rehearsals (Trancón 61). Sadowska-Guillon considers the production reflective of two of Nichet's typical attitudes: his interest in Spain and his willingness to experiment with texts not originally intended for the theatre ("Amado monstruo" 52). In 1989 the production traveled from Montpellier to other provincial centers in France and to the Théâtre National de la Colline in Paris. *Monstre aimé* was published in *L'Avant-Scène Théâtre* 842, and the Spanish translation of the French script, prepared by Tomeo himself, appeared in *Primer Acto* 230. Not only did the French script give rise to the Spanish one, but the publication in *L'Avant-Scène Théâtre*, which circulates internationally, coupled with the successful production in Paris, no doubt prompted stagings in other European countries. *El País* reported

German-language performances in Switzerland and Berlin as well as a Portuguese version (28 May 1990).

This two-actor play is a kind of grotesque, confessional dialogue between a job seeker and a personnel manager that revolves around each man's relationship with his possessive mother. Spanish playwright José Luis Alonso de Santos first saw *Monstre aimé* at the Théâtre National de la Colline and was instantly captivated by it. His enthusiasm grew with the subsequent stagings in Spain. He describes the text—with its reminiscences of Kafka, Buñuel, Poe, and Gómez de la Serna—as a kind of tribute to human frustration, and compares the closed, gray space of the set with the emptiness of two men who try to invent their own identities through the dark ghosts of their mothers (Alonso de Santos 64–65).

Le Mayordome myope, the Tomeo text included in the Festival Théâtral Ibéral, was first published as a novel, in Spanish, in January 1990. Before reaching Paris, the French stage version was performed by the Compagnie Providence at the annual Avignon festival, where it was well received. While Spanish playwrights have waited impatiently in the wings for years, ironically Tomeo is not the only Spanish novelist to gain a ready entrée to the French stage. In 1989 a French stage adaptation of *El pianista* by Manuel Vázquez Montalbán (b. 1939) was featured in Grenoble at the drama center codirected by Ariel García Valdés. The play, divided into three moments in time, spans a period of fifty years in Spanish history. The title character sacrifices his artistic career in Paris in order to join the Republican cause during the Civil War and then suffers the effects of the postwar era (Méreuze, "El viaje de Vázquez Montalbán" 57). The trajectory of *Historia de un idiota contada por él mismo*, by Félix de Azúa (b. 1944), is very similar to that of Tomeo's *Amado monstruo*. Christian Plézent read the novel, found it had dramatic possibilities, and invited Micheline Bourgoin to prepare a French stage version; Pasqual then included the play in the 1990–91 season at the Petit Odéon.

Arrabal observes that there is a current vogue of staging nondramatic texts. Although he has published almost twenty volumes of plays in French, recent productions of his works include other people's versions of his first novel, *Baal Babylone,* and even of his essay on El Greco. He waggishly theorizes that directors who choose to create their own theatrical texts can take full artistic credit for success but still blame the original author if there are any shortcomings (Personal interview 1992). Whatever the truth of Arrabal's explanation, Pasqual and the Petit Odéon were not fighting the trend. For the 1992 Avignon festival, Pasqual had prepared a collage, in Spanish, of Lorca poems, and the Hispanic Cycle in the Odéon's little theatre included *Entre las ramas de la arboleda perdida,* José Luis Alonso's staging of Alberti's memoirs, as performed by José Luis Pellicena.

The eighty-two-seat Petit Odéon was also the scene of a series of free staged readings over a two-week period in May 1992 of works by four Latin American and five Spanish authors. Along with five Spanish plays read several weeks earlier in the little theatre at the Théâtre National de la Colline, they represented a cooperative venture, Hispanité-Explorations, spearheaded by Irène Sadowska-Guillon. According to Sadowska-Guillon, the professional readings were recorded for broadcast on France-Culture and a selection of the texts, all translated by members of the Hispanic committee of France's International Center of Theatre Translation, will soon be published (Personal letter). An ambitious program of cultural exchange, apparently organized in competition with Ibéral, Hispanité-Explorations has announced additional translations in progress and forthcoming readings or stagings of Spanish plays in France and French plays in Spain (Newsletter).[5]

The quality of performance at the Odéon and the Colline was exceptionally high for staged readings: the actors were drawn from the two national theatres, and the texts were presented with lighting effects, background music, and a certain amount of movement. Audience reponse to those I attended (Sergi Belbel's *Caresses,* Juan Benet's *Agonia Confutans,* and Francisco Nieva's *Le Bal des ardents*) was strongly favorable.

Among authors and plays selected for the two cycles of Hispanic readings were some predictable choices: for example, Cabal's *Dernier rond* (*¡Esta noche, gran velada!*), at the Colline, and Nieva's text, which was read at both theatres. Cabal's tragic-farcical view of the boxing world was the winner of the Espectador y la Crítica best play of the year award for 1983. Long recognized as one of Spain's most imaginative set designers, directors, and playwrights, Nieva (b. 1927) was awarded the National Theatre Prize (1980) and the Prince of Asturias Prize for Literature (1992). *El baile de los ardientes* is an excellent example of his iconoclastic, surrealistic plays of "calamity and farce."

Given Hispanité-Explorations' expressed intention of promoting a representative selection of the best contemporary theatre, other choices were less obvious. A potentially broad cross section of Spanish playwrights was limited by the presentation of more than one work by two of them and by seeking out dramatic texts written by novelists. Two of Sanchis Sinisterra's Quincentennial plays were included: *L'Illustre théâtre de Eldorado* at the Colline and, at the Odéon, *Lope de Aguirre, le traître*, the same play that would receive a full-scale production there a few months later. Younger playwrights were represented, twice, by Sergi Belbel (b. 1963). His *Caresses* and *Lit nuptial* (*Talem*) were both done at the Colline, and *Caresses*, an episodic text inspired by Schnitzler's *La Ronde*, was repeated at the Odéon. Also included were *Sept cités de Cibola*, by novelist and poet Jesús Ferrero (b. 1952), and *Agonia Confutans*, one of three little-known plays published in 1971 by the celebrated novelist Juan Benet (1927–1993). If the total selection of texts was not likely to bring joy to the hearts of Spanish dramatists patiently awaiting fame in Paris, at the least *Agonia Confutans*, an intense two-character dialogue marked by role-playing within the roles, lent itself well to the format of a staged reading. Moreover, by the end of the cycle of readings, Sadowska-Guillon was able to announce follow-up productions of the two Belbel plays.

Hispanité-Explorations was also responsible for a shorter series of readings, scheduled in June and July 1992 in conjunction with a Catalan Month at the Atalante Theatre in Paris. The main attraction of the summer program was *Le Venin du théâtre*, François Rey's translation of the Rodolf

Sirera two-character metadrama previously presented at an Ibéral reading under the title *Le Poison du théâtre*. Directed by Agathe Alexis, *Le Venin du théâtre* was a coproduction of the Comédie de Reims and the Comédie de Béthune, the National Drama Center of the North. The accompanying readings were to include another Sirera play, *Indian Summer*, Belbel's *Lit nuptial*, and, rather surprisingly in that he is from Andalusia, not Catalonia, Gómez-Arcos's *Interview de Mrs Morte Smith par ses fantômes*. In the meantime, Ibéral was already at work on another festival of Hispanic theatre, to take place in spring, 1993, at the Espace Herault.

Recent stagings in France of Spanish texts, the involvement of Hispanic directors at the most prestigious theatres in France, the visibility given both Spanish and Latin American culture during the Quincentennial, and the ongoing activities of Ibéral augur well for an increased presence of Spanish playwrights on the French stage, but clearly much must be done to achieve the kind of integration, or even "penetration," that Torres Monreal outlined years ago. If the data in Alvaro's yearbook may be taken as a measure of actual French-language performances, then the key to stagings lies in the availability of translations. Almost without exception, the titles that crop up repeatedly in lists of works staged in France are precisely the texts published by *L'Avant-Scène Théâtre* or that appear in current catalogs. To be sure, a well-publicized, successful initial performance facilitates revivals, but the accessibility of the text may be essential for achieving either the first staging or subsequent ones.

The publication of play texts in France is far more difficult than in Spain, where there are several inexpensive series that actively promote playwrights, including ones who have not yet achieved any widespread recognition. But in France, even successful authors, like Manet and Roblès, indicate that their publishers prefer novels, which sell better (Personal interviews). French-language playwrights may find themselves obligated to write novels, whether they want to or not, in order to keep the door open to the publication of their dramas. *L'Avant-Scène Théâtre* has hence become an important source of texts but not primarily, at least in the case of full-length plays, for the purpose of developing new authors. In general the plays chosen, whether French-language originals or translations, have been ones that achieved critical and spectator acclaim in a recent production, probably in a major Parisian theatre. It is therefore interesting to note to what extent the Spanish plays made available through *L'Avant-Scène Théâtre*, including the lesser-known short texts, have been staged repeatedly in France. The suggestion is clear that if SGAE, as the representative of Spanish playwrights, wishes to promote Spanish theatre beyond the Pyrenees, the most effective mechanism may be the publication and dissemination of French translations of selected texts. They are fortunate in having such dedicated allies in this cause as Camp and Demarigny of Ibéral and, more recently, of Sadowska-Guillon and Hispanité-Explorations, and the directors of several major theatre centers in France, whose combined efforts are breaking down the traditional French image of Spain—baroque, dark, violent, passionate—to provide new perspectives on France's neighbor and economic partner.

Chapter 4

FRENCH THEATRE ON THE CONTEMPORARY SPANISH STAGE

In any discussion of interchange between the contemporary French and Spanish stages, it is a given that the cultural balance of trade favors France. Parisian hits may readily reach Madrid, but the reverse is not true. Major French playwrights of the postwar period—Anouilh, Sartre, Camus, Ionesco, Beckett, Genet—are well known in Spain, while major Spanish dramatists are rarely staged or totally ignored north of the Pyrenees. Among living Spanish playwrights only Arrabal, whose long residence in France has given him a dual national identity, has achieved full integration in the French theatre. In March 1989 Ibéral, a coalition of those interested in promoting Spanish theatre in Paris, organized a special week of activities for selected Spanish dramatists (see Chapter 3.) That they simultaneously announced a counterpart visit of three French dramatists to Spain (Victor Haïm, René de Obaldia, Eric Westphale) is more surprising. Can there also be a need for an affirmative action program in Spain on behalf of French dramatists?

Although there is no doubt that French theatre has been a dominant influence on the contemporary Spanish stage, that influence has varied over the years. In Madrid, the center of the Spanish theatrical world, it was more pervasive thirty years ago than today, when its impact is greater in Barcelona and in the provinces than in the capital. The Parisian hits that travel swiftly over the Pyrenees have tended to be precisely the "boulevard" comedy that for

97

mainstream Spanish playgoers is synonymous with French theatre. The French classics, with the notable exception of Molière, seldom reach the Spanish stage. The impact of the major postwar playwrights, cited above, continues to be significant, but the reception to their works in Spain has not always been a favorable one. Outside the area of comedy, other contemporary French playwrights are rarely staged, particularly in Madrid.[1] Indeed Haïm, Obaldia, and Westphale are hardly household names in Spain, where, according to available theatre annuals, Haïm has had but one major production, Obaldia several minor ones, and Westphale, none at all.

In 1973 Editora Nacional published for the Spanish center of the International Institute of Theatre (UNESCO) a panorama of the Spanish stage, 1940–1972. The section on contemporary international theatre placed the United States in first position, noting the unquestionable influence of such American authors as O'Neill, Miller, Wilder, Williams, and Albee (de la Hoz 161–162), and recognized Britain as the third major foreign presence (164). France came second, with the observation that the northern neighbor had maintained her reputation for creating good theatre and being an innovative leader for the world. Citing a long and diversified list of French dramatists (Claudel, Montherlant, Baty, Giraudoux, Cocteau, Anouilh, Sartre, Camus, Beckett, Ionesco, Adamov, Schéhadé, Genet, Weingarten, Adrien, Obaldia, Marceau, Artaud, Audiberti, Bernanos, Achard, Aymé, Guitry, Feydeau, Deval, Roussin), the entry concluded that there has been a continuous French presence on the Spanish stage (163).

From the perspective of 1990, the importance and even the constance of that French presence is not quite so clear. A primary source of information on the contemporary Spanish stage is the late Francisco Alvaro's theatre annual, *El espectador y la crítica*, 1958–1985. For each of these volumes, he selected significant productions in Madrid of Spanish and foreign works. A comparison of the early volumes, 1958–1960, and the ones from twenty years later, 1978–1980, reveals interesting shifts both in the dominance of foreign works on the Madrid stage and in the influence of French theatre in particular.[2]

For 1958, Alvaro highlighted 27 productions in Madrid of Spanish plays and 27 of foreign works. English-language theatre (British and American) accounted for 12 of the latter plays, while 9 were French. The following year, foreign works outnumbered Spanish plays, 26 to 20, but the French share had dropped to only 4. (British and American, combined, accounted for 18.) In 1960, however, French plays topped the list of foreign works. That year there were 29 Spanish and 27 foreign plays.[3] Of these, 13 were French, while the combined British and American total was 11. For the three-year period, French theatre thus represented almost a third of the foreign plays and a sixth of all important productions in Madrid.

Twenty years later, for the three-year period 1978–1980, French theatre represented only 6 percent of the foreign and only 2 percent of the total Madrid productions highlighted by Alvaro in his theatre annual. For 1978, revealing the new ascendency of national theatre, Alvaro included 18 Spanish and 12 foreign works. None of these was French. Half of the foreign plays were British or American, and the prize for the best foreign play of the year in Madrid (an award established in 1967) went to Chekhov's *Tío Vania*. The following year, Alvaro selected 17 Spanish and 12 foreign plays. Germanic texts tied the Anglo-American at 4 each, and the best foreign play award went to Wesker's *Sopa de pollo con cebada (Chicken Soup with Barley)*. French theatre was represented by the Catalan-language production of Haïm's *Abraham i Samuel*, given by the Teatre Lliure from Barcelona, and by Enrique Llovet's very free version of Molière's *El Tartufo*. In 1980, Alvaro selected 25 Spanish and only 9 foreign works, and the judges for the Espectador y la Crítica prizes declared that there was no winner in the best foreign play category. The entire group of foreign plays came from Anglo-American or Germanic texts.

Nor did the situation of French theatre in Madrid improve appreciably in the decade of the 1980s. Data published in *El Público* for the 1986–87 season reveal no French presence on the commercial stage and only a handful of brief runs at national or municipal theatres of three or four performances each by visiting troupes (49: 70–74). French theatre fared better the next season, but without any box office hits. In 1987–88, public theatres featured several productions with limited runs, and somewhat more important stagings of Molière's *Los enredos de Scapin* (*Les Fourberies de Scapin*), Giraudoux's *Ondina*, and Cocteau's *El águila de dos cabezas* (*L'Aigle à deux têtes*). Commercial theatres also produced comedies by Marc Camoletti and by Bricaire and Lasaygues. The only French texts to remain on the boards for fifty or more performances were the latter's *La señora presidenta* and the Molière (*El Público* 61: 63–65). Of the thirty-six productions running in Madrid in January 1989, only two were French: both revivals of comedies by Feydeau (*El Público* 66: 69). These achieved runs of over 100 performances, as did André Roussin's *La Mamma*, but the only other French presence during the 1988–89 Madrid season were two brief stagings on tour (*El Público* 73: 65–66).

In Barcelona, on the other hand, French theatre is more likely to be performed and more likely to number among the hits of the season than in Madrid. *El Público's* Barcelona correspondent, Jaume Melendres, has developed a formula to determine relative success of productions by considering the aggregate number of spectators, the average number per performance, and the percentage of the house that is filled. By his calcuations, three of the fifteen most successful productions of the 1986–87 Barcelona season were of French origin: Sarraute's *Per un si per un no* (*Pour un oui, pour un non*) at the Poliorama, Savary's *El tango de Don Joan* at the Romea, and Bricaire and Lasaygues's *El coronel . . . ?* at the Goya (*El Público* 49: 75–79). The impressive French presence continued in Barcelona the following fall. Of twelve theatres open in November 1987, three featured French works: Claudel's *L'intercanvi* (*L'Echange*) at the Romea, Giraudoux's *Ondina* at the Goya, and an adaptation of Musset's *Lorenzaccio* at the Lliure (*El Público* 52: 71). It should be noted that Claudel and Giraudoux had last received major productions in Madrid in 1965 and that Sarraute had not yet been performed in the capital. According to Melendres's formula, two of the ten most successful productions of the 1987–88 season were of French origin: both of them versions of Musset's *Lorenzaccio* (*El Público* 61: 71). The pattern continued in 1988–89, with three French works in the top dozen productions: Molière's *El misantrop* and Musset's *Lorenzaccio*, both at the Poliorama, and Beaumarchais's *Les noces de Figaro* at the Lliure (*El Público* 73: 69–71).

For its first issue published in 1991, *El Público* prepared a photo review: "1981–1990: Imágenes de una década." Taking into consideration the nation's theatrical history, which included more than 7000 productions in the ten-year period, the editors selected 250 moments that stood out in their memories. Foreign authors are well represented, ranging from Shakespeare and Goldoni to Dario Fo and Tadeusz Kantor. A total of twenty productions have a French connection, however tenuous. Six are by French companies on tour, and two of these are, in fact, French translations of Spanish texts discussed in the previous chapter: Vitez's staging of *La Celestina* and Nichet's of *Amado monstruo*. One is of *El rey de Sodoma* by the Spanish-French playwright Arrabal, and another is the Argentine-French Copi's last play, *Una visita inoportuna*, directed at the Poliorama by Argentine-French director Jorge Lavelli. There are two revivals by those associated with earlier, landmark productions: Genet's *Las criadas*, starring Nuria Espert, and Giraudoux's *La loca de Chaillot*, directed by José Luis Alonso. There are two plays by Bernard-Marie Koltès, both of which played to near empty houses in Madrid in 1990. The remaining eight productions, all of them successful versions of French authors (Jarry, Molière, Cocteau, Rostand, Sarraute, Musset, Beaumarchais) were staged in Barcelona.

There are doubtless a number of reasons that French theatre, which appears to have lost much of its impact in Madrid in recent years, nevertheless maintains a strong visibility in Barcelona. Geographically and linguistically, Catalonia is closer to France than is Castile. French troupes on tour can pass through Catalonia more readily and can anticipate that audiences will understand them with relative ease. It is thus not surprising that the Spanish-French actress Maria Casarès visited Barcelona for one-night performances, in French, of Copi's *La Nuit de Mme Lucien* in 1985 and of Nathalie Sarraute's *Elle est là* and *L'Usage de la parole* in 1987.

For cultural and political reasons, many Catalans identify themselves as European, rather than Spanish. During the Franco regime, Castilian language and culture were imposed upon Catalonia. Freed from that kind of repression in democratic Spain, influential Catalan theatre companies have turned readily to foreign works while ignoring those emanating from Madrid. Of the twenty-five productions staged by the Lliure during its first ten years (1976–1986), five Catalan playwrights were represented but the only text written originally in Spanish was *Fulgor i mort de Joaquín Murieta* by the Chilean Pablo Neruda. Plays by French authors, however, included Haïm's *Abraham i Samuel*, Genet's *El balcó*, and Molière's *Jordi Dandin* and *El misantrop*; these four productions put the French on a par with the Germanic and Anglo-American presence (*El Público* Cuaderno 10: 72). In 1986–87, the Lliure continued the pattern by adding Beckett's *Oh! els bons dies* (*Oh, les beaux jours*) to its repertory, and in 1987–88 the troupe's biggest box office success was G. J. Graelis's adaptation *Lorenzaccio, Lorenzaccio*. In February 1989, apparently in response to a crisis that threatened the Lliure's existence, the company returned to the boards with Beaumarchais's *Les noces de Figaro*.

Nowhere is the influence of the French stage more pervasive in Barcelona than at the Poliorama, the theatre directed by Josep Maria Flotats since 1985. Born in Barcelona in 1939, Flotats was educated at a private French institute there because his Republican father refused to send him to any school that would require him to sing Francoist anthems (Mignon 1980: 5). Already a fluent speaker of French, Flotats participated in the festival at Avignon in 1958 and subsequently went to Strasbourg to study theatre. His successful French acting career led to numerous roles in Paris at the Théâtre National Populaire, the Théâtre de la Ville, and the Comédie Française. He has brought to the Barcelona stage works of French authors, notably Sarraute and his creation of Rostand's *Cyrano de Bergerac*, but has also imported French theatre people and foreign texts that had been well received in France, such as Brian Clark's *El dret d'escollir* (*Whose Life Is It Anyway?*) in which Flotats had starred at the Théâtre Antoine in 1980. The Poliorama's 1987–88 season featured the Clark play and a version of Musset's *Lorenzaccio* that continued into 1989, when it was joined by an adaptation of Molière's *El misantrop.*

While the presence of French theatre may have been more apparent in Barcelona in the late 1980s than it was in Madrid, in both of these cities light comedy is the dominant fare. The majority of Spanish playgoers, like their counterparts in Paris or London or New York, go to the theatre to be entertained. Not surprisingly, the longest-running French play in Madrid theatre history is a farce: Robert Lamoureux's *La sopera* (*La Soupière*). In the Spanish version by Juan José Arteche, it opened in the Teatro Club on 20 September 1972 under the direction of the author. By the end of 1973, it had reached 1000 performances, and its run continued into 1975. Writing for *ABC*, critic Adolfo Prego categorized *La sopera* as a comedy intended for an audience that expects fifteen or twenty hearty laughs per act in return for the price of their tickets (qtd. Alvaro 1972: 187).

La sopera deals with a conspiracy to kill a rich old aunt and hence falls into a subgenre of mystery farce. Its success on the Madrid stage is rivaled by that of the romantic bourgeois comedy, *Flor de cactus*. Pierre Barillet and Jean-Pierre Grédy's *Fleur de cactus* (1964), also a major box office hit on Broadway, reached Spain rapidly. It opened at the Lara in September 1966 with a stellar cast, headed by director Alberto Closas, Julia Gutiérrez Caba, and María José Goyanes. It ran for more than 200 performances in 1966, returned to the Lara in September 1967 for an additional run of more than 400 performances, and, with a change in cast, was revived in May 1968, again at the Lara. Most Spanish critics brushed the play aside as an eminently forgettable, well-made comedy that was well staged and well acted. Alvaro himself, however, found deeper values in the text, as did the influential Pedro Laín Entralgo, who focused on "the psychological problem of a love relationship between people who come from different generations" (qtd. Alvaro 1966: 275).

This kind of serious subtext is much harder to find in most lighter French works that have achieved popularity, for more typically the Spanish have imported bedroom farces. Among the other longest-running French plays in Madrid are two by Jean de Letraz: *Una noche en su casa . . . Señora . . .* (*Une Nuit chez vous, Madame*) (1971) and *Enséñame . . . tu piscina* (1977), a revival of *Las mujeres nos asustan* (1964). Despite the unquestioned box office success of *Una noche . . .* , Spanish critics wondered what led director José Carlos Plaza to choose the French work when there were better comedies being written in Spain. Alvaro provides a partial answer in his commentary on *Las mujeres nos asustan*. He reports that Alejandro Ulloa has previously done that same farce in Barcelona in order to make enough money to keep staging classic Spanish theatre, which he personally preferred (Alvaro 1964: 252). The commercial stage could count on a certain French mystique to fill the house.

This is not to say that French comedy has been without detractors in Spain. F. C. Sainz de Robles once defined a school of "genuinely French comedy" by its "capricious psychology, minimal dramatic action, and a dialogue sprinkled with . . . clever double meanings"; he concluded that such plays are entertaining, frivolous, and readily forgotten (1952–53: 22). Later in the 1950s, when the rigid morality of "Nationalcatholicism" (the Spanish treat this as one word) was still in force, the negative review in *Pueblo* of André Roussin's *Bobosse* pointed out the inappropriateness of treating adultery lightly. Even if the topic were acceptable, Victoriano Fernández Asís further observed that in French theatre, in contrast to the Spanish tradition, dialogue takes precedence over action and the Spanish audience becomes restless (qtd. Alvaro 1958: 210). Whatever the general truth of the critics' reservations, actor-director Adolfo Marsillach won the National Theatre Prize for 1958, in part because of his staging of Roussin's boulevard comedy.

Roussin, it should be noted, remained a favorite on the commercial stage in Madrid throughout the 1960s and 1970s, with several plays that ran more than 200 performances each. Another popular boulevard author during the

Francisco Nieva's set design for *El Tartufo,* the 1969 Llovet-Marsillach free adaptation of Molière. (Photo courtesy of Manuel Martínez Muñoz)

same period was Françoise Dorin, represented by six titles in seven years.

At times the same criticism that was leveled at Roussin's *Bobosse*—namely, that dialogue and character dominate at the expense of action—has been directed at the comedies of Molière, but Molière in Spain, as elsewhere, is by far the most popular classic French playwright. Indeed Molière is the most staged French author south of the Pyrenees, with more productions in the 1965–1986 period than the leading twentieth-century figures: Ionesco, Beckett, Sartre, Genet, and Anouilh.[4] In 1973, Manuel Díez Crespo affirmed that Shakespeare and Molière were the most staged classics of world theatre during the previous three decades (de la Hoz 25). By the late 1980s, the pattern had not changed.

Among the notable Madrid productions of Molière is the 1967 version of *Las mujeres sabias* (*Les Femmes savantes*), directed by Miguel Narros; its run of more than 200 performances at the Teatro Español placed it among the most commercially successful plays of the season, and Víctor María Cortezo's set design was awarded the first annual Espectador y la Crítica prize in that category. Alvaro observed that the reception of the classic comedy was remarkable and attributed it in large part to the new, faithful translation by Enrique Llovet.

Llovet was also responsible, two years later, for a freer version of *El Tartufo*; with more than 450 performances, it ranks as the longest-running Molière text in Madrid theatre history. Adolfo Marsillach, who directed and played the title role, was awarded the Espectador y la Crítica prize for best director, and the stage designer, Francisco Nieva, also won the annual award. The box office triumph, however, was due not only to the brilliance of the acting and staging but also, and perhaps more importantly so, to the daring political message. Marsillach's Tartufo overtly satirized the technocrats of the Opus Dei who had emerged as a powerful force in the Franco regime. Some critics were appalled at the liberties taken with a classic, and others wondered why the play was not closed down by the censors. Alvaro, delighted by what he considered a magnificent attack on theatrical arteriosclerosis, declared *El Tartufo* to be the most spectacular and positive event of the season (1969: 201). Laín Entralgo, writing for *Gaceta Ilustrada*, affirmed that the comedy's well-deserved success was a result of its combination of high quality and contemporary relevance (qtd. Alvaro 1969: 208).

American scholar Wilma Newberry has provided us with a detailed description of this *Tartufo* in performance and with a history of the comedy's problems in Spain. Marsillach's innovative and energetic staging effectively broke down the barriers between audience and actors and between past and present. For example, at one point Marsillach as Tartufo leaped into a box seat, identifying its occupants as supporters of his cause, that is, of the Opus Dei; actors mingled with the spectators as they entered the theatre and stepped out of character in midaction (Newberry 925–926). These theatricalist, Brechtian strategies no doubt underscored the political intention of the play. Newberry reminds us that the 1969–70 production is only the latest in a series of polemical versions of the French satire of hypocrisy, which had been denounced at various times to the Spanish Inquisition until that institution was abolished in the nineteenth century (922).

Ten years later, Llovet and Marsillach teamed up again for another subversive *Tartufo*, this one aiming its barbs at political opportunists who had switched from right to center during Spain's transition to democracy. For me, a foreign spectator who had not seen the earlier version, it was a magical production, distinguished by Marsillach's comic exuberance and Nieva's ingenious set. For Madrid critics, it was not only déjà vu but a cheap political shot. Nevertheless, in 1979–80 it ran for more than 200 performances to delighted audiences, making it one of the most successful Molière plays on the Spanish stage.

Madrid's municipal Teatro Español, under the leadership of Miguel Narros, opened its 1987–88 season with an elaborate staging of *Los enredos de Scapin*, playwright José Luis Alonso de Santos's version of *Les Fourberies de Scapin*. In recognition of increasing cultural relations between France and Spain, Narros invited Daniel Soulier to direct the comedy. The result was surely one of the most curious productions Spain has seen of Molière. As mentioned in Chapter 3, in France in the 1950s and 1960s, there was a marked tendency to stage Spanish plays with strong doses of *espagnolade*, whether or not the stereotypical Andalusian costumes and music had anything to do with the particular text. The theory was that French spectators expected "Spanish" elements in a Spanish work. Soulier's approach to Molière in Spain was to superimpose *espagnolade*, apparently in the belief that Spanish spectators would welcome a flamenco touch on a classic French farce set in Naples. The French director recognized that the singing of the flamenco *cantaor*, which occurred at intervals throughout the performance, was "sorrowful and sad," but he justified it as "an admirable counterpoint" to the comedy ("Reflexiones" 18 September). Although he affirmed that he intended to respect the spirit of Molière and the seventeenth century and acknowledged that flamenco music would not do if the comedy were being staged in France or Italy, he justified the *cantaor* because the play was being done in the Spanish language ("Homenaje"). The audience on opening night, when I attended, logically failed to see the connection between Molière and the tragic tones of *cante hondo*.

Soulier's failed experiment notwithstanding, Molière enjoys continued popularity in Spain. *El Público's* recent theatre annuals, including data from the provinces, reveal a high level of interest in his comedies among smaller, regional troupes. Heading the list is *Le Médecin malgré lui*, with four productions in Castilian or Catalan during the 1985–1986 period. By contrast, the great authors of seventeenth-century French tragedies are conspicuously absent. Including touring French companies, there are only five references to Racine and Corneille in a quarter century of theatre listings. Of these, the production of greatest impact was the 1975 *Rodogune*, given in French at the María Guerrero National Theatre by a Parisian troupe. The various reviews excerpted in *El espectador y la crítica* praise the Artaudian staging of a baroque text that, in their view, could indeed be interpreted as barbaric ritual without violating the spirit of Corneille's work. The Oblique Théâtre was subsequently awarded the Espectador y la Crítica prize for the best foreign company performing in Madrid that year.

The great French playwrights of the eighteenth and nineteenth centuries fare no better on the contemporary Madrid stage than do Racine or Corneille, but in the late 1980s Beaumarchais, Musset, and Rostand have been performed in Barcelona by the Poliorama and the Lliure theatres. Flotats, as director and lead actor of the Poliorama, undoubtedly chose Cyrano and Lorenzaccio, roles with which he was familiar because of his years in France, as showcases for his own talents. His 1985 *Cyrano de Bergerac* was widely acclaimed throughout Spain; it was, in essence, a famous native son's long awaited homecoming. Although by 1987–88 Flotats had become a more polemical figure, he had also built a loyal audience. His version of the romantic drama *Lorenzaccio*, opening in May 1988, was the third staging of Musset that season in Barcelona; it followed the

Lliure's version *Lorenzaccio, Lorenzaccio*, directed by Lluís Pasqual, and Josep Maria Mestres's *Fantasio*. Playgoers in Barcelona were thus afforded the unique opportunity to compare, almost simultaneously, two major productions of Musset's masterpiece, a work long considered unstageable.

Writing for *El Público*, Gonzalo Pérez de Olaguer declared 1987–88 to be "the year of Musset" and expressed amazement that the early-nineteenth-century author could be so relevant for today's spectators (*El Público* 57: 20). Both the Lliure and the Poliorama productions pared the romantic text, emphasizing the situation of the individual rather than the historic setting. Flotats indicated that *Lorenzaccio, El misantrop*, in which he also starred, and *Tos assajant Don Juan*, a text by Elvire Jouvet, were intended as a tribute to Jean Vilar, the great director under whom Flotats had worked at the Théâtre National Populaire.

If Musset's masterpiece was once excluded from world repertory on theatrical grounds, the same can surely not be said of Beaumarchais's *Le Mariage de Figaro*. Nevertheless, except for the 1969 production by the National Drama Center of Caen which won the Espectador y la Crítica prize for best foreign company, the title does not appear in Alvaro's theatre annuals, and Pérez de Olaguer confirms that it has been seldom staged in Spain (*El Público* 66: 17). The pre-Revolutionary French comedy has, however, had its difficulties with censorship from time to time, for it lends itself to a subversive reading: the clever Figaro, champion of the underdog, outwits the oppressive forces of those in power. Director Fabià Puigserver (1938–1991) stated that he had chosen the text without political intent, but Barcelona spectators were not likely to ignore a potential subtext. When the play opened at the Lliure in February 1989, the theatre was in financial crisis and had threatened to close its doors because of insufficient government subsidies.

In 1967 Puigserver had been the set designer for an independent theatre staging of *Les noces de Figaro,* translated and directed by Francesc Nel.lo. The Lliure production used Nel.lo's translation, but Puigserver deviated considerably from the "very French, very Versaillesque adaptation of the text" that had seemed appropriate twenty years earlier (qtd.

El Público 66: 17). During the Franco period, the theatre troupe was less interested in the setting than in conveying a message on the overthrow of a dictatorship. The recent production, on the other hand, emphasized the human and social dimensions of the story, added original music by Arrizabalaga, and placed the action firmly in Andalusia. Puigserver observed that Beaumarchais knew Spain well, and he found the characters to be deeply immersed in Andalusian culture. For the director, Figaro was a "Goyesque and extremely Andalusian character" and the count was "an aristocratic Spanish gentleman whose fate it is to live in an era that is drawing to a close" (qtd. *El Público* 66: 18). Soulier's superimposing of flamenco onto Molière left Spanish spectators bewildered. Placing the barber back in Seville both surprised and delighted Barcelona audiences.

In the opinion of playwright Lauro Olmo, the twentieth-century French dramatists who have had the greatest impact on the contemporary Spanish stage are Jean Anouilh, particularly his early plays, Albert Camus, Eugène Ionesco, Samuel Beckett, Jean-Paul Sartre, and, somewhat later than the others, Jean Genet (Personal interview). Olmo's observations are confirmed by data in *El espectador y la crítica* and in F. C. Sainz de Robles's yearly anthology, *Teatro español.*

The first volume of Sainz de Robles's series coincides with the season that is generally recognized as the true rebirth of the Madrid stage following the Civil War: 1949–50. Sainz de Robles mentions three productions of Anouilh plays in the capital during 1949–50 (all of them in Teatro de Cámara and hence generally restricted to a single performance), two in 1952–53, and four in 1953–54. Ionesco's name first appears for 1953–54; Camus and Beckett, for 1955–56. Although Sartre's works were doubtless well known to Spanish theatre professionals and had unquestionably influenced some dramatists (notably Alfonso Sastre), for political reasons they were prohibited by the censors until 1967; indeed, Sartre was banned for an even longer period than Brecht, whose plays had finally been permitted in commercial theatres two years before. Sainz de Robles cites a chamber theatre production of Genet's *Las criadas* (*Les Bonnes*) as early as 1962, as well as a perfor-

Francisco Nieva designed the sets and costumes for Claudel's *El zapato de raso*. Directed by José Luis Alonso in an adaptation by Antonio Gala, the play was produced at Madrid's Teatro Español in 1965. (Photo courtesy of Manuel Martínez Muñoz)

mance by a group in Barcelona in 1965. Nevertheless, the real ascendency of Genet dates from the memorable Víctor García–Nuria Espert version of this same play in 1969.

For the years 1965–1986, there is a continued presence in the Spanish theatre of these six playwrights.[5] Ionesco heads the list with fourteen stagings, while Camus, with eight productions, is the least performed. Aside from light comedy, no other French authors are cited with this frequency, including those who developed Spanish and/or Catholic themes and enjoyed popularity in the early postwar period. Claudel and Montherlant, for example, virtually disappear, with only one title each, both directed by José Luis Alonso. Cocteau reappears, after a long silence, with four experimental productions in the 1980s. The only staging of Giraudoux reported during these same seasons was Alonso's production of *Intermezzo* in Agustín Gómez-Arcos's translation at the María Guerrero in 1965.

The revival of Giraudoux's *La loca de Chaillot*, coinciding with Madrid's Fall Theatre Festival of 1989, highlights both the status of this French playwright on the Spanish stage and the key role that José Luis Alonso (1924–1990) played in maintaining the cultural tie with France. As I suggested in a note published in 1969, Jean Giraudoux doubtless had an influence on Spanish authors early in the postwar period. Nevertheless, his plays are seldom performed and generally did not reach Madrid theatres until decades after they were written. Alonso's original production of *La loca de Chaillot*, opening at the María Guerrero in January 1962, is perhaps Spain's most notable staging of Giraudoux. Also translated by Gómez-Arcos and starring Amelia de la Torre, it was labeled a "magnificent work" by Sainz de Robles. The 1962 *Primer Acto* Larra prize for best director went to Alonso and for best actress to de la Torre, in part because of their work on the Giraudoux play.[6]

Alonso's name is closely linked to that of Anouilh in Spanish theatre history. On the occasion of Jean Anouilh's death in October 1987, Alonso recalled for *Primer Acto* his long involvement with the French writer, dating from a restricted chamber theatre production of the "pièce grinçante," *Ardele o la margarita*, in 1946. In tracing Anouilh's fortunes in Spain, Alonso concludes that mainstream theatregoers never really accepted him: for them, his fiction/reality, corruption/purity games were "too intellectual": "While in his country he was among the top authors of the boulevard, in Spain he was a writer for little chamber

Mari Carrillo as Joan of Arc in Anouilh's *La alondra*. Madrid, 1954. Directed by José Tamayo. (Photo by Gyenes)

theatres" (*Primer Acto* 221: 6). According to Alonso, some plays, like *Los peces rojos* (*Les Poissons rouges*) and *La salvaje* (*La Sauvage*) were critical successes but failed to draw audiences. He names two historical dramas as exceptions to this general pattern: José Tamayo's productions of *Becket o el honor de Dios*, in 1962, thanks to a stellar cast featuring Fernando Rey and Francisco Rabal, and the Joan of Arc play, *La alondra (L'Alouette)*, in 1954, for its "spectacular staging that, to be sure, had nothing in common with the austerity of the Parisian one"(6).

Alonso's selection of Tamayo's 1962 *Becket* as a memorable Spanish production of Anouilh is readily supported. Indeed, it was chosen as the best foreign play for the first Larra awards. Certainly there are also, as he suggests, critical successes that failed to attract audiences. One case in point is the 1975 revival of *Antígona*, directed by Miguel Narros at the Reina Victoria, a major commercial playhouse, with Ana Belén, one of Spain's most popular film actresses, in the title role. The critics had high praise for the cast and direction and some minor disagreement on the appropriateness of Lauro Olmo's version, which subtly shifted the action to contemporary Spain by his use of colloquial language. Alvaro concluded that the reviews were favorable and the production of unquestionably high quality, but the show closed after only fifty performances (1975: 67).

On the other hand, Alonso's general appraisal of Anouilh's reception in Spain is somewhat more pessimistic than the statistics would indicate. In the decade of the 1970s two Anouilh plays stand out as critical and box office successes: *Los peces rojos* (1973) and *Una orquesta de señoritas* (1977).

Directed by Gustavo Pérez Puig in a translation by A. Ruiz Funes, *Los peces rojos* opened at the Fígaro in October 1973 and ran for more than 400 performances. It shared the Espectador y la Crítica prize for best foreign play with Wesker's *La cocina* (*The Kitchen*) and led Alvaro to identify Anouilh both as "one of the most complete playwrights of the present generation" and as the living French author who had had the most plays staged in Spain (1973: 183). A revival the following September at Madrid's Bellas Artes

Jesús Puente and Licia Calderón in 1976 Barcelona production of Anouilh's
Los peces rojos. Directed by Jesús Puente. (Photo by Gyenes)

Theatre lasted for an additional 200 performances. The success of the Madrid production no doubt inspired actor-director Jesús Puente, whose own production of *Los peces rojos* reached Barcelona in January 1976. Anouilh's tragicomedy is a brilliant metaplay, focusing on the struggle of the dramatist-character against the mediocrity and resentment of those around him. Critic Fernando Lázaro Carreter compared Anouilh's satire to Quevedo and found the text to be "the desperate scream of a liberal man" under attack by a conspiracy of "weak, impotent dwarfs" (qtd. Alvaro 1973: 185–186).

There are traces of Anouilh's early plays, particularly the "pièces roses" and "pièces brillantes," in the comedies of Spanish authors like Víctor Ruiz Iriarte. In the case of *Los peces rojos*, there is an apparent direct influence on Jaime Salom's *La piel del limón*, an impassioned plea for divorce reform. The Barcelona dramatist's play opened in Madrid in September 1976 and remained on the boards for more than 500 performances. In a general way, Salom's text, like Anouilh's, mixes surface humor with an essentially tragic view of the human condition and places the liberal protagonist in a losing battle with the reactionary forces of his family and society. More specifically, however, there is a comic juxtaposition of the protagonist in childhood and middle age, with the adult actor doubling in both roles. Not coincidentally, that actor in the Salom production was Jesús Puente, who had played the counterpart Anouilh role in Barcelona some months earlier.

Una orquesta de señoritas, by the San Telmo company from Buenos Aires, was chosen for the inaugural production at Madrid's newly refurbished Príncipe Theatre in April 1977. It ran for more than 400 performances, as well as enjoying a successful provincial tour in 1978. The troupe, which featured male actors in all but one of the female roles, was awarded the Espectador y la Crítica prize for the best foreign company performing in the capital that year.

During the transition to democracy after Franco's death in 1975, there was a short-lived wave of cross-gender acting on the Spanish stage that ultimately included a 1976 version of Genet's *Las criadas* with male actors and a 1978 staging of

Beckett's *Esperando a Godot* with an all-female cast. At the beginning of the movement, Angel Facio's polemical version of Lorca's *La casa de Bernarda Alba*, with Ismael Merlo in the title role, had opened just a few months before Anouilh's sad little comedy reached Madrid.

In reacting to *Una orquesta de señoritas*, Spanish critics understandably tried to analyze why the portrayal by men of the "young ladies" of a touring provincial orchestra, in their story of frustrated loves, worked so well. Arcadio Baquero Goyanes suggested that it was an effective distancing device, and Lázaro Carreter thought that it served to heighten both the cruelty and the poetry within the text (qtd. Alvaro 1977: 83). Lorenzo López Sancho, reviewer for the conservative *ABC*, hastened to clarify that this was not a transvestite performance with dubious erotic intent but rather a return to a classic convention of male actors in women's roles (qtd. Alvaro 1977: 82–83). Alvaro was at a loss to know which to admire more: "the illustrious French playwright's funny, pathetic farce or the carefully measured, perfect interpretation" of the Argentinian actors (1977: 80). When *Una orquesta de señoritas* was revived in December 1985, a local critic in Saragossa labeled it "a classic play that continues to have audience appeal" (El Público Anuario 1986: 33). In the well-received production by Saragossa's Al Caracol company, the cross-gender acting had disappeared, nor were male actors used in a 1988 revival in Seville.

Camus's appeal in Spain during the early years of the Franco regime no doubt included a political undercurrent beyond the committed content of the works themselves. The Algerian-born author, whose mother was of Spanish descent, had strong ties to Spanish Republicans in exile in France, and this fact must have been known to many theatre people and playgoers. To stage Camus, then, was to make a political statement, even though the censors did not view him so harshly as they did such leftist writers as Brecht and Sartre. On occasion that historical context may still have its validity. Significantly, Taller de Teatro Gaditano in Cádiz chose his drama set in Spain, *Estado de sitio* (*L'Etat de siège*), for a July 1986 production that coincided with the fiftieth anniversary of the outbreak of the Civil War. The continuing interest in Camus, however, generally transcends the overtly political, and all four of the works that comprise his original theatre have been done in the past two decades.

One Camus text in particular has had a long and illustrious production history on the Spanish stage. Directed by José Tamayo, translated by José Escué Porta, and featuring José María Rodero in the title role, *Calígula* opened at the Bellas Artes in October 1963 to such wide acclaim that Tamayo included it in the repertory of his touring company for 1964, 1966, and again in 1970. Rodero, who had received a National Theatre Prize for his Caligula, revived the play in 1982 with director Luis Balaguer, once again to rave reviews. It was performed at the annual festival of classic theatre at Merida and chosen to reopen the capital city's Alcázar Theatre. There was agreement among Madrid critics that the success of *Calígula* is dependent upon the lead actor and that Rodero fulfilled the role magnificently, bringing even greater depth to his earlier performance. In acknowledging Rodero's triumph as the infamous Roman emperor, E. Haro Tecglen, writing for *El País,* described his complex Caligula as "cynical, mordant, capricious and, naturally, absurd, but also tragic, bitter" (qtd. Alvaro 1982: 197). Antonio Valencia proclaimed Rodero to be Spain's greatest actor and the revival of the Camus play to rival the best theatre of the contemporary world stage (qtd. Alvaro 1982: 198). Haro Tecglen's reaction was much less positive to yet another revival in 1990, this one directed again by Tamayo but starring film actor Imanol Arias (*El País* 3 September 1990).

The enthusiastic reception to the 1982 *Calígula* belies David Bradby's recent assessment in *The Cambridge Guide to World Theatre* that Camus's plays "no longer seem as innovative as they did in the 1940s and 1950s" (1988: 146). But it is possible that Camus, with his strong moralistic bent and his ties to Mediterranean culture, has tended to find a more responsive audience south of the Pyrenees than in France. Referring to Camus on the French stage, André Camp reports that his atemporal tragedy, *Le Malentendu* (1944), has seldom been revived. He moreover suggests that the tense atmosphere, the language consisting of short sentences, and the shadowy women dressed in black, all reflect the influence of García Lorca (*L'Avant-Scène Théâtre* 763: 51). Camp's perceptive comment may clarify why *El malentendido* has enjoyed multiple stagings in Spain, including a 1969 revival directed by Adolfo Marsillach and a 1970 one by actress Gemma Cuervo. Even *Les Justes*, which Bradby labels as more of an extended debate than a dramatic action (1988: 146), has fared well in Madrid. It was one of the plays done by the independent group TEI in 1973, the year their Pequeño Teatro Magallanes received the Espectador y la Crítica award for best programming. In spite of the amateurish cast, the play ran for more than a hundred performances and inspired a positive response to Camus's "marvelously human voice" (C. L. Alvarez, qtd. Alvaro 1973: 73).

Like Anouilh, Ionesco first became known in Spain through chamber theatre. In some respects, his theatre has now come full circle, for his continued popularity resides mainly with independent or regional groups and with his earliest plays: *La cantante calva* (*La Cantatrice chauve*) and *La lección* (*La Leçon*). For 1986 alone, *El Público's* theatre annual lists five productions of one or both of these plays in such places as San Sebastián, Jaen, and Cádiz, as well as Madrid province. For 1988, there are four productions of *La cantante calva*, in Salamanca, Sabadell, Alicante, and Madrid. The periodic directories of amateur and professional companies, also published by *El Público*, similarly reveal Ionesco's strong appeal.[7] They identify twelve plays ready for performance in 1985–86 and eight for 1988. In the theatre annual for 1988, Ionesco, with eight entries, is the most frequently cited French playwright, eclipsing even Molière, listed four times.

Establishment critics greeted the early chamber theatre productions of Ionesco with hostility. To Trino Martínez Trives and Manuel Gallego Morell's January 1955 staging of *La lección* and *La cantante calva*, Sainz de Robles responded that neither play was worth translating (1954–55: 19). The first Ionesco text to reach mainstream audiences, in January 1961, was *Rinoceronte;* it was translated by Trives, who by then had assumed a major role in promoting the French Theatre of the Absurd in Spain. Although the play had its defenders, Sainz de Robles's negative reaction, recorded in the pages of his *Teatro Español*, was typical of establishment critics. Declaring *Rinoceronte* to be "obscure, absurd and boring," he found Ionesco's work to be to theatre what bad abstract art is to painting: "something to bedazzle fools or charlatans" (1960–61: xxiii). When José Luis Alonso dared return to the María Guerrero National Theatre in November 1964 with more Ionesco, the French absurdist was greeted with enthusiasm. Alvaro captioned the entry for *El Rey se muere* and *El nuevo inquilino* (*Le Roi se meurt* and *Le nouveau locataire*): "Ionesco, absuelto" (Ionesco, absolved). José Bódalo received a National Theatre Prize and a Larra for his portrayal of the king. Alonso also received both of these awards that year, and Francisco Nieva was named best stage designer in *Primer Acto*'s Larra competition, in part for his work on the Ionesco production. The Ionesco texts, in Trives's translation, shared the Larra for best foreign play with Strindberg's *La sonata de los espectros*. The Madrid run was followed by a triumphant tour of Barcelona and the provinces.

This 1964 *El Rey se muere* may be the high point for Ionesco in Spanish production history. In 1973 his *Macbett*, under the direction of José María Morera, also was done at the María Guerrero, but to mixed reactions, in part because of an unwillingness on the part of audience and critics alike to accept a parody of Shakespeare. The cast, drawn from the Angel Guimerà national company of Barcelona, included Gemma Cuervo as Lady Duncan. Both set design and translation were by Francisco Nieva, whose long years of residence in Paris had given him the opportunity to see original productions of Ionesco and other French playwrights. In spite of the caliber of the people involved, *Macbett* was labeled a failure. In 1984, when the independent Sala Cadarso featured *La cantante calva* and *El maestro* (*Le Maître*), along with Obaldia's *El difunto* (*Le Défunt*), Alvaro was led to comment, "We have already forgotten the 'theatre of the absurd' that was so controversial and so interesting in the 50s" (1984: 104). José Monleón similarly observed that no one takes seriously any longer the crisis in language raised by Ionesco in his early plays (qtd. Alvaro 1984: 106–107). Nevertheless, the program of the three short French plays, under the direction of Manuel Canseco, ran for more than a hundred performances. Ionesco may no longer shock, but he still entertains.

Although his initial reception in the 1950s was also negative, the current status of Beckett in Spain is unquestionably high. On the occasion of Genet's death in 1986, Angel Fernández-Santos identified Beckett and Genet as the two outstanding, solitary rocks of the contemporary stage. Pointing out their common exploration of the tragic hell of human existence, Fernández-Santos declared that Beckett, who paved the way for Genet, "provoked short circuits in the logic of a theatre, like that of Spain, that had lost all contact with that essential question" (1986: 19). Nevertheless, Antonia Rodríguez-Gago was correct when she affirmed in early 1984 that Beckett had been conspicuously absent from the official Spanish stage (26). *Esperando a Godot* was staged in chamber theatre in Madrid in May 1955, and again in March 1956, by Pequeño Teatro Dido, under the direction of Trino Martínez Trives. It was chosen by José Monleón and his editorial board for publication in the inaugural issue of *Primer Acto* in 1957, where it appeared with an analysis by Alfonso Sastre. Monleón recalls that for young liberals, Beckett's dramatic world was quintessentially realistic, while for the dominant Franco regime, this Theatre of the Absurd epitomized the wrong thinking of those who had lost the Civil War (*Primer Acto* 206). Alvaro indeed reported that establishment critics had promptly labeled *Godot* as "arbitrary, confusing and boring" (1958: 171). In 1967 Alvaro confessed that initially he had not understood Beckett's play; his first reading, of an Argentinian translation, had left him angry and dismayed (1967: 262). Pequeño Teatro Dido's 1958 chamber theatre production of *Final de partida* (Luce Moreau de Arrabal's translation of *Fin de partie*) led to a similar response. *Final de partida* did not return to the Madrid stage until 1984. Even *Esperando a Godot* was seldom performed there, although revivals noted by Alvaro in the capital for 1967 and 1978 were enthusiastically received and ran for 50 and 100 performances, respectively. The only other Madrid staging of Beckett cited by Alvaro from 1965 through 1983 is Trives's revival of *Días felices* (*Happy Days*) in 1974; the text had premiered in 1963.

The year 1984, however, marks a renewed Spanish interest in the Irish-French playwright. With a January opening at the Sala Cadarso, Miguel Narros directed *Final de partida*, in a new version by Aitana Alberti. The following October, José Sanchis Sinisterra brought to the María Guerrero National Theatre in Madrid *Que hermosos días*, his version of *Happy Days* created by the Drama Center of Catalonia and starring Rosa Novell as Winnie. Juxtaposing reviews of the two Beckett plays, Alvaro chose comments that highlighted the changing audience response to Beckett and, indeed, the changing historical circumstances. E. Haro Tecglen of *El País* observed that what was once seen as a frightening, metaphysical tragedy could now evoke appreciative laughter (qtd. Alvaro 1984: 182).

Beckett specialist Rodríguez-Gago, writing for *El Público*, characterized the two 1984 productions as "magnificent." Before traveling to the National Drama Center in Madrid, Sanchis Sinisterra had staged *Happy Days* in Catalan, under the title *Oh! els bons dies*. It was Novell who had fallen in love with the role of Winnie and had therefore encouraged Sinisterra to take on the project. This Catalan-language premiere was accompanied by a series of cultural events in Barcelona related to Beckett's theatre: roundtable discussions, special expositions, and video showings. These activities were followed by a major Beckett festival in Madrid in the spring of 1985. Accordingly *Primer Acto* dedicated part of No. 206 to Beckett, including statements by the two directors.

Narros, who had just been named to head Madrid's municipal Teatro Español, considered *Final de partida*, with its limited physical action and economy of expression, to be an interesting challenge. He felt that his successful production had attracted a new audience, because of Beckett's appeal to university students, and that the play's dramatic situation continues to be relevant for contemporary playgoers (*Primer Acto* 206: 34). Sanchis Sinisterra agrees that "the famous 'absurd' is our daily reality" (*Primer Acto* 206: 37). While acknowledging Trives's previous contribution to Beckett performance in Spain, the Catalan playwright-director held that his new translations of *Happy Days*, like Beckett's own "rational" French version, *Oh, les beaux jours*, contributed to a better audience reception (37).

In the last half of the 1980s, interest in Beckett remained strong, particularly in Catalonia. Sanchis Sinisterra's own Teatro Fronterizo staged *Primer amor* in Barcelona in January 1986, and, as previously noted, the prestigious Lliure added *Oh! els bons dies* to its repertory in 1986–87. In 1987, Joan Anton Benach reported enthusiastically in *El Público* that the Centro Insular de Gran Canaria had created an exciting ballet based on Beckett's radio script *Letra y música* that was expected to tour throughout the Canary Islands and the Peninsula. Benach found the spectacle to be controversial but highly attractive, "capable of stimulating understanding of the exceptional contribution" that Beckett had made to world drama (*El Público* 50: 25). *El Público's* Guía Teatral de España for 1988 lists no fewer than five Beckett productions available for contract, including Fronterizo's *Primer amor*, Gran Canaria's *Letra y música*, a version of *Godot* by Jácara in Seville, and short plays by groups in Barcelona and Madrid. In 1989 Sanchis Sinisterra and his theatre group opened their own playhouse in Barcelona, calling it Sala Beckett. *El Público's* listing of theatres operating in September 1990 revealed that the Beckett's stagings for that month were indeed limited to works by that playwright (*El Público* 82: 170).

The production history of Sartre in Spain follows a very different pattern from that of Ionesco and Beckett. While the chamber performances of the Theatre of the Absurd left conservative critics bewildered and angry, the censors took a far more rigid stance with the leftist existential philosopher, whose works were completely silenced on religious and political grounds. On the other hand, once Sartre reached the Barcelona stage in October 1967, he gained more ready access to mainstream, professional theatre. At the end of the 1980s, however, Sartre's plays did not match the continuing popularity of Ionesco or Beckett with independent groups.

The long ban on Sartre created an aura of expectation for the premiere of Adolfo Marsillach and Nuria Espert's *Espectáculo Sartre* at the Poliorama Theatre. The production consisted of playwright Alfonso Sastre's translations of both *La . . . respetuosa* and *A puerta cerrada* (*La putain respectueuse* and *Huis-clos*), but it was the latter text that held the greater interest. Marsillach, Espert, and Gemma Cuervo, who played the third principal role, were enthusiastically received by audience and critics alike. After an extended run in Barcelona, the *Espectáculo Sartre* opened in Madrid's Reina Victoria in March 1968, remained there for more than 200 performances, and then enjoyed a provincial tour into the spring of 1969. This success is all the more noteworthy if one realizes that most plays performed by Espert's company in the 1960s ran only two months (Londré 1985).

The significance of the event led Alvaro to dedicate more space than usual to the production and to publish his own essay on Sartre and his work. Reflecting conservative Spain's bias against the French existentialist, Alvaro was quick to disassociate himself from the plays even while praising them. Having characterized Sartre as perhaps the most influential figure in postwar literature and theatre, and having said that the staging of his works, even with twenty years of delay, opened new vistas to the Spanish stage, Alvaro affirmed: "We should all congratulate ourselves, although we are not, absolutely not, in agreement with Sartre's ideas" (1968: 201). He attributed the favorable audience response to "circumstances, curiosity, a certain snob appeal," for the two plays, particularly *A puerta cerrada*, were "distasteful to the spectators who usually attend our theatres" (1968: 203). Alvaro nevertheless noted that Spanish playgoers had understood and appreciated the dramatic force and theatrical effectiveness of the work.

Underscoring several of the establishment critics' specific comments on *A puerta cerrada* is their attempt to reconcile Sartre's atheism with their own Catholic views. Lorenzo López Sancho found a "religious feeling" floating above Sartre's apparent atheism (qtd. Alvaro 1968: 213). Manuel

Díez Crespo, in almost identical words, also found religious feeling floating above the text, which he interpreted as an allegorical *auto sacramental* that proved the existence of hell (qtd. Alvaro 1968: 213). As for the importance of the play and the quality of the production, critical reaction was highly favorable. Alfredo Marqueríe labeled the drama "truly extraordinary," "a creation without peer in the tragedy of our time" (qtd. Alvaro 1968: 216–217).

The second professional production of Sartre in Spain came in 1970, the year after the *Espectáculo Sartre* ended its tour. The María José Goyanes company, directed by José María Morera, included Sastre's translation of *Las moscas* (*Les Mouches*) in its repertory for performances in more than thirty provincial cities, but the tour never reached Madrid.

The second Sartre play in the capital was *Los secuestrados de Altona*. Directed by Morera, translated by Sastre, and with a cast headed by Gemma Cuervo, Encarna Paso, and Fernando Guillén, it opened at the Beatriz in March 1972, ran for more than 200 performances before going on tour, and received the Espectador y la Crítica prize for best foreign play of the year. Designer Francisco Nieva also received the Espectador y la Crítica award, in part for his work on this production; his set, which emphasized blacks and grays, reflecting mirrors, huge engravings, and oversize furniture, created a deliberately unreal audience perspective on the characters. Alvaro reprinted an explanatory note by Sastre, and his collage of critical commentary, a well-balanced and fair assessment of the text, was quite different in tone from the Sartre section in his 1968 annual.

That *Los secuestrados de Altona* should have struck a responsive chord with Spanish audiences at the end of the Franco era is not surprising. Alvaro suggests in passing that some spectators interpreted the play as "an explicit attack on fascism" (1972: 148), and certainly it is. Although the action is set in postwar Germany, the symbolic tale of exploitation and guilt, torture and inner exile, madness and incest, is not far removed from the political and moral allegories created by Spanish authors to allude to their own historical tragedy.

The third major Sartre production, *Las manos sucias* (*Les Mains sales*), opened in November 1977, two years after Franco's death. It ran for more than 350 performances in Madrid, moving from the Esclava to the Bellas Artes Theatre in March 1978, when its contract with the former expired, and then making a provincial tour. Directed by José Luis Alonso and translated by Marsillach, *Las manos sucias* was named best foreign play of the year. José Luis Pellicena, in the role of Hugo, also received the Espectador y la Crítica prize for best actor. Critic Antonio Valencia proclaimed that he was tempted to stand up and cheer during the performance because he found the play to be so extraordinary, "a complete restoration of theatrical values" (qtd. Alvaro 1977: 111). The overt political theme of Sartre's text did not disturb Alvaro. Although newspaper advertisements for the play raised the question of whether the work was Communist or anti-Communist, he found that irrelevant: "The important thing is that we have before us a great dramatic work that deals with nothing less than human responsibility, as defined in Sartrian thought" (1977: 109). In the space of ten years, mainstream response to Sartre's theatre had moved from defensiveness to open acceptance; the transition, of course, was consistent with the changing political reality of Spain.

In the 1980s, Sartre virtually disappeared from major playhouses, the one exception being the 1985 production in Catalan by the Centre Dramàtic de la Generalitat of Sartre's version of Dumas's *Kean*. Nor does his popularity with provincial and amateur groups compare with that of Ionesco or, to a lesser extent, Beckett, although *A puerta cerrada* by itself was cited in *El Público's* directories as available in three separate productions in 1985–86 and two in 1987; the annual for 1988 similarly listed two stagings, one by a university group in Málaga and the other by a group in Madrid. Smaller companies with limited resources may, of course, be attracted to short plays that can be done with minimal props and sets. Sartre's longer works, like some of Genet's, may therefore be inaccessible to them. Relative number of productions among independent troupes is therefore not a true measure of a playwright's impact.

A puerta cerrada was the text chosen by director Angel Facio to revive Los Goliardos in the fall of 1989. The company had been one of the most influential of the independent theatre movement during the Franco regime but had disappeared fifteen years before. Facio stated quite clearly that he had chosen Sartre's play with its small cast because of budgetary restraints (qtd. Valiente 30). He created a "free adaptation," and chose actors with three very different accents: Spanish, Argentinian, and Polish. For actress Zywila Pieatraz-Wach, who played Estelle, this was her first role in Spanish; she clarified that the director had helped her to assume the frivolous attitude of young women of Madrid's high society (qtd. Valiente 29). At the play's premiere in Alcalá, Facio discovered from the audience's laughter that he was directing a comedy (qtd. Valiente 30). When the production reached Madrid the following summer, *El País* critic Haro Tecglen was dismayed at changes made to a masterpiece, ostensibly to enhance the text's theatricality. His review was titled "Revolt Against Sartre" (*El País* 2 July 1990).

Of the six major French authors of the postwar period, Ionesco is the most frequently staged, but the influence of Genet and Beckett is doubtless more significant. Genet, like Camus, touched a particularly responsive chord in Spain, albeit for different reasons. If Camus's existentialist analysis of guilt and responsibility appealed to the moralistic vein of Hispanic culture, Genet's iconoclastic unmasking of decadence from the vantage point of the Other spoke directly to another essential, if contradictory, aspect both of Spanish tradition and of contemporary Hispanic reality. There are traces of Genet's metatheatrical games, with their emphasis on exploiter and exploited, not only in such Spanish playwrights as Fernando Arrabal, Francisco Nieva, and Luis Riaza, but also in Latin American authors like the Argentine Griselda Gambarro and Cuban exiles José Triana and Eduardo Manet. Nieva, who acknowledges the impact that reading Artaud and Genet had on his own evolving theatre, affirms that Genet revealed to him not only the decadence of our civilization but also an appreciation of the beauty rejected by that civilization, of spectacle, and of tragic nightmares (Nieva 1978: 39–41). There is something essentially Hispanic in Genet's irreverent confrontation of taboos, his insistent probing of the seamy underside of society, and even in his baroque language, so far removed from classic French expression.

In her autobiography, the Spanish-French actress Maria Casarès discusses at length her search for her Spanish roots and her pleasure at finding opportunities within the theatre world to express her Hispanic identity. She pointedly mentions her role as the Mother in Genet's *Les Paravents* (1966) to be such an opportunity, encountered, quite surprisingly, "right in the middle of Paris." She cites Genet, along with directors Jorge Lavelli, who spoke to her in Spanish, and Maurice Béjart, who encouraged her to sing in Spanish for a spectacle based on San Juan de la Cruz, but does not clarify why it was Genet's text that forced her to uncover the land she had buried so deeply within herself that she had to make a supreme effort "to find it again, to recover my true reality" (*Residente* 393).

When I asked Casarès to explain her reference to *Les Paravents*, she recalled having difficulty finding the right approach to her character during early rehearsals. Genet himself offered the suggestion that she would find the key to the Mother within her Hispanic heritage: specifically within the picaresque novel. The actress, who several years later triumphed in her portrayal of La Celestina, a related character, said that Genet's observation opened a window for her that revealed the kind of vitality needed to transform thought into spirit. For her, Genet's anarchism was, indeed, closely related to Spain (Telephone interview). At the time of Roger Blin's controversial staging at the Odéon, Genet's grotesque vision of the French military involvement in Algeria evoked comparisons with Goya's portraits of the royal family (*Théâtre Acteurs*). That observation similarly places Genet within a satirical current that runs from the picaresque and Quevedo through Goya to Valle-Inclán.

Genet did, in fact, have a direct connection to Spain, for he worked as a prostitute in Barcelona's Barrio Chino for an extended period in the early 1930s and he visited the country with some frequency in later years. In an interview for *Primer Acto,* held in 1970 when he came to see the Víctor García–Nuria Espert production of *Las criadas* but not published, for political reasons, until 1981, Genet declared his socialist convictions. He added that he wished his ideological statement to be made first in Spanish, and in Spain (Genet 54). Expressing his love/hate relationship to the Spanish nation, he identified it in his own life as the place "where everything began about forty years ago" (Genet 52). He assured his listeners that his criticism of Spain was not that of a foreigner, but of someone who was one of them (Genet 54). Lluís Pasqual's Spanish reading of Genet's *Le Balcon* for his 1980–81 Lliure production was neither casual nor done without the author's consent.

Genet's enormous impact on the Spanish stage rests primarily on one play and, indeed, on one landmark production: the version of *Les Bonnes,* created by García and Espert in 1969. It was this work that made Espert "internationally famous" (Londré 1985). In comments to Carmen Compte for a 1975 study in *Les Voies de la Création Théâtrale,* the actress recalled that the Sartre plays, which she had loved, had given her the money to be able to stage the Genet text, which she found to be the most difficult and satisfying of her career (qtd. Londré 1985). The production won the grand prize at the 1969 international theatre festival in Belgrade and made a triumphant tour of major European cities. Fifteen years later it was still hailed as one of the most significant events in contemporary Spanish stage history (Pérez Coterillo *El Público* 14: 9).

Its long-term fame notwithstanding, the García-Espert *Las criadas* did not have an auspicious beginning. The intention was to stage it along with Arrabal's *Los dos verdugos (Les deux bourreaux),* and a set was designed that would accommodate both texts. On dress rehearsal night at the Reina Victoria in Madrid, the censors walked out indignantly after the Arrabal play. *Los dos verdugos* was banned but the censors, who left before seeing *Las criadas,* fortunately did not prohibit the Genet as well (Espert 1982: 44). The management of the Reina Victoria, however, refused to let the show go on. The Espert company thus moved to Barcelona, where the Poliorama had become available. It was there that the premiere took place in February.

For his production—which featured Espert and Julieta Serrano as the two maids, Claire and Solange, and Mayrata O'Wisiedo as the lady—García concentrated on the visual and physical elements rather than the verbal text. He ignored Genet's suggested set design of Louis XV furniture, creating instead a barren, curved space with reflecting panels, an angled floor, and a circular bed with black sheets where the ritualistic sacrifice could be carried out. To the black uniforms of the maids, he contrasted elegant dresses in pure white and an equally symbolic red cape. He carefully led the actresses into a new kind of aggressive expression that emphasized the rhythms in language, gesture, and movement. The result was the oneiric atmosphere of a Black Mass. Critical reaction in Barcelona was mixed, but *Las criadas* played for three months, reaching 148 performances.

The Madrid staging of *Las criadas* finally opened in October, at the Fígaro, where it ran for 250 performances. The theatre management allowed the Espert company to set up a kind of cultural center, with book exhibits, lectures, and poetry readings (Londré 1985). Recognizing the significance of the production, Alvaro devoted a double section to it in his annual and published several photos. Nevertheless, his own ambivalence is readily apparent. In the dialogue he created from critical excerpts, he introduced comments from an unidentified spectator who found the play boring. A recurrent theme in his excerpts of published reviews is that *Las criadas* is a defense of evil. The casual reader of these eleven pages of commentary might never suspect that they describe a production of more than fleeting interest. Alvaro's conclusion to the critical response he cites is that he does not know what to make of it (1969: 230).

The same conservative/liberal dichotomy, evoked by the early productions of the Theatre of the Absurd, surfaces again in this mixed response to the García-Espert *Las criadas*. Of the thirteen critics who cast votes for the Espectador y la Crítica awards, four selected *Las criadas* as best foreign play of the year. (The winner, with five votes, was Sean O'Casey's *Red Roses for Me*, in a version by Alfonso Sastre, directed by José María Morera and with set design by Francisco Nieva.) Although no one associated with the Genet text won a prize, García also received four votes as best director and the three actresses collectively garnered five votes. Obviously a minority of critics responded positively. Moreover, the Madrid run was followed by a successful provincial tour in 1970.

Paradoxically the original García-Espert *Las criadas* not only received wider acclaim outside Spain than within but was well received abroad precisely because of the Spanish quality of the interpretation. In an interview with Evelyne Ertel in Paris, Espert emphasized that the Argentine-born García "had very strong ties to Spain," that he had relished the opportunity to work in his native language, and that the Spanish troupe had not considered him a foreigner. Raymonde Temkine, in a review of the production on tour in France in April 1970, stressed both the extraordinary dramatic impact of this particular staging and its underlying Hispanism; in spite of its being done in a foreign language, the French critic found the performance superior to earlier productions in France, including those of Louis Jouvet and Jean-Marie Serreau (Temkine 1: 47). Temkine attributed such aspects as the sense of ritual, passion, and violence to the company's Hispanic roots; the Spanish language lent itself particularly well to the syncopated rhythms García wished to evoke (1: 48). When García later attempted to recreate *Les Bonnes* in French with French actresses, he was far less successful (Londré 1985). Perhaps a lingering impression that *Les Bonnes* is a "Spanish" play explains why in 1984 Angel Facio became the first Spaniard invited to direct a play in Poland; the text in question was, of course, Genet's. The Polish version of the French work, directed by a Spaniard, ran two nights a week for over a year in the experimental Jaracza Theatre of Lodz (Koniecpolski).

When Víctor García died in Paris in October 1982, at the age of forty-seven, Espert decided that she would revive his production of *Las criadas* in homage to him. She reassembled the original cast, and they went through the process of recreating the staging as outlined by García. The only change was in the choice of translation. Substituted for the earlier Manuel Herrero version was a new one by Armando Moreno, Espert's husband and manager, that had previously been used for the 1976 revival with the all-male cast. The production opened in Valencia in February 1983 and continued on tour well into 1985, including a run of more than 150 performances at the national Sala Olimpia in Madrid, starting in November 1984. *Primer Acto* highlighted the revival while it was still in rehearsal and identified the original production as one that had had a major influence on the European stage of the 1970s (*Primer Acto* 196: 42). *El Público* featured the return of *Las criadas* to Madrid as the cover story for No. 14, published that month.

In an interview for a newspaper in Oviedo, Espert declared that the spectators as well as the performers had matured during the fifteen-year interval; as a result, *Las criadas* had lost its shock effect and political connotations but had gained in universality (qtd. El Público Anuario 1985: 172). Her comments are supported by the generally favorable response of the Madrid critics. Alvaro no longer expresses ambivalence but rather declares *Las criadas* to be one of the fundamental works of our times (1984: 136). Lorenzo López Sancho, writing for the conservative *ABC*, labels the play "a classic" and finds García's oneiric staging to be appropriate for such a magical, baroque ceremony (qtd. Alvaro 1984: 139). José Monleón, as always the liberal champion of innovative theatre, proclaimed the revival to be "incredibly fresh and vigorous," a homage not only to Víctor García but also to "talent and hope" (qtd. Alvaro 1984: 139).

Next to the García-Espert *Las criadas*, the most influential staging of Genet in Spain is doubtless Pasqual's production of *El balcó*, in Carme Serrallonga's translation, which opened the Lliure's 1980–81 season in Barcelona. In an extensive interview with the director, published in *Pipirijaina* before the premiere, Joan Abellán expressed reservations about many of Pasqual's decisions, including the set design and his casting of Rosa María Sardá as Mme. Irma. To Abellán's criticism, Pasqual responded that the spectators would have the last word (*Pipirijaina* 16: 68). And they did. Pasqual received both the Serra d'Or Critics Prize and the Adrià Gual Prize for his direction of *El balcó*. In his subsequent review for *El Público* of the first ten years of the Lliure, Abellán called Genet's text one of contemporary drama's challenges for ambitious directors (Cuaderno 10: 59).

In his retrospective commentary, Abellán defines *El balcó* as a "brutal metaphor of reality" and finds in this iconoclastic, denunciatory work all of censorship's greatest taboos (Cuaderno 10: 59). The allusion is aimed more to the censors of Francoist Spain than to France. Genet's metatheatrical games, set in a brothel against the background of revolution, present a satirical attack on conservative Spain's untouchable subjects: morality, religion, and the military. Genet's stage directions explicitly call for a Spanish crucifix in the opening scene. Within the world of illusion revealed there, neither the Bishop nor the young woman who has come to confession are what they seem. They are a prostitute and her client engaged in role-playing. Given the subversive potential of metadrama, the scene suggests an underlying hypocrisy in the outer world as well, that is, in Spain's Nationalcatholicism.

In his production notes, Pasqual indicates his awareness of this intentional Spanish connection. He affirms that for Genet Spain is a kind of bridge between Europe, the great Western cemetery, and the Arab culture, which he considered the vital force of the future. As examples within the play, Pasqual points out that the character Carmen not only has a Spanish name but is reminiscent of Lorca's protagonists. The Police Chief bears a strong resemblance to Franco himself, and there is a direct textual reference, in Spanish, to *El Valle de los Caídos*, the mausoleum Franco had prepared for himself years before his death. The director asks himself how he can visualize Genet's "decontextualized Spanish background" within *El balcó*'s universal poetics. Among the several changes Pasqual made, all with Genet's approval, were two that foregrounded the Spanish essence: the first prostitute, appearing with the Bishop, was to be played by a boy in a girl's first communion dress; the fourth prostitute would be a Spanish lady wearing a mantilla, dressed as if she were going to an audience with the Pope (Notas de lectura 56). Pasqual added both an extra layer to the role-playing and, in the choice of typical Spanish costumes, another visual sign of the constant Spanish background.

The Lliure production of *El balcó* and the Espert revival of *Las criadas* are the stagings of Genet that have achieved the greatest visibility in Spain, but his works are also done on occasion by provincial theatres and amateur groups. The texts most frequently staged in Spain are the short ones, *Les Bonnes* and *Haute surveillance*, but in 1985–86 the Catalan-language Teatre del Maresme, in the province of Barcelona, undertook the challenge of staging *Les Nègres*. Three years after Genet's death, in June 1989, *El Público* featured his picture on the cover and affirmed that his work was gaining in international significance (*El Público* 69: 1). The following October, *Cuadernos el Público* 41 was a monograph dedicated to Genet and including Facio's translation of the previously unpublished play *Elle*.

There is no single measure that can establish a playwright's impact. In France, for example, Alejandro Casona is no longer staged in any major playhouse, yet his plays are popular with certain community theatres. French authors, including key figures of the postwar stage, are seldom produced in Madrid but retain an important presence in regional theatres. For example, *El Público's* Cartelera for the 1985–86 fall-winter season, which includes 1348 titles, cites 14 plays produced of Ionesco, the highest number for any foreign playwright. Other French authors included in a chart of 19 foreign playwrights, represented by 4 or more titles, are Molière (8), Beckett (6), Saint-Exupéry (5), Boris Vian (5), and Sartre (4). By contrast, the Spanish playwrights represented by the most plays produced are García Lorca (35), Arrabal (15), Alonso de Santos (14), and Valle-Inclán (13). *El Público's* Guía Teatral for 1988 lists 840 titles by more than 400 authors. Of the 19 authors with 4 or more citations in the index, 10 are Spanish or, as in the case of Chilean Jorge Díaz, a longtime resident of Spain, and 5 are French: Ionesco (8), Beckett (5), Anouilh (4), Genet (4), and

Molière (4). The only foreign playwright cited as frequently as Ionesco is the Italian Dario Fo, and the only Spanish playwrights that equal or better his number of productions are Lorca (13), Arrabal (10), Valle-Inclán (9), and Calderón (8). There are 3 entries for Camus on this 1988 list, and Sartre is represented by 2 productions.

Another measure of impact is the number of articles and reviews devoted to a particular author in *El Público*, the influential government-subsidized theatre monthly. The indexes for the first four years of publication (1984–1987) place Genet at the top of the list of the six major postwar playwrights with eleven entries. There are six entries for Beckett, four for Ionesco, two each for Anouilh and Sartre, and none for Camus. One may thus conclude that Ionesco is favored by little theatre groups but that Genet, with fewer productions, nevertheless has greater prestige among theatre professionals.

No matter what measure is used, it is difficult to identify a significant impact of any serious French playwright who emerged after Beckett, Ionesco, and Genet or, indeed, who was born after the First World War. Analyses of available theatre annuals reveal no new Trino Martínez Trives doggedly introducing a younger generation of French authors to experimental theatres and no José Luis Alonso clearing the path for them to major commercial or public playhouses. To be sure, this relative absence of new playwrights is explained in part by theatre trends in France that first decentralized the stage and then emphasized collective creation, spectacle, and the role of the director, rather than the literary text of an individual author. Even so, there are many younger dramatists who achieved visibility on the French stage in the 1970s and 1980s but whose names do not appear in the lists of Spanish productions.

This is not to say that Spanish theatre professionals are unaware of current developments on the French stage. We have already noted the liaison between the two countries provided by directors like Flotats and Pasqual, and there are other indicators of strong interest from Spain. *Pipirijaina* (No. 21, March 1982), featured a series of five articles on the contemporary French stage, including interviews with the

Minister of Culture Jack Lang, with directors of several of the decentralized national drama centers, and with critic Bernard Dort. The following September, Angel Berenguer organized a week-long seminar to focus precisely on the contemporary French stage and its projection in Spain. Among the participants invited to the seminar in Sitges were key figures from both national stages. José Monleón marked the occasion by publishing in *Primer Acto*, No. 197, an interview with Antoine Vitez on forty years of French theatre, from Charles Dullin to Jack Lang. When the Théâtre du Soleil toured Spain for the first time in the fall of 1986, *El Público* dedicated Cuaderno 16 to Ariane Mnouchkine's company and noted in the preface that the Parisian theatre group had already had a noticeable influence in Spain on certain productions by Miguel Narros and Lluís Pasqual (Cuaderno 16: 5). Moreover the cultural ties between the two countries are strengthened by the presence in France of influential Latin American directors. *El Público's* Cuaderno 31 (March 1988) on the work in Europe of directors Alfredo Arias, Jorge Lavelli, Alejandro Quintana, and Raúl Ruiz is primarily a look at innovative theatre in France.

One younger director and author who has achieved popularity in Spain is Argentine-born Jérôme Savary (b. 1942) and his Magic Circus. On 20 April 1974, the independent group Tábano filled Madrid's largest theatre, the 2800-seat Monumental, for Vicente Romero's Spanish version of Savary's *Les Derniers jours de solitude de Robinson Crusoé*. Although the spectacle had only a short run, the opening night, which attracted an exuberant, youthful audience, was a memorable one. Some of the establishment critics were less than enthusiastic about the circus parody; Andrés Amorós even suggested that the production might have been rated for audiences under a certain age (qtd. Alvaro 1974: 128). But Fernando Lázaro Carreter summarized the appeal of *Los últimos días de soledad de Robinson Crusoe* by declaring that the youthful performers displayed such joyful imagination that they converted the old Monumental into a brilliant fiesta that could make the spectators forget their worries (qtd. Alvaro 1974: 127).

Savary's Magic Circus troupe, without his participation, was subsequently chosen to open the 1982–83 season of Madrid's municipal Teatro Español with *Histoire du Soldat*, performed in French. In June 1984, Savary himself returned for a production of *Bye Bye Show Biz* at the María Guerrero. In his role as master of ceremonies, the Argentine-French director spoke Spanish for the benefit of his Madrid audience. Although some critics suggested that Savary had run out of new ideas and Haro Tecglen lamented the ascendancy of spectacle over text, M. Diez Crespo praised the production for its "ingenuity, poetry and tenderness, magic, illusion, beauty and joy," and Adolfo Prego congratulated the National Drama Center for staging this example of French "ingenuity, skepticism, and culture" (qtd. Alvaro 1984: 120). The playful *Bye Bye Show Biz* toured Barcelona, Palma de Mallorca, Pamplona, and more than a dozen other Spanish cities.

When Savary collaborated with Quim Monzó to create, in Catalan, a Don Juan spectacle for the Centre Dramàtic de la Generalitat de Catalunya in Barcelona, *El Público* chose the production for its cover story (No. 38, November 1986). *El Tango de Don Joan* exemplifies two currents of the contemporary European stage: musical spectacle and international cooperation. Savary's modernization of the universal Don Juan myth, set in a clichéd Barcelona of the 1960s with a touch of Argentine tango, was coproduced by the Catalan Drama Center and the Carrefour Européen du Théâtre of Lyon, France. For the set and lighting design, Savary sought the collaboration of Serge Marzoiff and Alain Poisson, who had been brought to Barcelona from France by Flotats. Before reaching Barcelona's Romea Theatre on 1 November, traditional Spanish date for staging Zorrilla's *Don Juan Tenorio*, the spectacle played for a week in Hamburg, Germany. The reaction of Barcelona critics, cited in *El Público's* Anuario Teatral was mixed, but none doubted that the work would be a box office success (1987: 60–61).

Gildas Bourdet, an author-director who, like Savary, heads a national drama center in France, has also collaborated on a Spanish production of one of his works. The

Drama Center of Valencia, in cooperation with the National Center for New Tendencies of the Stage (CNNTE) of Madrid, brought Bourdet to Spain in 1988 to codirect Gonzalo Martínez Fresneda's version of *Le Saperleau*. Bourdet's approach to theatre is quite different from that of Savary. His farce not only highlights the dramatic text but is an exploration of language and its meaning. Bourdet acknowledges a certain influence of Beckett, particularly in the figure of the dog-narrator (*El Público* 56: 14). *El Saperlón* opened in Valencia in April and then received ten performances at the Sala Olimpia in Madrid, starting in late May.

Among the scattered stagings of contemporary French playwrights in Spain, the case of Savary is not the only one with a Hispanic connection, although, next to Arrabal, Savary is clearly the best-known of the Hispanic-French writers. When Trives premiered his version of René de Obaldia's comedy *Du vent dans les branches de Sassafras* in 1968, *ABC* critic López Sancho and Alvaro were both quick to identify the author as half Panamanian (1968: 192); commentaries in France on this novelist-playwright (b. 1918) often omit that information. The production of *Viento en las ramas del sasafras* in Madrid's small Valle-Inclán Theatre ran for some 75 performances and introduced a series of contemporary French plays, sponsored by the French embassy, that also included works by Ionesco, Romain Weingarten, and Felicien Marceau. The play was received as an amusing but insignificant parody of westerns. In France Obaldia is a playwright of stature; in 1987, for example, his *Genousie* was revived at the prestigious Odéon. But in Spain, subsequent stagings of his plays have had even less visibility than the first: *El gran visir* at the Lady Pepa cafe-theatre in 1970; two short plays in Barcelona in 1973, directed by Alberto Miralles; *El difunto*, done by the Teatro Universitario de Madrid, along with two plays by Ionesco, in 1984. Ibéral, the group organized in Paris to increase cultural relations between the Hispanic and French stages, is quite justified in placing Obaldia on their list of French authors needing promotion south of the Pyrenees.

Another Hispanic-French playwright who has barely penetrated the Spanish stage is Cuban-born Eduardo

Manet. Manet's first play written in French, *Les Nonnes*, is a grotesque farce that expressly calls for male actors in the title roles. Premiered in Paris in 1969 under the direction of Roger Blin, it has been translated into twenty-one languages and staged around the world, including two unsuccessful productions in Spain: 1977, in Madrid, and 1983, in Barcelona. The first of these was directed by actor Antonio Corencia, who had also directed and acted in the all-male version of Genet's *Las criadas* the previous year. Manet's metatheatrical games, in which the cigar-smoking nuns kill a wealthy lady for her jewels only to find themselves under siege because of the black revolt in Haiti, met with a negative response from Madrid critics. Nevertheless, Pablo Corbalán recognized *Las monjas* to be a "baroque parable about fascism," and Angel Fernández Santos lamented that a performance so filled with "passion, talent and dignity" should pass unnoticed (qtd. Alvaro 1977: 79).

El Público has valiantly attempted to keep some later productions of French plays from being similarly ignored, although it is doubtful that younger authors like Michel Deutsch, who came into prominence in the 1970s, and Bernard-Marie Koltès (1948–1989) have had any significant impact in Spain as yet. Deutsch's *L'Entrainement du champion avant la course* was done by a company in Aragon in 1982 and 1983, and Jordi Mesalles directed *Partage*, a violent portrayal of the tragic death of Sharon Tate, at Barcelona's Regina Theatre in 1984. Both Catalan-language productions of the playwright from Strasbourg were featured in the pages of *El Público* (3: 25, 10/11: 28–29), as was the first production of Koltès in Spain in 1988 (62: 28–29). *Combat de negre i de gossos* (*Combat de nègre et de chiens*) is the second of Koltès's plays and was directed in France by Patrice Chéreau. The Barcelona director Carme Portaceli had become familiar with Koltès's theatre when she worked in Paris under director Antoine Vitez and had struggled for two and a half years to bring his "brutal reflexion on our society of victors and vanquished" to Spanish audiences (qtd. Durán i Domenge 28). *El Público* recognized the premiere of Koltès at the Mercat de les Flors Theatre as an event of enough importance that they chose to publish the text, in Castilian translation, as the third in their new series of plays. But the number of spectators who actually saw the production in Barcelona was low; the play had few performances and played to a 250-seat house that averaged less than 20 percent capacity.

In the spring season of 1990, after the author's death from AIDS, two of Koltès's works were on stage simultaneously in government-subsidized theatres in Madrid: *Combate de negro y de perros* at the María Guerrero National Drama Center, and *En la soledad de los campos de algodón* (*Dans la solitude des champs de coton*) at the experimental Sala

Pilar Bayona and Antonio Valero in *Combate de negro y de perros*, by Bernard-Marie Koltès. Directed by Miguel Narros, Teatro María Guerrero, 1990. (Photo by Antonio de Benito; courtesy of the Centro Dramático Nacional)

Pilar Bayona and Alain Lukusa in *Combate de negro y de perros*, by Bernard-Marie Koltès. Directed by Miguel Narros, Teatro María Guerrero, 1990. (Photo by Antonio de Benito; courtesy of the Centro Dramático Nacional)

Olimpia. Both were translated by the promising young playwright Sergi Belbel. *El Público* prominently featured the late playwright and his two works in No. 79.[8] The official stage was making a concerted effort to bring a "European revelation" to Spanish spectators. The effort failed. Attendance in Madrid, like that earlier in Barcelona, was very low. The Sala Olimpia, with its emphasis on "new tendencies," often plays to empty houses, but the María Guerrero, a showcase with elaborate productions, excellent acting, and attractive prices, generally does not lack spectators.

A key problem with *Combate de negro y de perros* is its length. The production, directed by Miguel Narros, originally ran three and a half hours. Haro Tecglen reported that some spectators left at intermission (*El País* 30 April 1990). The text was then cut to under three hours, but the audience stayed away. The action is set in Africa, at an enclave of white Europeans who are overseeing the building of a bridge by black laborors. The text deals with racism, but perhaps more so with loneliness. In spite of a hyperrealistic staging that included a moving jeep, "real" rain, and quantities of mud, the set—dominated by a huge bridge and surrounding darkness—took on metaphorical values. The four characters, prone to monologues and long duets, may be perceived as archetypes. The play is both long and static, requiring a supreme effort from the actors to sustain it. In this respect, it is typically French. Lope de Vega pointed out centuries ago in his advice on writing theatre—and avoiding neoclassicism—that the seated Spaniard becomes bored very quickly. While the playing time of the two-character *En la soledad de los campos de algodón* was only an hour and twenty-five minutes, the work seemed, at least to this spectator, more static than the longer text. Moreover, the acting was uneven. The existentialist dialogue, directed by Guillermo Heras, ran without an intermission, but even so spectators walked out in the middle.

Molière and Ionesco are holding their ground, but, Arrabal and Savary excepted, there is no wave of popularity in Spain at the moment for younger generations of French playwrights. Perhaps the Spanish stage simply no longer looks to the north for theatrical leadership, as it once did, or perhaps the slow acceptance of writers like Beckett, Ionesco, and Genet will repeat itself with Deutsch, Koltès, or others. Perhaps the increased exchange of directors between the Spanish and French stages will lead to a renewed exchange of dramatic texts as well. In the meantime, the affirmative action efforts of Ibéral deserve applause.

Metatheatricalism and Intertextuality

Chapter 5

JUANA LA LOCA AS DRAMATIC FIGURE: *UN CHATEAU EN NOVEMBRE* BY EMMANUEL ROBLES

It is not surprising that the historical figure of Spain's tragic queen, Juana de Castilla (1479–1555), should continue to attract the attention of playwrights. Nor is it surprising that Emmanuel Roblès in particular should choose the theme. Martha T. Halsey has noted the fascination that Juana, the mystery of her madness, and her long incarceration at Tordesillas have had for such diverse nineteenth- and twentieth-century Spanish writers as Manuel Tamayo y Baus, Benito Pérez Galdós, and José Martín Recuerda (Halsey 1978–79). Manuel Martínez Mediero's demythologizing and somewhat controversial *Juana del amor hermoso*, staged in Madrid in 1983, has given rise to renewed critical interest in the subject of Juana la Loca in Spanish drama (DiPuccio, Lamartina-Lens, Zatlin). It is by coincidence that Roblès's *Un Château en novembre*, 1984, should appear immediately after the Mediero text, for Roblès's interest in Spain is neither recent nor casual. Although his extensive oeuvre is written in French and he was born in French Algeria, Roblès has always identified strongly with his Spanish ancestry on both sides of his family. As Martha O'Nan and others have observed, Spanish themes are recurrent in his works. He has read widely in Spanish history (Personal interview) and recalls from his university days "a passionate immersion in the Spanish Golden Age" (Depierris 70–71).

The interest that Juana la Loca holds for dramatists is multifaceted. There are certain moments in her life that offer

147

the potential for intense dramatic development: Juana's forced separation from her husband Philip (Felipe I el hermoso), her response to his death, her potential liberation by the Comuneros after a decade of imprisonment. While the majority of the plays dealing with her concentrate on a particular episode, at least two works attempt to recreate the total experience of love, betrayal, jealousy, martyrdom, and madness: Mediero's *Juana del amor hermoso* and Gian Carlo Menotti's opera, *Juana, La Loca,* written for Beverly Sills in 1979 and revised in 1982. In his review of the 1984 production at the Spoleto Festival USA (Charleston, South Carolina), Tim Page correctly notes that Juana's story provides enough material for several operas. But in finding that the Menotti opus "was not history, it was hysteria," perhaps he overlooks how incredible the historical reality was.

Juana's story lends itself to interpretations at the individual or political levels. At the extremes, she is either a woman whose obsessive love and jealousy degenerate into madness or the hapless victim of the Machiavellian conspiracies of her husband, her father, and her son, all of whom need the myth of her insanity in order to retain their own political power. Official history, as sanctioned by the Franco regime, opted for the former version, even going so far as to imply that Juana shut herself up in Tordesillas voluntarily: "La pobre reina loca no pintaba nada. Muerto el esposo, fuése a Tordesillas y se encerró-en sí misma, negándose obstinadamente a todo contacto con el exterior" (The poor mad queen was out of it. Once her husband was dead, she went to Tordesillas and shut herself up, obstinately refusing any contact with the outside world) (Revuelta 7).

Contemporary historian Townsend Miller convincingly refutes this version along with a number of hypotheses of the past, particularly those related to the secrecy surrounding Juana's almost half-century of captivity. "For centuries, while Juana was little more than a legend, popular belief held that what Charles wished to conceal was his mother's madness—in other words, that the veil drawn around Tordesillas was one of filial shame" (T. Miller 319). The American historian asserts, however, that Charles could only reign as long as his mother, the rightful queen, were known to be mad. According to Miller, the mystery of Tordesillas was that "Juana had repented of her decision to relinquish the government, and that she was being held by brute force to keep her from getting out and claiming her trampled rights" (T. Miller 321). Although Spanish history books teach that Carlos I was king of Spain from the death of his grandfather Fernando in 1516 until his abdication in favor of his son Felipe II in 1556, technically Juana de Castilla was still queen when she died in 1555.

At the other extreme, Miller also rejects the theory that Juana was completely sane even after years of imprisonment and torture. Although a "strong case can be made out for the thesis that Juana's mind was far more sound than unbalanced during her dealings with Philip and Fernando, and that the labeling of her as mad by those two former persecutors was a gross example of political foul play" (T. Miller 320), Miller establishes that the theory of Juana's continued total sanity is as much fantasy as the initial myth of her going mad from love.

In her discussion of Tamayo y Baus's *La locura de amor* (1855), Galdós's *Santa Juana de Castilla* (1918), and Martín Recuerda's *El engañao* (written in 1976 and staged in 1981), Halsey carefully observes how the modern dramatic figure evolved: "Whereas Tamayo underscores the individual tragedy of Juana, Galdós and Martín Recuerda both emphasize the collective tragedy of Spain which her fate comes to represent" (Halsey 1978–79: 56). The mid-nineteenth-century work, in presenting a complicated intrigue revolving around Philip's infidelity, only hints at social or political themes. The two later plays, on the other hand, highlight both Juana as victim and her empathy for Spain's oppressed people. In *El engañao* Juana becomes the symbol "of a helpless Spain" (Halsey 1981: 44); Juana further underscores "the division between the 'two Spains,' " identifying herself with the Spain that loves liberty (Halsey 1988: 12). It is worthy of note that these three playwrights, to achieve their respective purposes, invent characters or episodes far removed from historical accounts.

Tamayo's *La locura de amor*, which was translated to several languages and widely staged throughout Europe, provides a romanticized, even melodramatic version of Juana. The action of all five acts takes place in Burgos in 1506, ending with Philip's unexpected death and Juana's concomitant retreat to madness. In the final scene, the bereaved Queen first emotionally proclaims that her husband's cadaver is hers alone and then, in suddenly tender tones, that the King is merely asleep. Tamayo has, of course, accepted the myth that allowed Fernando to usurp the throne that his daughter had inherited from Queen Isabel. From the standpoint of Roblès's *Un Château en novembre*, however, two aspects of *La locura de amor* are of particular interest: the portrayal of Aldara and the introduction of a Pirandellian approach to Juana's madness.

In creating the complicated intrigues of a love rectangle (Felipe pursues Aldara, who pretends to love him but secretly loves Don Alvar, who loves Aldara but pretends to court Juana in order to help the Queen make Felipe jealous), Tamayo invented the character of a Moorish princess. The mysterious Aldara, who has come to the Court under the assumed name of Beatriz, confides her identity to the Queen and ultimately converts to Christianity when she recognizes Juana's moral superiority. Juana is an angel, and therefore "this woman's God is the true God" (*La locura de amor* 133). Tamayo is once again consistent with official myth, in this case the religious one supporting the Catholic Monarchs in their forced Christianization of the Peninsula.

Tamayo's *Un drama nuevo*, 1867, is often identified as an antecedent of Pirandello's treatment of illusion and reality, art and life. The climactic scene of the third act of *La locura de amor* likewise falls within the Pirandellian mode by placing in doubt the line between madness and sanity. Juana declares herself mad as preferable to accepting Felipe's infidelity: "What happiness, oh eternal God, what happiness! I thought I was wretched, but it wasn't that: I was mad!" (*La locura de amor* 114). While Tamayo presents the possibility of feigned insanity as a means of foregrounding Juana's all-consuming love for Felipe, Miller's historical analysis points out the possibility that a number of Juana's apparently irrational acts were strategies she used in her ill-fated struggle to maintain her freedom.

At the other extreme from Tamayo, Galdós and Martín Recuerda both portray an idealized Juana at the end of her half-century imprisonment. Galdós's series of historical novels, the *Episodios nacionales,* have become a virtual history text for generations of Spaniards. In *Santa Juana de Castilla,* however, written near the end of his own life, Galdós departs totally from historical reality in creating a saintly Queen who, on the eve of her death, goes out to visit humble people in a nearby village. Similarly, Martín Recuerda (b. 1925) invents a grotesque but still noble Juana who escapes from Tordesillas and travels to Granada, where she identifies herself with Juan de Dios and his charitable labors on behalf of Spain's disenfranchised. The playwrights' purpose is to demythologize official history, that is, the image of Spain's period of grandeur that bypasses the suffering of the masses. Noting that there is no historical basis for Martín Recuerda's encounter of Juana and Juan de Dios, Halsey provides a rationale for both Galdós's and Recuerda's fictionalized queen. If Juana felt compassion for the Comuneros, then she might well have sympathized with the outcasts whom San Juan de Dios tried to help and would have embodied the pure Christian principles expressed in *Santa Juana de Castilla* (Halsey 1978–79: 54).

The Comuneros, who rose up against Carlos I (Carlos V of the Holy Roman Empire) and his foreign (Flemish) advisers in 1520, are in themselves an attractive subject for historical drama. As Halsey points out, had they been successful in restoring Juana de Castilla to the throne that was rightly hers, they might have established a constitutional monarchy in the early sixteenth century (Halsey 1988: 12).

In her 1974 expressionistic chronicle play, *Los comuneros,* Ana Diosdado (b. 1938) presents a powerful and, to some extent, accurate portrait of Juana. When the Comuneros forcefully enter the castle at Tordesillas to see their Queen, her laugh and her disheveled appearance immediately connote the effect of a decade of imprisonment and mistreatment. In her mind, past and present merge. Her reminiscences of Flanders, in contrast with Spain, are almost verbatim those found in her biography by German Hispanist Ludwig Pfandl: "No hay tomillo ni romero en Flandes. Ni espliego, ni laurel, ni ciprés. Pero está lleno de encinares, y hay chopos, pinos y hayas en inmensas arboledas" (In Flanders there is no thyme or rosemary. No lavender or bayberry or cypress. But it is filled with oak groves, and there are huge woods of poplars, pines, and beech trees) (*Los comuneros* 65). "Para ellos (los españoles) era la tierra donde no había romero, espliego ni tomillo; no se daban el tejo, el laurel ni el ciprés . . . . También se asombraron . . . de las arboledas de encinas, pinos, olmos, chopos y hayas . . . " (For them [the Spaniards] it was the land where there was no rosemary or lavender or thyme; yews, bayberry, and cypress did not grow there . . . . They were also astonished . . . at the woods of oaks, pines, elms, poplars, and beech trees...) (Pfandl 45).

Pfandl, to be sure, supported the official myth of Juana by characterizing her as a woman "of limited intelligence" (60) who, even before Felipe's death, "had fallen for the rest of her days into a dull state of idiocy" (61). Miller, on the other hand, points out that Juana "had a bold and penetrating mind—before its tissues were destroyed" (T. Miller 347) and that she was initially quite lucid when she received the Comuneros. Although to some extent Diosdado tends to agree with Pfandl's now discredited assessment of Juana, her character does identify herself with the ideological positions that Martínez Mediero and Roblès were to foreground in their later plays. In essence she supports love, not war. "Should we not replace hatred with love?" she asks, and adds that it would be "hermoso" (beautiful) (*Los comuneros* 59). She finds no reason to hate the French, whom her mother considered enemies, declaring them to be people just like the Spaniards. She openly assumes a pacifist stance: "No one can claim justice and right when there is war" (*Los comuneros* 60). Juana's madness becomes quixotic, both in the words of one of the Comunero leaders and in her own declaration of idealism: "Do you know who is mad? Those who believe in something that seems impossible, those who are capable of seeing what the others do not" (*Los comuneros* 66).

It is Juana, the idealist, and the potential she held for a better Spain, that also attracted the attention of José Martín Elizondo (b. 1922) in his one-act *Juana creó la noche*, 1960. Martín Elizondo, who lived in France from 1947 to 1989, has directed and authored plays in both Spanish and French. In his original works he frequently draws upon Spanish art, literature, and history for his themes. His unpublished text is prefaced by two lines from Federico García Lorca's "Elegía a doña Juana la Loca": "En el cofre de plomo, dentro de tu esqueleto, / tendrás el corazón partido en mil pedazos" (In the lead coffin, inside your skeleton, you will have a heart broken into a thousand pieces). Indeed it is a brokenhearted Juana who recalls her sorrows (the absent King, the daughter stolen from her, the conspiracies to drive her mad, the execution of the Comuneros) in her rambling speech to an unknown man, the Desconocido, who may exist only in her imagination. The disheveled, ragged, barefoot Queen writes poetry and is accused by the Desconocido of deliberately assuming the role of madwoman. Juana does not disagree that she has, in essence, created her long night. She reads from her poem: "Juana, como por juego, creó la noche . . . Y los cielos entonces dijeron, 'qué gozo, seguir dándole voz, que dialogue con su sombra'" (Juana, as if it were a game, created the night . . . And the heavens then said, "what pleasure, to go on letting her speak, to have her talk to her shadow") (*Juana creó la noche* 15). The shadow in this case, vaguely recalling a line from the *Poema del mío Cid*, proclaims: "Juana, que gran reina si quisiérais" (Juana, what a great queen if you wanted) (*Juana creó la noche* 24). Although much closer to historical reality than the Juana la Loca of Martín Recuerda's *El engañao*, Martín Elizondo's portrayal, too, is a lament for what might have been.

Although Roblès is a full generation older than Martínez Mediero (b. 1939), of the Juana la Loca plays discussed here the one to which his *Un Château en novembre* is most closely related is *Juana del amor hermoso*. Unlike Roblès's emphasis on a single episode in Juana's life, Mediero created an expressionistic chronicle play with action flowing from one temporal plane to another over a span of years. Nevertheless, both works make use of anachronisms for humorous effect and are overtly theatricalist. Moreover, while relatively faithful to historical reality, they provide a vindication of Juana from the standpoint of contemporary ideology.

Martínez Mediero's Juana goes from a bubbling adolescent to a broken woman who has been subjected to years of imprisonment, torture, and rape. The text makes clear that she is a victim of patriarchal political interests, as represented by her family, the Church, and the State. In this respect *Juana del amor hermoso* both falls readily into Herbert Lindenberger's definition of the martyr play and lends itself to a feminist reading. Juana incarnates love, ranging from her passion for Felipe to her devotion to the Spanish people. In opposition to her parents, the Catholic Monarchs, Juana is liberal in her political and religious beliefs and stands for individual freedom. Ultimately, however, she does not join the Comunero effort to restore her throne because she cannot take sides against her own son. The freedom she finds, again consistent with a model of the martyr play outlined by Lindenberger, is an inner one, in this case one that comes from a conscious, Pirandellian decision to assume madness: "I want to remain mad, Juan Padilla, forgive me . . . . To do everything you want to do . . . one has to kill, and I don't know how to do that . . ." (*Juana del amor hermoso* 143). "When there are feelings in a story, then what happens is what has happened to me . . . Everything, everything is materialism and one is either materialistic or one is simply mad . . ." (*Juana del amor hermoso* 144).

Although Juana may be viewed as the tragic heroine of a martyr play, *Juana del amor hermoso* is marked by a surface humor, both in the introduction of deliberate anachronisms and in the treatment as caricatures of certain figures, notably the Catholic Monarchs and Cardinal Cisneros. Queen Isabel even reappears after her death to express her righteous indignation at Fernando's activities (his remarriage to a Frenchwoman and his treatment of Juana) and to inform Juana of the wisdom she has acquired in Heaven—where, she says, "in the afternoons now we're reading Erasmus's

Praise of Madness" (*Juana del amor hermoso* 134). In spite of the earthly Isabel's religious fanaticism, rigid political views, and role in setting the stage for Juana's martyrdom, Martínez Mediero does establish a bond between mother and daughter. Juana recalls her mother nostalgically (perhaps the ghost is the expression of her need to compensate for the mother's absence) and indeed calls out to her for help when Fernando arranges her imprisonment at Tordesillas. The ghostly Isabel, in turn, voices tender support for her daughter, whom she characterizes as one of those "seres tan hermosos . . . que sirven de enseñanza a toda la humanidad" (beings so beautiful . . . that they serve as a model for all humanity) (*Juana del amor hermoso* 133).

The hint of a tender mother-daughter relationship, as well as the demythologized Isabel, is not repeated in Roblès's *Un Château en novembre*. The protagonist of the French-language text finds herself in a generational conflict with her mother, whom she repeatedly accuses of never loving her. For this Jeanne de Castille, love is more important than politics or religion. According to the author, the psychology of the character is deliberately contemporary (Personal interview). She is like many young people today who reject their heritage and their parents' values in order to pursue their own happiness. In an epilogue scene, Jeanne self-consciously declares to a present-day audience: "The truth is that I've lived in a dark century where love was enslaved. And I already belonged to your century, with today's women who assert themselves and live according to their hearts. What risks one runs when one is ahead of her time!" (*Un Château en novembre* 344).

Roblès's perspective on Juana la Loca is overtly revisionist, and his portrait of the Church's representative, Bishop Fonseca, is thoroughly negative. But the author felt no need to caricature Queen Isabel, a figure for him of undisputed grandeur (Personal interview). Martínez Mediero, on the other hand, grew up in Francoist Spain where Isabel la Católica had been turned into the model wife and mother: what A. P. Foulkes has termed an "exemplary myth," that is, a national legend propagandized by the dominant ideology in a post-revolutionary period as part of the effort to resist opposition or change (Foulkes 13). Roblès does not hesitate to subvert official Spanish history, but he is understandably distanced from some of the concerns that underscore the younger Spanish writer's work.

For his Juana la Loca play, Roblès chooses the moment in November 1503 when the anguished Princess finally receives word from Philip, who had set out for Flanders without her the previous December. She hastily prepares to leave Spain only to discover that the Catholic Monarchs have determined to prevent her departure from La Mota castle. In what official history has labeled the first scandalous indication of her madness, she clings to the iron bars of the castle gate, remaining out in the winter cold for days in protest, until Queen Isabel gives in to her demand that she be allowed to rejoin her husband.

The particular episode in the historical Juana la Loca's life, when she is forced either to act or to accept the sacrifice imposed upon her by an absurd world, is well suited to the dramatic formula found in several of Roblès's major plays: *Montserrat*, 1948; *La Vérité est morte*, 1953; *Mer libre* and *Plaidoyer pour un rebelle*, 1965. Georges-Albert Astre defines this formula as being "a paradox that tackles and destroys all reassuring conformity: it is through the most provoking and quixotic madness that the unacceptable absurdity of social norms and, beyond them, the ontological absurdity of the world are vanquished" (Astre 1987: 72). In a separate commentary on Roblès's literary world, Astre observes a repeated pattern of heroes confronting an existential choice: "Gripped by a passion for life that implies action, problematic heroes par excellence, they question all things, and above all themselves. Sooner or later, they inevitably confront an hour of choice which is likewise their hour of greatest solitude" (Astre 1983: 13). Juana la Loca then, in November 1503, is a quixotic figure caught in her time of decision.

Various critics have pointed out Roblès's propensity for Hispanic or Mediterranean characters, settings, or themes, and his preoccupation with the Spanish tragic sense of life; but the form of his dramatic texts is classically French. For example, *Montserrat*, perhaps his best-known play and one that continues to be staged around the world, conforms to the three unities and the rule of *bienséance*. The emotional level of the drama is intense, excruciatingly so, but the physical action—the execution, one by one, of innocent victims that Montserrat can save only by betraying a cause in which he believes deeply—takes place off stage. The core of *Un Château en novembre* likewise falls within this traditional French mold, although the action does extend beyond the classic twenty-four hours.

Act I, predictably, serves as exposition. Jeanne, in the solitude of La Mota, waits with increasing anguish for a letter from Philippe, whose reputation as a womanizer is quickly revealed. Jeanne is subject to wild mood swings but is patiently served by two ladies-in-waiting and a Moorish slave. Through the reports that the loyal Diégo brings her from the court, she realizes that she is a pawn in a political game of chess.

Act II begins with a moment of hope for Jeanne. The letter has arrived, and she and her companions begin preparations for her journey to Flanders. But the Bishop and the Queen herself, who makes the trip to La Mota in spite of her failing health, conspire to keep Jeanne a prisoner. The act ends in a climactic scene of confrontation.

In the third and final act, Diégo realizes that he has been duped by the Bishop into aiding Jeanne's antagonists, but the Princess has feigned calm so that the armed guards are removed from her quarters and even her loyal attendants believe that she is sleeping peacefully. Thus she escapes to the gate to create, offstage, the scandalous scene which forces the Queen to agree to her eventual departure.

In *Un Château en novembre* Roblès deviates from the classic structure that marks his theatre by introducing an anachronistic prologue. A television reporter, who confesses that he has no background for this theatre assignment, has come to interview the characters. They speak in contemporary, colloquial language as they provide him with information on past events and their interpersonal relationships, but they remain in character, that is to say, they respond self-consciously as Jeanne or Isabelle. In their eagerness to tell their story, they recall Pirandello's six characters rather than a theatrical troupe, that is, a group of actors with identities of their own. Roblès provides two endings for the text, one of which reintroduces the television reporter, who elicits answers on what will happen to Jeanne after the action he has just seen.

Astre relates this prologue to the common technique of the play-within-the-play, "a sort of mise en abîme," but rejects the "perhaps unfortunate dissonance" of the parallel epilogue in favor of the alternate ending which remains in the historical past (Astre 1987: 96). The prologue, however, and the related epilogue that gives to the text a certain structural unity, do not really establish *Un Château en novembre* as a play-within-a-play, for the frame is not a separate play but a clarification of the text at hand. It is theatricalist in the sense that, at least briefly at the beginning and end, it distances the spectator from the action and calls attention to itself as theatre. But more important than this self-reflexive aspect are two other functions of the framing device: It makes clear the contemporary reading that can be given to Juana la Loca's story and it provides a lesson on Spanish history to a French audience. In the prologue, when Jeanne asks a reporter what he has read about the characters and their story, he responds, "Please go on as if I had read nothing" (*Un Château en novembre* 257). In essense the prologue serves as an entertaining explanation for spectators who might well respond the same way.

Un Château en novembre is linked to *Juana del amor hermoso* by the tone of the prologue and by its contemporary view of the protagonist. Her ideological stance is revealed most directly in her confrontation with Queen Isabel and Bishop Fonseca in the climactic scene of Act II. Like Mediero's Juana, Roblès's Jeanne opposes the patriarchy, which she considers repressive at personal and political levels. When she learns that she is being held prisoner because those in power (the Catholic Monarchs and the Church) fear that she and Philippe will ally themselves with the French, with whom Spain is at war, she asserts, "I'm personally not at war with anyone" (*Un Château en novembre* 310). She rebels against a system that has exploited her and denied her freedom of choice: "You have always subjected me to your will. Throughout my childhood all I received from you were orders, reprimands, and restrictions" (310). "And I have no intention of assuming duties that I have neither chosen nor approved" (311). To Jeanne's passion for Philippe, the Queen counters that her passion is "the grandeur of Spain." "A passion, Madame, that kills a great many people," Jeanne responds (312). Nor is Jeanne moved by references to God's will; like Roblès's heroes in general, she expresses no belief in God. She repeatedly disparages the Bishop for his role in the Inquisition and deplores religious fanaticism: "God and Spain are too heavy a burden for me! You have expelled the Moors, expelled the Jews, proclaimed the glory of God here, in Africa, and in the Indies, and that crown carries the weight of the whole world"(314).

Roblès's Jeanne and Mediero's Juana are closely related in their vocal rejection of the repressive ideology of Church and State. They differ in their defense of love, in part because Mediero's play spans Juana's lifetime and allows a gradual shift in the protagonist's attitude. Jeanne's dramatic moment comes before she is willing to acknowledge her husband's betrayal. Thus her focus on love and happiness is individual rather than collective. Love for Jeanne, that is, passionate love, is true radiant beauty: her concept of "soleil," the sun (*Un Château en novembre* 314). Happiness, not God or country, is the greatest good. At the opposite pole, Bishop Fonseca, as defender of Church and State, affirms, "we are not here on earth to be happy" (311). The battle lines are clearly drawn.

As Camille R. La Bossière has noted, Roblès frequently deals with the theme of happiness, but happiness that is difficult to achieve or maintain within the context of an irrational world. When faced with the choice between happiness and responsibility, Roblès's protagonists tend to choose the latter, for the individual is "*solidaire* even as he is *solitaire*" (La Bossière 34–35). Giuliana Toso Rodinis similarly observes that the *ailleurs* (freedom, happiness, escape from mediocrity)—the elsewhere sought by Roblès's heroes—may take the form of love for humanity. She cites the case of Juárez in *La Vérité est morte* and "the generous sacrifice of his personal happiness for the love of his people'' (Toso Rodinis 67). Although Toso Rodinis points to secondary female characters who ''aspire to a completely individual *ailleurs*'' (68), her description of Juárez could be applied equally to Vanina, the young female hero in *L'Horloge*, 1962. Consistent with his ties to French existentialism, Roblès turns repeatedly to this pattern of personal sacrifice by committed individuals who realize both that they must choose and that they must assume the responsibility for their acts.

In this regard, Jeanne of *Un Château en novembre* appears at first glance to be the antithesis of Roblès's typical protagonist, for she places her own happiness above all other concerns and her love is focused on Philippe, not on humanity. Nevertheless, Jeanne, in her refusal to submit to her victimization, is closely linked to Roblès's other, less self-centered, heroes. Hers is, once again, what Astre has termed with respect to Magellan in *Mer libre*, the ''rebellion of ardent souls, the demand to overcome in spite of all prohibitions . . . a thirst for the absolute'' (Astre 1987: 79). Some twenty years ago, Jean-Louis Depierris found that all of Roblès's work was ''the expression of a single truth: that of the sun and that of death'' (Depierris 167). For Jeanne, Philippe's love is the sun, in contrast to the darkness and death of the Spanish court. ''All my childhood memories are gray and black'' (*Un Château en novembre* 324), she declares. She equates both the Bishop and her mother with death, against which she lashes out passionately: ''I am alive, alive, do you hear? And you are killing me!'' (340). Although by the end of the play, Jeanne is portrayed as having crossed the line into madness, the use of Roblès's usual symbolism suggests that her irrational fight against absurdity is not essentially different from that of his earlier dramatic heroes.

It was not Roblès's intention in *Un Château en novembre* to be faithful to historical reality; he affirms that Jeanne's psychology is strictly his own invention (Personal interview). While there is a valid historical basis for much of the action, he has, in fact, blurred some of the chronology of the real Juana la Loca's life. For example, he suggests that one of her other famous ''mad'' scenes—shocking the Flemish court by angrily cutting off a rival's hair—had already taken place by the time of the La Mota scandal. As a result, he shows a more emotionally disturbed Jeanne than she would have been in November 1503. But through his four fictional characters and his portrayal of a hypocritical, fanatic Bishop Fonseca, he carefully supports as true much of what Jeanne says, particularly her criticism of a repressive regime and her charges that her enemies are conspiring against her. Certainly there is the suggestion that the scandalous scene at the castle gates is one she stages deliberately, in Pirandellian fashion, in order to manipulate the Queen, who is motivated by Spanish honor and what others will say. However, Maria's description of Jeanne, clinging to the iron gates, like "a great crucified bird" (334), casts her clearly into the role of martyr.

Diégo and the two ladies-in-waiting, Maria and Cristina, reinforce the dichotomy established by Jeanne between Spain (death and repression) and her *ailleurs* (Philippe, love, Flanders). Jeanne's opposition to religious fanaticism is voiced as well by Diégo in the prologue and again in Act III. His affirmation that Fonseca had burned heretics alive and destroyed five thousand Korans (262) effectively undermines the Bishop's credibility even before the action of the main play begins. Moreover, for Diégo and Maria, themselves lovers, and for Cristina, Flanders also beckons as a place of freedom. Diégo recalls the attractions of Brussels for the Bishop, and then feels compelled to add, hastily, that he will not forget his religious obligations as a Spaniard: "I'll take along my blackest clothes, the ones that make me look like a crow!"(301).

This opposition between Isabelle or Fonseca and Jeanne, between the enclosure of the castle and the *ailleurs*, between the forces of repression and the desire for freedom, between maintaining the status quo and rebelling in order to seek love and happiness, are reminiscent of Federico García Lorca's *La casa de Bernarda Alba*, 1936. The equation of Jeanne with Lorca's Adela, whose passion for life and love is likewise doomed to failure, is perhaps not coincidental, for Roblès's strong interest in the Spanish playwright and poet dates from the 1930s. It is, in fact, in terms of Lorca's familiar symbolism (water = sexuality) that Jeanne expresses her desires: "Ah, the happiness of water that runs and mingles with another! I only want some water . . . Nothing but water" (341).

If the intertextual reference to Lorca underscores Roblès's Spanish roots, it is the character of Aïcha, the Moorish slave, who signals his Arab ties. Eric Sellin points out that Roblès is one of two French Algerian writers admired in contemporary Algeria for their positive portrayal of Arab figures. As one might expect, Roblès's Aïcha does not follow the pattern of Tamayo y Baus's Aldara with her ready conversion to Christianity. Rather, in her defense of Jeanne, she proclaims, "In our country, in the land of the true faith, the mad are holy" (*Un Château en novembre* 335). From the opening moments of Act I, she is identified as someone exiled from the land of sun to the snow of Castile. The key Roblès symbols, *soleil* and *ailleurs,* are both introduced in the two women's initial dialogue. Jeanne declares: "It sometimes seems to me that winter only exists in this region, and that all of the cold of the earth is concentrated here and that everywhere else the weather is fair" (265). Jeanne's *soleil* (Philippe, love, Flanders) is mirrored in that of Aïcha (her dead lover, Marrakech). The princess and the slave are "sisters in the same prison" (270), entrapped by religious and political absolutism.

Even though Jeanne as a character is more preoccupied with self and with her own happiness than Mediero's Juana or many of Roblès's other protagonists, *Un Château en novembre* does use the tragic story of Juana la Loca as a vehicle of social and political protest. In some superficial ways, it bears a structural similarity to Tamayo's *La locura de amor,* but ideologically it falls with the contemporary Spanish works that link Juana la Loca with the victims of a repressive regime. Even though Jeanne does not create her own night, like Martín Elizondo's protagonist, she is none the less a martyr, forced closer and closer to madness by the representatives of the patriarchy so explicitly satirized in Mediero's *Juana del amor hermoso.*

Chapter 6

VINDICATING RUIZ DE ALARCON: *L'AUTRE DON JUAN* BY EDUARDO MANET

In the prologue to his *L'Autre Don Juan*, Eduardo Manet explains that he was invited to prepare a French adaptation of a Spanish Golden Age play for an international theatre festival. After reviewing texts by the best-known dramatists of the period, Lope and Calderón, he selected instead Juan Ruiz de Alarcón's *Las paredes oyen*, "a minor, but charming work" (Avant-Propos 8). Neither the request nor Manet's response is surprising. As discussed in Chapter 3, Spanish Golden Age theatre has enjoyed considerable popularity in France over the centuries. Manet's choice of Ruiz de Alarcón has another dimension, however, for this particular "Spanish" author was actually Mexican, and his contemporary French adapter is Cuban. Born in Santiago de Cuba in 1930, Manet first went to France in 1950 to study but then remained in Europe for ten years as a voluntary exile from the Batista regime.[1] He returned to Cuba in 1960, at the invitation of Castro, and in 1968 left his homeland again, in a second exile. Osvaldo Obregón affirms that Manet has since become the most successful Latin American playwright of the French stage (Obregón 37). Although he writes his plays and novels in French, Manet reveals his Hispanic origins directly, like Emmanuel Roblès, through his choice of theme, or indirectly, through the structure and style of his works, which tend not to fit the classic French molds. Among his plays with obvious connections to Latin America and the Caribbean are the three published together by Gallimard in 1985 under the label "théâtre et révolte":

163

The rapid action and role-playing within the role have made Manet's *L'Autre Don Juan* popular with young theatre companies in France. (Photos courtesy of Eduardo Manet)

Un Balcon sur les Andes, Mendoza, en Argentine . . . , and *Ma'Déa*.

Manet's prologue to *L'Autre Don Juan* makes clear that this comedy is intended as a vindication of a Mexican-born writer whose important influence on Corneille and Goldoni has not always been recognized and whose Latin American origins have often been obscured. The "very free version" of *Las paredes oyen* was completed in December 1972, published in France in 1973, and premiered in Montreal in 1974. According to the author, who achieved international recognition with *Les Nonnes* (1969), this play based on Ruiz de Alarcón is among his most frequently staged works, especially by young theatre companies (Letter 1989).

As we shall see, *L'Autre Don Juan* is not merely a French translation or adaptation of the Spanish-language comedy but rather a complex metaplay that blurs geographical and chronological borders by introducing Don Juan Ruiz de Alarcón both as an author-character within the frame play and as an actor-character within *Les Murs ont des oreilles*, the play-within-the-play (this despite the fact that the performance is ostensibly taking place in France in 1800, and the historical Alarcón died in Spain in 1639). Eventually the author and actor facets of the character merge when Don Juan, much to the consternation of the French troupe, insists upon delivering his lines verbatim from the original Spanish text.

The strategy of placing the original author as a character within the adapted text is not unique to Manet in the 1970s. Earlier in 1972 in France it was tried by Denis Llorca in his revival of Corneille's *Le Cid* at the Théâtre de la Ville in Paris. Llorca added to the cast the figure of Guillén de Castro, the often unrecognized author of Corneille's source text, and had him speak lines in Spanish; the production "provoked passionate and contradictory reactions" (Willey 93). In Spain, in 1976, Francisco Nieva accepted an invitation by the María Guerrero National Theatre to modernize Larra's *No más mostrador*—itself a reworking of Scribe's *Les Adieux au comptoir*—but created instead an original metadrama, *Sombra y quimera de Larra*. Nieva made Larra, the nineteenth-century author of the play-within-the-play, a character within the frame play. (*Sombra y quimera de Larra* is discussed in Chapter 7.)

The West Indian poet and playwright Derek Walcott responded in a somewhat related fashion when commissioned by the Royal Shakespeare Company to write a modern version of a Spanish Golden Age masterpiece, Tirso de Molina's *El burlador de Sevilla*. His *The Joker of Seville* places the frame action in Trinidad where, to the sound of calypso music, a local troupe is performing the traditional Don Juan play. The frame that separates the play-within-the-play from the fictional reality dissolves, and Don Juan dies at the hands of the "real" statue, not the actor-character playing the role. Walcott leaves occasional songs and isolated words in Spanish, hence underscoring the original text's origins, but his vindicatory approach has a more specifically Caribbean political message. He shifts part of the action to a West Indies island and turns Don Juan's servant into a black slave. When Don Juan seduces Tisbea, now a "fishergirl of mixed blood," the scene metaphorically becomes the rape of the New World by the Old. Although Walcott's entertaining musical, which premiered in Port of Spain, Trinidad, in 1974, has been enthusiastically received by audiences in various stagings, fifteen years after commissioning it, the Royal Shakespeare Company had yet to produce the play (Hamner 110).

Accepting the basic story outline of the Tirso play, Walcott melded it with the rhythms and music of Trinidad to create a new, essentially West Indian text. Manet also introduces dances and songs—some in Spanish and some in French—and is even more faithful in his scene-by-scene recreation of the Ruiz de Alarcón play-within-the-play, but his melding process is more complicated than Walcott's. Exuberantly Brechtian in its theatricalism, *L'Autre Don Juan* combines traditional elements of French farce, repeated cinematic images, a parody of the typical French approach to Spanish culture, and a running commentary on theatre and the theatre world. Although Manet's work is generally metatheatrical, his only other text to incorporate such an extensive use of theatre within theatre and theatre about theatre is his 1979 political satire of Latin American history,

Un Balcon sur les Andes. In his *Drama, Metadrama, and Perception*, Richard Hornby defines five manifestations of the metadramatic: the play-within-the-play, ceremony within the play, role-playing within the role, literary and real-life reference, and self-reference. *L'Autre Don Juan* contains examples of all of these, carried to farcical extremes.

The three texts mentioned above that become the play-within-the-play of their respective metaplays are all metatheatrical in themselves for their extensive use of role-playing within the role. Larra's *No más mostrador*, like the Scribe comedy on which it is based, is structured on mistaken identities resulting from characters' pretending to be other people. Tirso's Don Juan puts on someone else's costume—and identity—in one of his seductions and freely invents fictions to facilitate others. Alarcón's didactic comedy is filled with examples of such role-playing and self-serving fictions: noblemen disguised as coachmen, lies used in amorous pursuits, false tales spread to discourage rivals. The result when these texts are placed within the frame of a theatrical troupe performing them is a dizzying *mise en abîme*: actors playing actor-characters who play characters playing someone else. Manet further complicates this structure with real-life references: extratextual allusions to the historical Alarcón and, through the figure of the *Alguacil,* a constable who becomes the audience within the play, to external censorship.

In the published dramatic text, Manet carefully separates his frame play from his version of Alarcón's text. *Les Murs ont des oreilles* is presented in acts with numbered scenes: Act I has 20 scenes, Act II has 13, and Act III has 14. The scenes and their basic action coincide quite closely with the original play. Manet merely omits an occasional brief scene or combines two into one until he nears the end of Alarcón's third act. Like Nieva's handling of Larra's *No más mostrador*, Manet eliminates the conclusion of the play-within-the-play. In place of Alarcón's scenes XVII through XIX, Manet creates a musical number in which the singers offer several possible endings and invite the spectators to choose among them. This grand finale lightheartedly also ignores the resolution of the intrigues of the frame play.

The frame play, dealing with Marius, his troupe of French actors, and their interactions with the author-character Don Juan (including the rivalry of two actresses for Alarcón's affections, a situation mirroring the love intrigues of the play-within-the-play), is presented in specially designated sections: prologue, supplement to Act I (divided into a bullfight and an intermission), and supplement to Act II. Given this structure, there are no real intermissions. In Pirandellian fashion, the disjunction between actors and spectators, performance and rest period, disappears. One of Marius's repeated themes is that his "poor" troupe will only survive by selling food and drink on the side.[2] Manet suggests in the stage directions that the actors follow Marius's advice by hawking refreshments during the prologue and "intermission."

In his preface to *L'Autre Don Juan*, Manet describes the language of Alarcón's text as brilliant and his versification as graceful and resonant; he declares himself incapable of recreating the same effect in French. Recalling the old Italian expression, "Traduttore, traditore," he says that he will not half betray the original through a deficient translation but will rather "trahir *tout à fait*," betray it completely, by adopting only the internal action and sense of spectacle that attracted his own interest (Avant-Propos 8). In spite of his prose rendition (with occasional rhymed couplets at the ends of scenes), in some ways Manet is far more faithful to the original dialogue than his comment would indicate. On the other hand, he systematically subverts Alarcón's dramatic text through the other theatrical signs that make up the performance text. The Golden Age play, typical of its period, limits stage directions essentially to "exit" and "enter"; Manet creates extensive stage directions, including detailed instructions to the actors for their gestures.

Among Golden Age dramatists, Alarcón was the one with the greatest affinity for the decorum of French neoclassicism. His comedies not only avoid the swashbuckling action of Spanish cape-and-sword plays but have a moralistic bent.[3] In contrast to the rather austere *Las paredes oyen*, Manet's *Les Murs ont des oreilles* is a bawdy French farce—or a return to Renaissance Spain's own *La Celestina*—filled with sexual innuendoes and exuberant physical action. In particular, the servants in the play-within-the-play, from the first scene on, add meaning to their lines by obscene gestures. They appear laughing at upstairs windows while their masters are delivering serious lines and they engage in love play behind the protagonist's back. Mendoza, the character played by Don Juan, is physically deformed—a hunchback, like the historical Alarcón. The maid Celia wickedly suggests that he has other, less visible, physical attributes that her mistress Doña Anna should consider in choosing him over his rivals. Interference from the frame play grows throughout the play-within-the-play, in part because the author-character becomes increasingly angry at Marius and the blatant change in the tone of his comedy. To be sure, Don Juan's anger is also treated as a stock device of farce.

To facilitate rapid physical action, Manet calls for a stylized set, made of lightweight boxes. These are to represent houses with two or three levels for doors and windows. Characters not only enter and exit quickly and eavesdrop with ease but also appear at windows to add their comments to the scene in progress. Marius and three other actors from his troupe double in two or more roles of the play-within-the-play; the multiple houses speed costume changes—some of which take place in full view of the audience—and, through association of particular units with particular roles, help identify the emerging character. As a playful reduction in Alarcón's cast, Manet substitutes a puppet for a human actor; a house window becomes a puppet theatre for the intervention of that servant.

The obvious use of doubling functions metatheatrically in several ways. In one sense, it is a Brechtian technique that winks at the audience, calling attention to the play as fiction. This function is akin to the direct narration—supplied by Marius, Don Juan, or occasionally another actor-character— that informs the spectators about the work to be performed or about the scene in progress. In a self-referential way, the doubling allows the actors to reveal their histrionic tricks. And, because the doubling involves cross-gender acting, it prompts the *Alguacil* to voice a traditional bias against theatre.

Martin Esslin, in his "Actors Acting Actors," has pointed out the metadramatic implications for the audience of an actor-character within the text. He states that the attraction of all the variations on actors acting actors resides precisely in the chance to compare and appreciate the levels of "theatricality" and "naturalness" displayed side by side (Esslin 75). The technique inevitably "highlights the problem of acting itself" (77); it thus breaks the illusionism of the performance by calling attention to theatre as theatre. Manet fully exploits this potential. In his metatheatricalist approach, spectators not only "see double"—Hornby's requisite—but triple. For example, Marius is not only his "natural" self (the troupe's director) but also his "theatrical" roles: the Count and the Duke. When Marius plays the Count, we see double. But the Count in Act I, Scene 16, relates to Doña Lucrèce a conversation he has had with Don Mendo; in so doing, he changes his voice to reenact their dialogue. We "hear triple" as Marius plays the Count playing Don Mendo. Manet expands upon the strategy in Act II, Scene 9. The actress-character Lola normally plays Don Mendo; in this scene, she simultaneously assumes the role of Léonardo, Don Mendo's friend. Through changes of voice and stance, Lola moves back and forth between her two characters. Lola's Léonardo and Marius's Don Mendo will be noticeably more theatrical than their respective interpretations of Don Mendo and the Count, which, in turn, will be less "natural" than their portrayals of the actor-characters themselves.

Manet incorporates a related progression in cross-gender acting. In Act III, Scene 3, the servant Beltran thinks that Mendoza has gone mad when he overhears him having a conversation with himself, using his natural voice (that is, the voice Don Juan has assumed for playing Mendoza) and his imitation of Doña Anna's female voice. Later in Act III, the actress-character Eunice, who has played the maid Celia up to this point, suddenly appears in Scene 11 in a male role, that of Marcello. After slipping out of character entirely—becoming again the actress-character Eunice—she reappears in Scene 12, back in the role of Celia. At the same time the actress-character Lola continues to play Don Mendo, but wearing her own female costume. The snowball effect in the rapid role/gender changes leads to a total breakdown of the play-within-the-play: that is, to the kind of disruption that Hornby has identified as essential to metadrama.

It should be noted that Manet does not overlook the possibilities presented by the cross-gender acting for comic irony in his dialogue. For example, in a scene between Doña Anna (played by the actress-character Bella) and her cousin Lucrèce (played by the actor-character Pascual), Lucrèce welcomes the opportunity to chat "woman to woman." When Lucrèce confesses that she is burning with passion, Doña Anna expresses in an aside her shock at a lady using such language (*L'Autre Don Juan* 69). The audience, fully aware that the "lady" is being played by a man, will doubtless laugh at such double-edged comments.

The two characters within the frame play who are most distressed by the doubling are the author-character Don Juan and the *Alguacil*. One of the catalysts for Don Juan's reverting to the original Spanish text is excessive doubling, which, he says, destroys his intended comic rhythm. He accuses Marius of greed: "You could have hired another actor for the role of the Duke" (*L'Autre Don Juan* 114). Hornby informs us that self-reference is an extreme, intense form of metatheatre, even more so than the play-within-the-play. Don Juan's complaints about Marius's handling of the play in progress are among many self-referential commentaries on *Les Murs ont des oreilles*; he affirms that his text has been so distorted that he will not defend it to the censor. The *Alguacil* is particularly offended by the erotic elements and by the cross-gender acting; he allows the play to go on only because of Lola's physical charms and Marius's bribes.

Beyond the satire of censors and censorship (implicitly Hispanic-style censorship, given the Spanish word used for the law enforcement officer), the *Alguacil's* discomfiture reflects an important aspect of Manet's theatre about theatre. With respect to role-playing within the role, Hornby alerts us that cross-gender acting raises questions of sexual identity and that bisexuality, traditionally viewed as a threat, therefore is one reason for an antitheatrical prejudice (Hornby 68–70). When the *Alguacil* enters in the supplement to Act II to close down the show, he labels the production "subversive and porno." He complains that the nobles are portrayed as idiots and the servants as wise, but he is even more alarmed that Marius has "changed the men into women and the women into men" (*L'Autre Don Juan* 97). After Lola reveals her breasts (the stage directions allow a peep but recommend a full view), he expresses his admiration for the actress's femininity and accepts her playing a male role. (From this point on, Lola will play directly to the *Alguacil,* who will applaud her repeatedly.) In Act III, however, he becomes enraged again at Pascual's portraying Lucrèce: "Une femme peut jouer à l'homme, c'est mignon, c'est sain . . . mais un mâle ne doit jamais faire la femelle" (A woman can play a man. That's clever and healthy. But a male should never play a female) (121). He is quick to shout insults at Pascual, questioning his sexual orientation. His response is realistic; Western theatre audiences and society in general are less threatened by women in pants than men in skirts.[4]

When Lionel Abel created the term "metatheatre," he identified Calderón as one of the earliest exponents of this theatrical mode. Manet cites the baroque master to justify the deliberate anachronisms in his own metatheatrical farce: "La vie (le temps) n'est qu'un songe et les songes ne sont qu'illusion" (12). Time, like life, is but a dream, an illusion. Manet's playful twisting of the famous line from *La vida es sueño* ("que toda la vida es sueño, / y los sueños, sueños son") nevertheless reveals a recurrent characteristic of metadrama, at least of the works mentioned in this chapter. In the approaches taken by Llorca, Nieva, and Walcott, chronology is indeed blurred: Guillén de Castro (1569–1631) can become a character in a contemporary production of a play written five years after his death; Larra's ghost appears before the theatrical troupe begins its performance but commits suicide at the end; the slaves on the ship accompanying Don Juan to the colonized New World sing, "Hey, hey, hey! / Is the U.S.A. / Once we get dere, / we gonna be O.K.!" (*The Joker of Seville* 34). Manet's most consistent anachronism in *L'Autre Don Juan* is found in the performance text's intertextuality with film. The use of cinematic devices is, along with the superimposed eroticism and cross-gender acting, a key method of subverting Alarcón's *Las paredes oyen*.

The playwright admits to being a lifelong movie fan. As a child, he often skipped school to see the Hollywood films that reached Havana. It was his intention, when he first went to Paris in 1950, to study at the Institut des Hautes Etudes Cinématographiques. Although he arrived in France too late to register there and switched to acting school, he later directed films when he returned to Cuba after Castro took power. The richness of Manet's theatre is dependent upon cinematic devices and film images for its brilliant technical effects. Indeed he perceives a pervasive intertextuality with film in the work of the major Latin American directors residing in France: Jorge Lavelli, Alfredo Arias, and Jérome Savary (Mambrino 361).

Film imagery in *L'Autre Don Juan* at times is incorporated in the actors' movements, which are intended to simulate camera and editing effects. For example, at Don Juan's first entrance, during the prologue, there is a drumroll and the five members of the acting company freeze: "se figent comme au cinéma dans une 'image arrêtée' " (*L'Autre Don Juan* 20). Similarly, at the beginning of Act III, Marius narrates what had occurred at the end of Act II, and the actors return to that moment first by freezing and then by coming out of the freeze with jerky motions: "ils font des gestes saccadés comme s'ils sortaient d'une 'image arrêtée' " (103). At other times, specific gestures recall stock film images. In Act I, when Don Mendo promises to ask Doña Lucrèce's father for her hand in marriage, the two engage in a long kiss in the style of Hollywood films of the 1930s (47). When the Duke intervenes to prevent a sword fight between Don Juan and Don Mendo, the stage directions indicate that the pantomimed scene should recall silent movies (59). The sudden reversal in the *Alguacil's* attitude when Lola bares her breasts should be inspired, not by Stanislavski, but by cartoons (98).

Another cinematic strategy that underscores *L'Autre Don Juan* is the use of a soundtrack. There is a musical motif associated with Don Juan: a soft theme played by flute, harpsichord, and guitar (20). The stage directions specifically call for a soundtrack to accompany the bullfight that takes place in the supplement to Act I (61). When Don Mendo plots to kidnap Doña Anna by bribing her coachmen (really Don Juan and the Duke in disguise), Marius intervenes with a narration that evokes captions from silent movie melodramas: Will the villain succeed in his dastardly plans? (85) The chase scene itself, of the horseman pursuing the carriage, calls for a soundtrack from an American western (86).

Some of these cinematic elements may also be related to Manet's parody of *espagnolade*. As discussed in Chapter 3, the French stage has not always welcomed contributions from Hispanic countries and has tended, in the case of Spain, to superimpose on plays imported across the Pyrenees all the stereotypical trappings of Andalusia, whether they were appropriate or not. In her review of fifty years of production history of Lorca in France (1938–1988), Felicia Hardison Londré points out that the commercial success of major stagings could be attributed to a "tourist-bureau vision of Spain." To be sure, Federico García Lorca came from Andalusia, placed the action of his major tragedies there, and thus invited flamenco background music and traditional costumes from the south. Valle-Inclán, on the other hand, came from Galicia, and his northwestern region with its green forests, coastal mists, Celtic superstitions, and bagpipe music is far removed from Andalusia's parched plains and gypsy dancers. Nevertheless, the Parisian premiere of Valle's *Divinas palabras* in 1946 gratuitously shifted the action from Galicia to Andalusia in order to exploit *espagnolade*. In his study of Spanish theatre on the French stage (1935–1973), Francisco Torres Monreal asserts that playwrights, like Mihura and Sastre, whose works could not be molded into the accepted folkloric images, were doomed to failure. Manet's free version of *Las paredes oyen* is a reaction to this cultural context.

As already noted, Manet suggests a leitmotif for the Alarcón figure: the soft blend of flute, harpsichord, and guitar subtly evokes Spain, not flamenco, of course, but perhaps the music of Manuel de Falla. The costumes for the play-within-the-play are logically Spanish: Lucrèce carries a fan, and several characters will wear capes. Other elements are more exaggerated. The swordplay, which the neoclassical Alarcón would not have presented on stage, is added by Manet and doubtless meets audience expectations for a swashbuckling Spanish play. The most blatant example of *espagnolade*, however, is the bullfight: it has no relationship whatsoever to either the play-within-the-play or the frame play. Understandably, the furious author-character emerges at its conclusion, waving his text and shouting at the director.

The brief bullfight scene, done in pantomime to the accompanying soundtrack, is described in the stage directions as satiric but carefully structured. The actress-character Eunice appears as the bullfighter, and Marius, with an appropriate mask, is the bull. Their movements are to follow the rhythm of the castanets associated with the clicking heels of flamenco dancers. Significantly, the death of the bull is to be played against the music of Bizet's *Carmen* (61). That French opera, based on Mérimée's French story, is the epitome of *espagnolade*: a Gallic fictionalization of Andalusia that has come to be a universally accepted image of Spain. By parodying it, Manet anticipates Carlos Saura's ingeniously metafictional 1983 film in which he effectively reclaims *Carmen* for Hispanic culture.[5]

That France has freely borrowed from Spain's creative genius is an overt theme of *L'Autre Don Juan*. In the prologue, Marius introduces Alarcón as the source for Pierre Corneille's *Le Menteur*. "Pierre who?" asks the author-character. He expresses mild surprise but generously agrees to lend his intellectual talents to France. After all, there is an obligation to help "under-developed" countries (25). The dialogue inverts French pride in Corneille and ignorance of the original Hispanic author. Eventually Don Juan can no longer tolerate the way his text is being distorted by the French theatrical troupe. At that culminating point in the action (Act III, Scene 9), he announces that the play will go on, but only in Spanish, in order to put an end to his anxiety (115).

The linguistic strategy Manet develops here is similar to the one found in his *Un Balcon sur les Andes;* in the later play,

French actors perform in their native language to Spanish American audiences, with the aid of a running consecutive interpretation by a bilingual character. In *L'Autre Don Juan,* Alarcón delivers his character's lines verbatim from *Las paredes oyen* (lines 2506–7; 2526; 2529–36; 2538; 2543–44; 2546; 2573–75). Marius instructs Pascual to respond in French with Beltran's lines and at first attempts to provide a rapid consecutive interpretation to Alarcón's dialogue. In a snowball effect, Marius then switches to a simultaneous mode, partially drowning out Alarcón's Spanish. When Pascual gives up, Marius takes over the role of Beltran, becomes hysterical himself, and begins responding with the original Spanish lines to Alarcón's speeches (lines 2545; 2547–48). Lola and the *Alguacil* call out for a translation, Pascual spouts Grotowski's theories on the need for a laboratory theatre, and the scene finally ends on the brink of chaos.

The extended bilingual scene is built on the accelerating rhythm of farce and should provoke laughter from the audience for that reason. The use of the foreign language within the dialogue may also have a comic effect. Those who understand Spanish will receive pleasure from their linguistic skills and those who do not will be pleased to discover how well they can follow the action anyway. When Marius switches from French interpreter to Spanish-language actor, his reversal functions as another stock comic device. While the scene at some deeper level satirizes French appropriation of Spanish-language intellectual property, on the surface it entertains through its linguistic games. There is a related comic effect from the occasional interpolation of familiar French literary quotations and, even more so, in Act III, Scene 11, from Pascual-Lucrèce's adoption of a tragic style. Audiences will receive pleasure from recognizing the familiar, superimposed lines, and they may be expected to laugh at the inappropriate use of a Racinian mold to convey a Spanish comic message.

L'Autre Don Juan is a metatheatrical *mise en abîme,* starting with its very title. Spectators may well think initially of Spain's most famous Don Juan, the one Walcott revives in his *The Joker of Seville.* Don Juan Ruiz de Alarcón is clearly not that Don Juan, but another one. Moreover, Manet's text deals directly with the question of Alarcón's identity. The playwright has stated that his work is intended as a kind of "fanciful biography" (Interview 1990), and in that context he attempts to uncover the Mexican-born author's inner world as revealed in his text.

At the author-character's first entrance, he delivers a verse soliloquy rich in intertextual references: to the philosophical ponderings of Descartes ("Comment savoir si je suis / quand je me pense . . . " [How can I know that I am / when I think . . .], 20), to Calderón's Segismundo ("Que le rêve ne soit pas rêve, / ni la vie un mensonge" [Let the dream not be a dream nor life a lie], 22), and to Shakespeare's Hamlet ("être soi ou ne pas être" [to be oneself or not to be], 22). He concludes that life would be a heavy burden without the hope that others might see him as he wished to be: Juan Ruiz is the shadow of another Don Juan (23). The author-character of the prologue is not the deformed hunchback described by history but rather a romantic leading man. To become the character Mendoza for the play-within-a-play, he must don a jacket with built-in humps and a boot with a special heel to create his limp.

In theatricalist fashion, this transformation takes place in full view of the audience, and the visible use of a mirror here, as in other scenes throughout the play, draws attention to the mirroring effect of the metaplay itself. The physically deformed Mendoza is a false reflection in two ways. The outward appearance of the character in the play-within-the-play conceals his moral and—in Manet's bawdy farce—physical virtues. At the same time, the audience will "see double," realizing that this Mendoza is but the creation of Don Juan, an actor-character with the physical appearance of a romantic hero.

The historical Alarcón very probably created the Mendoza figure of his *Las paredes oyen* as an idealized self-image. As Walter Poesse observes, the victorious protagonist is poor, luckless, deformed, and homely: "In this character, appropriately called Don Juan de Mendoza, Alarcón is undoubtedly portraying himself, and wishes to 'prove' that nobility of family and soul should triumph over wealth, handsomeness, and a mean spirit'' (Poesse 42). Manet takes this idealization process one step further, inventing a Don Juan whose handsome body matches the soul that Alarcón imagined as an expression of himself. In the process, the Cuban-French Manet places the anxieties of the Mexican-Spanish playwright at center stage in his modernized version of *Les Murs ont des oreilles*. *L'Autre Don Juan* may be a French farce, but the constant presence of the author-character and the interlingual games are guaranteed to keep audiences aware of the original source of this complex metatheatrical text.

Chapter 7

SCRIBE TWICE REMOVED: *SOMBRA Y QUIMERA DE LARRA* BY FRANCISCO NIEVA

The dominant current on the Spanish stage in the early 1950s, when Francisco Nieva (b. 1927) began writing theatre seriously, was realism/naturalism. The innovative socially committed dramas, like Antonio Buero-Vallejo's *Historia de una escalera* (1949) and Alfonso Sastre's *Escuadra hacia la muerte* (1953), were certainly within this mode, as were psychological dramas like Joaquín Calvo-Sotelo's *La muralla* (1954), and even the metatheatrical comedies of Víctor Ruiz Iriarte and José López Rubio. Settings and acting style envisioned for these plays were invariably representational; the audience was to accept the illusion that what they saw was "really" happening. Nieva's theatre then—and now— is diametrically opposed to realism/ naturalism. In his own terms, it is "teatralizante," an overtly theatricalist stage. Often it is both theatricalist and metatheatrical, a self-conscious and self-reflective theatre that likewise mirrors life as theatre through a *mise en abîme* of metatheatricalist devices.

That Nieva's original plays of the 1950s have little to do with the dominant mode in Spain is not surprising. Finding his own aesthetic values more in keeping with what was happening in France, he lived in Paris for a dozen years, arriving there somewhat earlier than Fernando Arrabal. While he was initially drawn to France because of his work as a painter, Nieva's interest in theatre has been constant throughout his life. He attended the original productions of such revolutionary works as Ionesco's *La Cantatrice chauve,*

179

Beckett's *En attendant Godot*, and Genet's *Le Balcon*. Genet's work, both his novels and plays, was a great revelation for Nieva; at the time of the French author's death, he proclaimed that Genet had "shattered the old society" (Nieva 1986: 3). Before establishing himself permanently in Madrid in 1968, Nieva also spent extended periods in Italy and Germany and became an admirer of Brechtian theories of staging and set design.

It is with good reason that Nieva is widely considered the most European dramatist of contemporary Spain. His *Tórtolas, crepúsculo y . . . telón*, subtitled *Variaciones sobre el teatro*, was written in Paris in 1953; it is both one of Nieva's most complex approaches to metatheatre and, as José A. Hernández has demonstrated, a fine example of Artaudian Theatre of Cruelty. Indeed this early text takes Artaud's metaphor of the theatre as a plague and develops it concretely by portraying a theatrical troupe that has been quarantined. Emil Signes has related Nieva's works in general to the surrealistic Theatre of the Marvelous, as defined by Gloria Orenstein. (Her analysis of this international movement, albeit with strong roots in France, includes Arrabal, the Spanish playwright with whom Nieva doubtless has the most in common.) Signes points out that Nieva's theatre is "one of magical transformations achieved by the commingling of opposites," and that it is characterized by both the "magic of language" advocated by André Breton and an Artaudian "alchemy of the event" (Signes 133). In her overview of Nieva's theatre, Katarzyna Gorna-Urbanska similarly identifies ties with various French and Eastern European playwrights and philosophers. Nieva, however, seldom forgets Spain and Spanish literary traditions in his theatre. Certainly his use of metatheatricalism in particular, while not unrelated to Pirandello or the self-conscious stage of contemporary France, inevitably involves intertextual references to Spanish authors.

The impact of the French stage on Nieva's theatre takes two forms. Beyond the pervasive, indirect one that Signes has linked to the Theatre of the Marvelous, some plays have direct thematic ties to France. Notable among these are recent, short works that parody nineteenth-century melodrama as filtered through cinema. For example, *Te quiero, zorra* (1988) owes an obvious debt to Alexandre Dumas *fils* and his *La Dame aux camélias*. The action is set in Paris in 1850 and the opening scene is of Zoé languishing in her bed. While the spectator may initially draw upon remembered images of Greta Garbo in the 1936 film version of Dumas's work, Zoé is not suffering from tuberculosis. Her lamentable state results from discovering that she has suddenly grown a fox tail. This magical transformation carries a metaphorical connotation that underscores the comedy: in Spanish, a female fox is a woman of easy virtue. Zoé's appeal for her aristocratic lover is only enhanced by her new physical attribute.

Starting in the 1950s, Nieva began dividing his original theatre into two groups: *Teatro Furioso* (Furious Theatre) and *Teatro de Farsa y Calamidad* (Theatre of Farce and Calamity). By the time he achieved the first major production of any of his plays, in January 1976, he had written almost twenty titles in those two categories. This first production, however, was not of any of these but rather *Sombra y quimera de Larra (Representación alucinada de "No más mostrador")*, a text that has sometimes been passed over quickly by scholars who do not consider it among his original works. Indeed Nieva, by then recognized as Spain's foremost stage designer, had been invited to prepare a modernized version of *No más mostrador*, by Mariano José de Larra (1809–1837), for the María Guerrero National Theatre. He accepted the opportunity but rejected the limitations. He explains in the introduction to the first edition of his adaptation that after the second act, Larra's nineteenth-century comedy gets lost in farcical entanglements; to maintain high standards, a modernized stage version would have reduced it to a short, simple *sainete*, a popular comedy of customs (Nieva 1976: 16–17).

In a parallel to the strategy of Eduardo Manet for his adaptation of Ruiz de Alarcón's *Las paredes oyen*, Nieva chose instead to treat *No más mostrador* as a play-within-a-play. Drawing upon Larra's essays, Nieva created a portrait of the satirist and his sociopolitical context and invented a frame play dealing with the actors and their relationships to

Larra. He placed the two planes of reality (the fiction of *No más mostrador* and the "reality" of the frame play) within a third, oneiric level of reality. The resulting text stands apart from Nieva's Furious Theatre and Theatre of Farce and Calamity—he has labeled it *Teatro de Crónica y Estampa* (Theatre of Chronicles and Engravings)—but in its own way it is no less original than *La detonación*, Buero-Vallejo's 1977 treatment of Larra.[1] Significantly it also introduces Nieva's subsequent series of free adaptations, including his *Los baños de Argel*, based on Cervantes, for which he received the National Theatre Prize for 1979.

Nieva's *Sombra y quimera de Larra*, like Manet's *L'Autre Don Juan*, exemplifies all five of the general varieties of the metadramatic identified by Richard Hornby: the play-within-the-play, the ceremony within the play, role-playing within the role, literary and real-life reference within the play, and self-reference. The complex structure of Nieva's work includes an oneiric level in the beginning and concluding scenes that function as prologue and epilogue to the frame play. The action begins with a ceremony that is, in itself, an example of both literary and real-life reference: the reading of José Zorrilla's poem of homage at Larra's tomb. Larra-Fígaro, the "sombra" (shadow, in the sense of ghost) of the title, enters and directly addresses the audience, alluding not only to the life and times of the historical figure but also, in a self-referential way, to the performance of *No más mostrador*. The author-character declares that this daring new, corrected version, of which he does not approve, has been done by another "frustrated writer" of today (*Sombra y quimera* 73).[2] The figure of a wailing woman, seen by Larra's tomb at the beginning, gives a circular structure to the play by reappearing at the end in a "dance of death."

At the prologue's end, the Larra figure takes his place in a box seat. The oneiric level merges with the fictional reality as Larra becomes the author-character of the frame play. Fictional time has shifted back to a fluid moment, prior to Larra's death, that combines the staging of *No más mostrador* and the visualization of the essay "El Día de Difuntos de 1936." By joining the spectators, the Larra figure also blurs the division between actors and audience. The conventions of realism/naturalism and representational staging will be further undermined throughout the play. The actor-characters of the frame play, while ostensibly performing in the play-within-the-play, will step out of character and address the spectators of *No más mostrador,* who will, in turn, shout comments at them from the upper gallery.

Metadrama is, of course, drama about drama. In that respect, Nieva's (meta)theatricalist approach to his subject is both surprising and appropriate. It is surprising because Larra, in his own theatre criticism, favored authenticity in costumes and period settings and, above all, a realistic acting style, anticipating, as José Monleón has noted, Stanislavski and twentieth-century Method acting. Nieva's concept of theatre is, in some ways, diametrically opposed to Larra's and influenced specifically by Brecht's nonrealistic stage design. Like Brecht, Nieva favors extending the playing space to include the audience, thus destroying the very illusionism that Larra applauded. On the other hand, Larra wrote a great deal about theatre. Nieva incorporates some of those opinions into his text and invents actor-characters who react to them, in essence rebelling against the author within the play and, through their acting style, subverting his theatrical theories. *Sombra y quimera de Larra* is theatre about theatre, self-referential in terms of Nieva's play and externally referential to the real-life Larra and his writings.

In various respects the very choice of Nieva as author of a text based on Larra and of *No más mostrador* as the play-within-the-play is rich in metatheatrical implications. The actor-characters of *Sombra y quimera de Larra* frequently criticize the author of *No más mostrador* for being "afrancesado" (Frenchified), but to some degree the charge could refer to the author of the frame play as well. Both Nieva and Larra lived in France for years and absorbed French cultural models. Moreover Larra, the author-character within the play, like Nieva himself, is accused of not having written an original play. Nieva's *Sombra y quimera de Larra* is a version of Larra's *No más mostrador,* and Larra's play in turn is a version of Eugène Scribe's *Les Adieux au comptoir.* The comments about French influence and borrowed texts thus have a double metatheatrical function, referring directly to the historical Larra and obliquely, in a self-referential way, to the author of the play in progress.

A French-Spanish connection is present not only in the play-within-the-play but also in the historical Larra's famous pen name, Fígaro. Nieva gives to his author-character both names, thus recognizing that Larra's most lasting works are the satirical essays written by his Fígaro persona. Larra explained the rationale for his new pseudonym in an 1832 essay, "Mis nombres y mis propósitos." The name is, of course, borrowed from Beaumarchais's character in *Le Barbier de Séville* and, as noted in Chapter 1, the eighteenth-century French comedy drew its inspiration from Spain. Larra was struck by the comment of Beaumarchais's barber that he laughed quickly for fear that he might otherwise cry. In dealing with Larra's life and tragic suicide, Nieva, too, plays with facile humor and underlying pathos.

The accusation within the frame play that Larra had merely translated a French work is not true, any more than one could accurately speak of uncreative borrowings in referring to Manet's version of Ruiz de Alarcón's *Las paredes oyen* or Nieva's version of the Larra text. *No más mostrador* (1831) was a free adaptation of Scribe's *Les Adieux au comptoir* (1824). Larra shifted the original text from a *comédie-vaudeville* to a comedy by eliminating the songs, and he expanded it from one act to five by adding a number of characters and situations.

Role-playing within the role—built on the stock comic technique of letting the audience, but not all the characters, in on the game—is a common strategy of farce, and not surprisingly forms the basis of the action in *Les Adieux au comptoir*. Scribe, we must recall, was the father of the well-made play and hence of modern bourgeois comedy; *Les Adieux au comptoir* evinces his usual skillful manipulation of plot. The social-climbing wife of a rich merchant wants their daughter to marry an aristocrat, but the father prefers a hardworking middle-class son-in-law to a good-for-nothing count. Functioning in Lionel Abel's terms as a would-be dramatist, the father has the young man of his choice pretend to be a nobleman; the role-playing within the role leads to several comic situations based on mistaken identity. Ultimately the daughter falls in love with the bourgeois in disguise, daughter and mother recognize that true worth—financial and moral—are not necessarily related to social class, and all ends happily. If Larra's theatre theories are far removed from Nieva's, it is even harder to imagine any kind of play more in opposition to Nieva's aesthetics than Scribe's *Les Adieux au comptoir.*

In nineteenth-century France, Scribe's predominantly middle-class audience would have found their own values mirrored within the play, but his satire of the nobility is gentle. Larra, on the other hand, in *No más mostrador,* while increasing the complexity of the metatheatrical games, sharpened the social satire. Under the surface humor, his comedy presents a more negative view of the nobility but also a harsher criticism of the bourgeoisie. Virtually all of the expanded cast of characters are engaged in role-playing within the role: the father Deogracias invents the farce of Bernardo pretending to be the Conde del Verde Saúco and later spreads the lie that he has lost his own fortune. Bernardo plays the count, but the count also plays Bernardo—at least until he gains an inheritance and no longer has to pretend that he loves the middle-class Julia, whom he would marry only for money. The mother Bibiana, another would-be dramatist, tries to create a script in which her name is Concha, her life-style is elegant, and her friends are aristocrats. And the offstage aristocrats pretend to be her friends only until they believe Deogracias's lie. Within the dramatic world, the characters play their parts in response to their personal interests. The implication of such metatheatrical games is that the "real" world, the world of the spectators, is not much different. As in Jacinto Benavente's prototypical metaplay *Los intereses creados* (1907), the hypocrisy and materialism within the farce mirror the defects of external society.

The reflection of life as theatre implicit in the role-playing within the role of *No más mostrador* surely did not escape Larra, who stingingly attacked hypocrisy in such articles as "El mundo todo es máscaras, todo el año es carnaval." The real-life Larra's suicide was doubtless caused more by his bitter disillusionment with a false, self-serving society than by unrequited love. Hornby suggests that the most fully developed variety of metadrama, the play-within-the-play, is used when society is cynical. Theatre becomes a metaphor of life. If the play is but an illusion, then "by extension, the world in which we live, which also seems to be so vivid, is in the end a sham" (Hornby 45). Nieva's choice of structure is thus doubly appropriate, reflecting both the context of our own postmodernist era and the cynicism of the historical Larra.

Nieva's frame play involves the acting company that is performing Larra's *No más mostrador*. The real stage is divided into two dressing rooms and the playing area where the troupe actually does stage part of Larra's comedy, including an only slightly modified version of the first two acts. Initially the action alternates between backstage and onstage; gradually, as the frame play dominates, the action becomes simultaneous and the "real" drama of the actor-characters merges with the play-within-the-play. Larra, author of the play-within-the-play and object of the actor-characters' growing hostility, is largely hidden from view in his box seat. It is his suicidal shot that brings an end to the performance.

If Scribe's *Les Adieux au comptoir* and Larra's *No más mostrador* follow the conventions of farce, Nieva's frame play borrows techniques of melodrama, with reminiscences of Shakespearean tragedy (at least as it would be viewed by a French neoclassicist). Nieva does not mention Tamayo y Baus's *Un drama nuevo* (1867) in his introduction, but there are some unmistakable surface parallels between his own metadrama and the nineteenth-century work. The actor Romerito, deeply resentful of what he considers personal allusions in Larra's satirical articles, arouses the hatred of the other actors. He plants an anonymous letter (written, he says, by dramatist Manuel Bretón de los Herreros) in Antonia's dressing room to make her believe that Larra, with whom she is in love, has been making fun of her. He leads Antonia's father, Don Pedro, to believe that Larra has dishonored his daughter, while also fanning the older man's hostility to the modern plays that have replaced his beloved Calderón. Romerito, like Shakespeare's villainous

Iago or Tamayo's treacherous Walton, obviously is motivated by envy. His role-playing within the role of the frame play mirrors the role-playing within *No más mostrador* but shows the dark side of the game. In the final scene of the first part, the distraught actress-character finds her father's gun and shoots her reflection in the mirror. The sound of the shot, alluding as it does to the suicide of the historical Larra, who may indeed have been the victim of the envy of Bretón de los Herreros and others, blurs the line between fiction and reality.

This blurring of the line between fiction and reality, between art and life, is precisely the function of metadrama. In essence metadrama breaks the frame that establishes the boundaries between the play in progress and the external reality of the spectators. In Nieva's complex structure, his Chinese boxes of metatheatrical devices, the various "frames" disintegrate as the multiple levels of reality gradually merge.

By juxtaposing the action of *No más mostrador* with the fictional reality of the actor-characters, Nieva quickly destroys the separation between the two levels. "Reality" imposes itself upon the "fiction." The actress Antonia misses her cue as Julia because she is upset by the anonymous letter she has found "backstage"; the other actors must improvise. Later when Julia-Antonia is "onstage," she responds to the dialogue of *No más mostrador* by references to the author-character Larra. Deogracias–Don Pedro enters when he should, but he carries along a wine bottle, index of his "offstage" role in the frame play. The frame play in turn blurs with the oneiric level and with real life. At the beginning, stagehands visibly remove Larra's tomb, and at the end, it is revealed that the wailing woman from the prologue is Petrita, a member of the same theatrical troupe. The line between the frame play and real life disappears when the actor-character Bernardo becomes the counterfigure of Larra, speaking the anguished words of "El Día de Difuntos de 1836."

Historical references within the frame play—to the first Carlist War, to political and literary figures, to Larra's personal life—further break down the division between fiction and reality and also provide the basis for allusions to the external reality of the spectators by foregrounding the parallels between the post-Fernando VII and post-Franco eras. Like *La detonación*, which Buero had already drafted when *Sombra y quimera de Larra* was staged, Nieva's text, underscoring Larra's relevance to the contemporary world, self-consciously reflects the political and cultural context in which it was created: the end of a repressive regime, disillusionment with the progress of liberal reforms, the presence of terrorists in the Basque provinces, the continuation of censorship, and even the reluctance of actors and audiences alike to accept any new approach to theatre.

Although Nieva does not use the term "metatheatre" in his own commentary on the play, he is clearly aware of the techniques he is using and their Spanish literary antecedents. When the actor-character Saúco-Romerito openly rebels against the dramatist-character, his words allude to Miguel de Unamuno's 1914 metanovel *Niebla* and to Cervantes's *Don Quixote*: "A mí no hay autor que logre matarme si yo no quiero, ni me asusta con sus quebrantos ni sinsabores. Hijo soy de mis propias obras" (No author can succeed in killing me if I don't want it, nor can he scare me with his afflictions and his sorrows. I am the son of my own works) (*Sombra y quimera* 115). Deogracias–Don Pedro, already quite drunk by the third act of *No más mostrador*, likewise departs from Larra's script to recite lines from Calderón, precisely the Golden Age dramatist identified with "el gran teatro del mundo" (the great theatre of the world). In his self-conscious use of the metadramatic, Nieva has not overlooked the implications of the mirror: fiction and reality reflect one another at all of the multiple levels. In this light, the visible mirror of the stage set takes on symbolic values.

As already noted, the shot that Julia-Antonia fires at the end of the first part alludes to Larra's death; it refers back to the speech of Larra's ghost in the prologue and foreshadows the author-character's suicide at the play's end. The "melodrama" within the frame play prepares the spectator for Julia-Antonia's desperate act. She has been frantically seeking some object between her "onstage" scenes, finally locating the revolver behind her father's dressing room mirror. The surprise of her subsequent action is not that she fires the gun but that she chooses her reflection as the target. Whose image does she shatter? Julia of *No más mostrador*? Antonia of the frame play? Julia-Antonia of *Sombra y quimera de Larra*? The actor-characters are not alone in having multiple identities. So did the historical figure whose life and works form the axis of the play. Indeed, after the shot rings out from the theatre box, Saúco-Romerito underscores the nineteenth-century satirist's duality by crying, "¡Muerto Larra, viva Fígaro!" (Larra is dead. Long live Fígaro!) (133). The possible interpretations, fittingly enough, are at least double. In pulling the trigger, Larra-Fígaro killed his image, but not his "reality"; Fígaro lives on. But if one views Larra's death as caused by the society of his time, a society—represented here by the actor-characters—that objected to seeing itself reflected in his satirical writings, then society in essence pulled the trigger—shattering its image in the mirror but leaving the reality, with all its flaws, intact.

In his introduction, Nieva suggests another, expressionistic reading, of his text. He indicates that Larra's appearance at the beginning, in what I have called the oneiric level, "gives us the clue that the performance is being produced in his own head" (Nieva 1976: 22). Such an interpretation foregrounds the *quimera* (delusion) and *representación alucinada* (hallucinatory performance) of the title and anticipates Buero's *La detonación*, where the action is largely screened through the consciousness of the protagonist. It extends the *mise en abîme* by making the frame play itself a play within a play—with the inside of the deceased Larra's head serving as the theatre. To be sure, it also makes "another frustrated writer" (a certain Franciso Nieva?) a creature of Larra's imagination. The metafictional games this implies call to mind Carlos Rojas's novel *El ingenioso hidalgo y poeta Federico García Lorca asciende a los infiernos*, winner of the Nadal Prize for 1979, which, probably coincidentally, establishes a surreal theatre of the mind in the afterlife. Nieva's intention notwithstanding, it is unlikely that the audience gave this interpretation to the play. The Larra figure is mostly out of sight in his theatre box, thus leaving the fictional reality of the frame play uninterrupted. The reviews of the stage production that I have read are strongly favorable but make no reference to such an interpretation.

Even without this additional level of Larra's ghost as the author-character in the process of creating in his mind the *representación alucinada* that unfolds before our eyes, *Sombra y quimera de Larra* is a rich example of metatheatricalism, a play that explores and interweaves a variety of meta-dramatic devices for the purpose of laying bare not only the world of the theatre but the theatre of the external world.

Sombra y quimera de Larra is also a curious case of a Spanish reworking of a French text. Scribe's short, well-made farce became Larra's longer and more acerbic well-made comedy, but still within the restraints of the realistic, representational theatre in vogue in France at the beginning of the nineteenth century. In Nieva's hands, the Scribe-Larra text becomes a play-within-a-play subverted by the overt theatricalism of the actor-characters and the hallucinatory state of the ghostly author-character. To the extent that Nieva's concept of theatre has been shaped by surrealism and an Artaudian theatre of cruelty, the "frustrated writer" of today has used a contemporary French inspiration to undo the influence on Larra of the French theatre of his time.

Chapter 8

A SPANISH-FRENCH PLAYWRIGHT: THE THEATRE OF CARLOS SEMPRUN-MAURA

Of the Spaniards who have become authors of the contemporary French theatre, Fernando Arrabal has undoubtedly achieved the greatest visibility. He has lived in France since the mid-1950s, initially publishing and staging most of his works in French, but, particularly since the death of Franco in 1975, has been an active participant in Spanish cultural life as well. He is known throughout the world as both a French and a Spanish playwright and novelist. While Arrabal's fame as a bilingual, bicultural Spanish-French author may set him apart, he is not a unique case. Emmanuel Roblès, whose recent Juana la Loca play is discussed in Chapter 5, is also a playwright and novelist of international stature. Born in French Algeria of Spanish parents, he is a Frenchman who considers himself to have a dual heritage; he speaks fluent Spanish and often deals with Hispanic characters and themes in his works. Agustín Gómez-Arcos left Spain in the mid-1960s after the controversy surrounding the staging of his *Diálogos de la herejía*. In France he has had a modest involvement in theatre and considerable success as a novelist; in his narrative, he frequently writes of Spain. Yet another example is Carlos Semprun-Maura, a playwright, novelist and essayist who left Spain as a young child at the beginning of the Civil War in 1936 but still considers himself a Spaniard:

> En lo que se refiere a mis raíces nacionales—o geográficas—reconozco ser esquizofrénico. Soy un español de París. Capaz de escribir temas franceses, como es-

191

> pañoles. Capaz de escribir en las dos lenguas. No me
> duele en absoluto. A mi modo de ver, dos culturas
> valen más que una. Y si hubiera podido tener cuatro o
> cinco, qué maravilla! [As for my national—or geo-
> graphic—roots, I admit to being schizophrenic. I am a
> Spaniard from Paris. Able to write about French
> themes, like Spanish ones. Able to write in the two
> languages. I don't regret it at all. From my way of
> looking at it, two cultures are better than one. And if I
> could have had four or five, that would have been
> wonderful!] (Letter 1988).

Carlos Semprun-Maura was born in Madrid on 23 November 1926. At the outbreak of the war, his family was in
the Basque country. His father, until then a university
professor, was named ambassador to Holland by the Republican government. The family thus went to Holland in
1936 and then later to France. It was in the Hague that the
young boy began reading literature in French; there were
no Spanish books in the library, and, while he knew a little
French, he could not read Dutch at all. The first book he
read in French was Fournier's *Le grand Meaulnes*, followed
by a police novel, Saint-Exupéry's *Vol de nuit*, and a work by
Blaise Cendrars: hardly typical reading either for an eleven-
year-old or for anyone learning a second language! The
young boy's oral skills initially were not on a par with his
reading; Semprun-Maura recalls having a terrible accent
when he first arrived in France (Interview 1987). His formal
education, however, was primarily in France, and he soon
became completely bilingual.

The children of exiles often become so assimilated into
the host country that they lose their sense of identity with
their national origin. Even in Toulouse, the French city with
the largest Spanish emigré population, by the late 1950s the
younger generation was rapidly losing Hispanic culture
and in danger of being ideologically illiterate (Domergue
and Laffranque 94). Not so in the Semprun family. Like his
older brother Jorge (b. 1923), Carlos became an active
participant in the clandestine anti-Franco movement. As a
political militant, he made the first of many trips to Spain in
1954 and ultimately spent fifteen years of his life in the

cause. In 1976 he returned to Spain legally and collaborated for two years in the leftist newspaper and magazine *Diario 16* and *Cambio 16* (Interview 1988). Jorge Semprun, whose novels written in French have gained him an international reputation, in 1988 was named to President Felipe González's cabinet as Spain's Minister of Culture.

Carlos Semprun-Maura's interest in theatre spans several decades but is not his only literary activity nor even the one most directly related to his Spanish roots: "How strange. I've just realized that my books (novels and essays) almost always deal with Spain, but in my theatre only two works . . . speak of that theme" (Letter 1988). To date, he is the author of six novels and three book-length essays. Among his narrative works of Spanish theme are *Un Chapeau qu'on met le dimanche pour voir les siens*, 1968, his first published novel; *L'An prochain à Madrid*, 1975, which, touching upon his personal reality, deals with the exile's return; and *Les Barricades solitaires*, 1985, one of two novels thus far that Plaza y Janés has had translated and published in Spanish editions. (Although Arrabal does his own Spanish versions of works originally published in French, other Spanish-French authors generally write in French and are translated into Spanish by someone of the publisher's choosing.) Three of Semprun-Maura's essays relate to Spanish history: *Révolution et Contre-Révolution en Catalogne*, 1974; *Ni Dios, ni Amo, ni CNT*, 1978 (written directly in Spanish); and *Franco est mort dans son lit*, 1980.

Much of Semprun-Maura's professional and creative work has been directed to French radio. He has done programs, in Spanish, that have been produced in France for international broadcast, aimed at Spain or Latin America. In addition to adaptations and documentaries, in a twenty-five-year period from the early 1960s to the late 1980s he wrote thirty-eight original plays in French that were aired on France-Culture or France-Inter. In June 1988 he was awarded a prize by the Société des Auteurs et Compositeurs Dramatiques for his total contribution in the field of radio. Almost without exception, Semprun-Maura's radio plays are not specifically written for a listening audience but rather have stage directions that call for visual effects. The scripts, therefore, can be read like any other dramatic text.

Semprun-Maura's original theatre has consisted primarily of his radio plays, but the work he has done for the legitimate stage has had a significant impact. His two major plays, *L'Homme couché*, 1971, and *Le Bleu de l'eau-de-vie*, 1981, accompanied by a selection of strongly favorable reviews, were both chosen for publication in the influential *L'Avant-Scène Théâtre*. The former, staged at the Théâtre Lucernaire in the Montparnasse section of Paris, was directed by Laurent Terzieff, who also created the lead role. *Le Bleu de l'eau-de-vie* premiered at the Petit Odéon, the experimental theatre associated with the Comédie Française. It was directed by the late Roger Blin, widely considered to have been France's foremost *metteur en scène* of the avant-garde. For Guy Dumur, the reviewer from *Le Nouvel Observateur*, this Semprun-Maura play had given actor Patrick Chesnais "the best role of his career" (qtd. *L'Avant-Scène* 703: 21). With the same actor, the play ran for several months the following year at the Petit-Montparnasse theatre and also was presented at the Off-Avignon festival (Interview 1988). In November 1990 it was revived in Paris at the Théâtre de Nesle in conjunction with the Festival Théâtral Ibéral.

Besides these two major plays, Semprun-Maura is the author of several short original works and adaptations, some of which were also published in *L'Avant-Scène Théâtre* starting in the 1950s. These include an early text, *Sur une plage de l'ouest,* which he wrote in Spanish and published in his sister's French translation under the pseudonym Carlos Larra (the Larra, of course, in honor of the nineteenth-century Spanish writer). His adaptations of two plays by Léonide Andreiev were staged by Terzieff, and his translation of *La noche de los asesinos* by Cuban dramatist José Triana was produced by Blin. Three of his own short works were both staged outside Paris and produced for national radio (Office de Radio et Télévision Français) under the direction of Jean-Marie and Dominique Serreau.

Given the critical success of his two major stage plays and his connections with French theatre circles, it is surprising that Semprun-Maura has not had more of his works produced. He attributes this to his own disposition, his unwillingness to make the necessary effort to get a play staged; he prefers the relative tranquillity of the radio world (Interview 1987). It is perhaps for this reason that his radio scripts are closely linked to his stage plays rather than representing a separate genre. Both facets of his theatre reflect the same repeated techniques and themes. He turns frequently to metadrama and to the fantastic mode. He creates a series of characters who manifest extreme ennui or agoraphobia. His texts from the 1980s may be considered psychological drama, with probings of guilt or destroyed illusions. Often he sets up conflicts between brothers or former friends, conflicts that may revolve around a love relationship or have political implications or both.

Semprun-Maura's early short plays (*Sur une plage de l'ouest*, 1959, and *La Salle d'attente*, 1967) are antirealistic, allegorical pieces that relate to surrealism and the Theatre of the Absurd. The former is of particular interest for its overt metatheatricalism. Groups of characters come and go, commenting on but offering no help to a drowning man. Upset by this portrayal, the actors rebel against the author-within-the-text, accusing him, among other things, of having written "a work lacking in realism and altruism" (*Sur une plage de l'ouest* 41). In both the play-within-the-play and the frame play, they find escape from their reality in the tango music of Tino Rossi. In *La Salle d'attente* groups of characters similarly comment on the train that cannot depart because of a body on the tracks. The text foreshadows Semprun-Maura's mature theatre in its introduction of a passive character: in this case, a man who has been arrested for draft evasion. Handcuffed to two policemen, he explains that he simply forgot about his military service. He always dropped his mail into the wastebasket, unread, because he never turned his eyes away from the window in front of his desk.

L'Homme couché, the first of Semprun-Maura's major stage plays, develops logically from these early short texts in its connection with the Theatre of the Absurd, its potential allegorical meaning, and the passivity of its title character. It is, as the critics quoted in *L'Avant-Scène Théâtre* reveal, a text open to multiple comparisons and interpretations

(*L'Avant-Scène* 474: 22–23). Not unexpectedly, most critics found connections with plays originally written in French, notably those by Ionesco, but Georges Lerminier of *Le Parisien Libéré* recalled a Hispanic antecedent, Ricardo Talesnik's *La fiaca* (1967) (qtd. *L'Avant-Scène* 474: 22). The Argentine's satirical comedy had been staged in Paris as *La Flemme*.

Talesnik's Nestor decides to stay home from work one day, and then another, and then another, as a kind of rebellion against the daily routine. His lethargy springs from a desire for personal freedom. His surprising ailment at first shows signs of being contagious, but ultimately he is "cured" by economic pressures and his boss's ultimatum. Semprun-Maura's play is more complex and less superficially humorous than the Argentine work, lending itself to deeper psychological, philosophical, or political readings. Matthieu Galey, writing for *Combat*, found it to be nihilistic, a "critical satire of everything, of love, of couples living together, of political commitment, of the lack of communication." For François-Régis Bastide, of *Les Nouvelles Littéraires*, the playwright "achieves a curious blend of the unexpected, of humor and of emotion, without ever worrying about logic. But one would say that his characters exist, have always existed somewhere, who knows where, even before he dreamed of bringing them together in a perfectly surrealist plot" (qtd. *L'Avant-Scène* 474: 23).

Boris, the title character, has been in bed for a year. He claims to be tired and to have lost the use of his legs. He is cared for by Marie, who lives with him. His attic flat is constantly invaded by unannounced visitors. A series of sailors arrive to leave mysterious packages that will later be claimed by cabdrivers. Joseph storms in, looking for Nada, who has abandoned him. He leaves, and Nada herself arrives; she is Boris's former lover who says she has lost the use of her arms. News from the outside is alarming. Diseased sailors, carrying mysterious packages, have caused an epidemic. Their ship is destroyed. The last sailor to enter Boris's room is dying. Joseph, too, has died, probably from poison. Boris remarks that Nada always tries to kill her ex-lovers; when she departs again—after recovering the use of her arms—the coffee she prepared smells funny to Marie, who throws it out. To Marie's desperation nothing has changed, and Boris, who had gotten up when Nada was there, has now returned to his original state.

Semprun-Maura suggests that his play is a simple love story. Without Nada—whose full name is María Nadario—the world no longer exists for Boris. When she returns, he is able to get up. When she leaves, he succumbs again to lethargy. At the same time, he adds, the play is "to some extent a picture of the world at that time" and the nickname Nada was inspired by the famous Goya engraving (Interview 1988).

The playwright's comments about the love story notwithstanding, *L'Homme couché* invites other readings. Nada, as the text clarifies, is Spanish for "Nothing." That nothingness, or the realization of the absurdity of human existence, proves to be a fatal attraction for Joseph and a debilitating one for Boris. The absurdity of life is reinforced by the sailors and their meaningless task of delivering boxes. The contents of the boxes are unknown to them, to Boris, and to the cabdrivers. Yet the sailors and the cabdrivers go through the monotonous routine, even when faced with death. Boris has become aware of the absurdity of life and has retreated passively from it. On another level, however, the sailors and the cabdrivers may be responding to orders from an international political movement. (The ship that brings the disease-bearing boxes comes from Hong Kong.) Nada speaks to one of the sailors in just these terms, reminding him, in essence, that it is his function to obey orders from above, not to question Boris. The meaningless—or menacing—tasks are imposed through an unidentified chain of command.

The character of Boris bears a close relationship to that of Pierre in *Le Bleu de l'eau-de-vie*, but the later play, in spite of its comic moments, is an intense psychological drama, far removed in tone from the absurdist, allegorical *L'Homme couché*. The critics quoted in *L'Avant-Scène Théâtre* found that intensity reminiscent of Chekhov and variously termed the work "a masterpiece," "a rare pleasure," "an event" (qtd. *L'Avant-Scène* 703: 21). In a somewhat less extreme way, Pierre, like Boris, has retreated from the world. He no longer works, he spends his days in his apartment, and he has apparently become an alcoholic who cannot remember what he has done while drunk. He receives an unexpected visit from his old friend Alain. Gradually the visit becomes a confrontation in which Alain forces Pierre to face reality, including the fact that he has been making obscene phone calls to Laure, his estranged wife. At the play's end, Alain leaves Pierre with a recording of his own voice and the

Marc de Brebisson and Ollivier Arrighi in the revival of Semprun-Maura's *Le Bleu de l'eau-de-vie*, Paris, 1990. (Photos courtesy of *L'Avant-Scène Théâtre*)

Marc de Brebisson and Ollivier Arrighi in the revival of Semprun-Maura's *Le Bleu de l'eau-de-vie,* Paris, 1990. (Photo courtesy of *L'Avant-Scène Théâtre*)

admonition that "all the scotch in the world will not be enough . . ." (*Le Bleu de l'eau-de-vie* 20).

Alain's motivation is not altruistic. Pierre is doubtless right that Alain has become Laure's lover. If Boris's lethargy may be explained by the loss of his love Nada, Pierre more obviously has embarked upon a path of self-destruction because of the loss of Laure. The implicit rivalry between the two former friends, however, also relates to their response to other lost illusions: their revolutionary political ideals and their literary ambitions. Alain has, in essence, sold out to the establishment; rather than being a politically committed novelist, he has turned into a newspaper writer who churns out routine assignments. Pierre, the would-be poet, has responded to his unfulfilled ambitions by turning his back on the system, by becoming an outcast. Alain, like the sailors in *L'Homme couché*, plays the game and obeys the rules. Pierre refuses to conform and hence retreats from reality.

There is a Pirandellian aspect to Pierre's characterization; the line between his real world and his fantasies remains unclear. Alain suggests that Pierre's alcoholism, along with the concomitant memory loss, is feigned and that his stories about the golden-hearted prostitute next door are made up. He reminds Pierre that he once had all his friends convinced that he was having a romance with a nonexistent woman. The possibility of Pierre's role-playing within the role is mirrored in Alain. Upon his arrival at Pierre's apartment, he clearly acts out a carefully planned scene that is intended to disguise his real motives. Pierre rips away Alain's mask just as Alain attempts to tear away his.

The role-playing within the role and the identification of both characters as would-be writers are not the only metatheatrical devices in the play. The dialogue includes a number of allusions to film. For example, in talking about Alain's job, Pierre repeatedly evokes the image of the newspaperman as portrayed in American movies, and he describes Alain, because of his efforts at tracing the obscene telephone calls, as "a real Hitchcock" (16). As metadrama, *Le Bleu de l'eau-de-vie* is related not only to the early one-act play, *Sur une plage de l'ouest*, but also to several of Semprun-

Maura's favorite radio scripts, all of which include a writer as character: *Magnifique la luxure* (1981), *Nuits ouvertes comme des lits* (1983), *C'étaient des tilleuls, je me souviens* (1985), and *Ma chanson la plus triste est espagnole* (1987). These several plays were directed for France-Culture by Jean-Pierre Colas. *Ma chanson la plus triste est espagnole* premiered as a stage play in January 1990, running for a month at José Valverde's Théâtre Essaïon but without attracting the attention of the critics; a stage production of *C'étaient des tilleuls, je me souviens* has also been planned by a different director (Letter 1990).

Of all his dramatic texts, *Ma chanson la plus triste est espagnole* is the one that best reveals Semprun-Maura's deep identification with Spain. Both in theme and technique, it is a Spanish work, one that recalls to the Hispanist numerous other texts—of fiction, theatre, or film—many of them unknown to the playwright himself. In several respects, however, it is also the most representative of Semprun-Maura's plays, for it incorporates almost all of the most characteristic tendencies of his theatre.

The action of *Ma chanson la plus trieste est espagnole* takes place in an isolated house in a little town in Spain at some unspecified time after Franco's death. There are three characters: Juan, a writer of stage and radio plays; María, his wife; and Pablo, his brother—who died seven years before the fictive present. The story, as it gradually develops, is one of frustration, guilt, and the brother-against-brother conflict fostered by the political aftermath of an inevitably fratricidal Civil War. Pablo had fought the Franco regime; as a result he had spent years in Carabanchel prison where he was tortured and died. In the course of his improbable evening visit, he accuses Juan of having been the one who denounced him to the police. Juan denies his complicity until María makes the same assertion: "You collaborated with the government. You helped the police to dismantle a clandestine group of students . . . " A sobbing Juan responds that he broke under torture (45).

At the core of the story from Juan's past is a historical reality—the confrontation of the clandestine anti-Franco student movement with the police brutality of a repressive regime—that has been used by scores of Spanish writers including, for example, novelists Juan Goytisolo in his landmark *Señas de identidad* (1966)—prohibited in Spain until after Franco's death—and Montserrat Roig in her recent novel, *La voz melodiosa* (1987). To be sure, it is a reality with which Semprun-Maura, because of his own political involvement, has a personal familiarity. But the French-language text has a decidedly Spanish ring in aspects far removed from the author's own family experience—for example, when Juan proclaims the generational crisis of the children of the victorious right: "Nous étions les fils des vainqueurs, vaincus par la victoire de leurs pères" (We were the sons of the conquerors, conquered by the victory of their fathers) (*Ma chanson la plus triste est espagnole* 44). Other historical and political references within the text, to Franco's death or to terrorist attacks, give to the fictive present an authentic Spanish context. Indeed, it is not unreasonable to place the action in the late 1970s, when the playwright had returned to Spain, or to see certain parallels in the Juan-María-Pablo relationship with Antonio Buero-Vallejo's expressionistic *Jueces en la noche* (1979), a psychological and political drama with a somewhat related treatment of the love triangle and of the phantoms arising from guilt. Even the nostalgia Semprun-Maura's characters express for Madrid and the Retiro park is authentically Spanish with antecedents, both literary and personal: from his childhood, the playwright remembers the Retiro as a "magic place" (Interview 1987).

Within the historical-political context (represented here quite typically by a conflict between brothers), there is the other story, that of *desamor*, of a marriage succumbing to frustrated dreams and boredom. The phantom Pablo is evoked by Juan's remorse and by María's desire. Was she ever really the lover of her husband's dead brother or is that idealized relationship as much a product of fantasy as her flirtation this evening? In Pirandellian fashion, the question is never answered. Pablo is, for both of them, the symbol of the unrealized dream, of the distance that lies between present reality and the image they once had of themselves.

"Ce n'est pas mon frère qui est mort," Juan declares. "C'est moi. J'étais idéaliste, je suis devenu un coffre à chaussures" (It isn't my brother who died. I did. I was an idealist. I've become a shoebox) (30). In separate scenes and in almost identical words, the husband and wife accuse each other of having killed the speaker's youth, beauty, and talent. Juan summarizes the blame thus: "Indeed, living together kills everything. Inspiration, love, desire . . . " (43). In this respect Pablo is the phantom of what might have been, evoked by a disenchanted couple's midlife crisis.

Semprun-Maura's treatment here of a disintegrating marriage, while universal in theme, is one that evokes any number of plays from democratic Spain, such as Jaime Salom's empassioned plea for divorce reform, *La piel del limón* (1976), or his husband-wife confrontation, *Una hora sin televisión* (1987). But even more in tune with recent Spanish theatre and cinema is the intensive use of the metadramatic in *Ma chanson la plus triste est espagnole*. Perhaps, in this respect, the closest parallels lie with the films of José Luis Garci, most notably with his 1987 *Asignatura aprobada*, whose protagonist, like Semprun-Maura's Juan, is a writer of radio plays whose scripts merge with the frame reality.

The metatheatricalism of *Ma chanson la plus triste est espagnole* is apparent beginning with the title, an intertextual reference to a Spanish poem by Jaime Gil de Biedma. (Semprun-Maura has used lines of poetry for titles on other occasions. "Magnifique la luxure" is from a poem by Rimbaud, and "Le Bleu de l'eau-de-vie" is both an intratextual reference to a poem written by the character Pierre and an intertextual one to an unpublished poem the adolescent Semprun-Maura wrote in Spanish.) María and Juan cite the poem "Ma chanson la plus triste est espagnole" as an example from a truly talented writer, in a conversation in which they both disparage Juan's talent. Juan attempts at other moments to convince himself of his worth as a playwright by recalling triumphant opening nights and referring to the enthusiasm of Nuria (an apparent allusion to famed Spanish actress Nuria Espert), but his work now is primarily for radio, and María tells Pablo that Juan "is still writing those horrible little plays" (15). Juan's one chance at being staged in Paris ended in failure; he rationalizes that "there are practically no Spanish authors performed in Paris" (25).

At the play's beginning, Juan reads to an uninterested María a scene he has just written. The play-within-the-play is a husband-wife dialogue about the husband's clandestine trips as an anti-Francoist militant and the fact that Franco is now dead. While the acrimonious relationship between the spouses mirrors that of the frame play, Juan's character, as someone actively fighting a repressive regime, is the antithesis of Juan, that is, he serves as the author-within-the-text's idealized self. Pablo, too, is the image that Juan would like to project upon himself. He describes his "real" brother (not the phantom who visits them that evening) as a sparkling person and brilliant writer. The phantom may be "a hallucination that's come straight out of one of my plays" (29). The line between illusion and reality, art and life, further blurs with a second play-within-the-play. When Pablo has left, Juan turns on the television. To his shock the play he hears (spoken by the same actors who create María and Juan) is, in fact, the play he is in the process of writing.

Semprun-Maura has blended the metadramatic here with the fantastic to create an ambiguous, "Twilight Zone" atmosphere. There is no explanation within the text for the arrival of Pablo nor any clarification for the television broadcast of Juan's play in progress. Different levels of reality within the dramatic world simply coexist. The playwright acknowledges that the fantastic has had a continuing appeal for him: "For me, theatre is the art of the double, of the mirror" (Letter 1988). In *Derrière la nuit, la nuit* (1972), an isolated house is the place of encounter for characters living in three different moments in time, two of them involving clandestine freedom fighters: the Second World War, the Algerian War, and the present. In *Personne, ici* (1974), the fantastic takes on a science-fiction tone as mysterious voices first cause a husband and wife to lock themselves in their high-rise apartment and then lure them to their death. In *C'étaient des tilleuls, je me souviens,* the ambiguity of fantasy and reality is ultimately clarified when the setting is identified as a psychiatric hospital in which the "nurse" and "doctor" are patients, along with the other two characters, an actress and a journalist. All four of them, in essence, are prisoners.

In Semprun-Maura's theatre in general, as in many contemporary Spanish plays, the characters are entrapped, psychologically if not physically. Sometimes, like Pablo in *Ma chanson la plus triste est espagnole* or Natacha in *Derrière la nuit, la nuit,* who was killed by the Gestapo, they are imprisoned or assassinated because they have actively opposed the dominant regime. Sometimes there is an outside force, imaginary or real, that creates the enclosure or precipitates their death (*Personne, ici, C'étaient des tilleuls, je me souviens*). More likely they have retreated to fantasy, alcohol abuse, or lethargy because of their failure to remain true to the revolutionary ideals and/or career ambitions of their youth (*Le Bleu de l'eau-de-vie, Ma chanson la plus triste est espagnole*). Juan, in this last play, is haunted by both frustration and guilt. An intense feeling of emptiness, failure, or guilt may immobilize characters to the point that they can no longer leave their rooms (Boris in *L'Homme couché* and the actress-characters Suzanne in *Nuits ouvertes comme des lits* and María in *C'étaient des tilleuls, je me souviens*). The memory of someone's death or the threat of one's own underscores most of Semprun-Maura's work, as it does much of Spanish literature. Indeed the most optimistic, almost Casonian, of the scripts mentioned in the present study is *Magnifique la luxure:* Nadia, who had been prevented from committing suicide by Serge, plans to kill herself when he is arrested but then changes her mind, because she might be able to help him. Love, atypically in this case, has not followed the path of other lost illusions.

Semprun-Maura's forte is the psychological analysis of character, but his works transcend the individual case study to offer a metaphor of contemporary life. In his use of the metatheatrical, as in his earlier experimentation with the absurd, he presents a dramatic world that reflects external society, providing a mirror for frustration and disillusionment. While his recurrent themes and techniques belong to dominant currents of French or world theatre, *Ma chanson la plus triste est espagnole* makes apparent their underlying Spanish connection, thus inviting intertextual readings with Hispanic authors.

Chapter 9

CONCLUSION

In the present study, we have looked at cultural exchange between the contemporary Spanish and French stages from two basic perspectives: the collective, in terms of production history in the two countries, and the individual, in terms of bicultural interests of particular playwrights. While these approaches are obviously dissimilar, there is a repeated strand in the two sections of the book; that of exile, manifested as geographical displacement and as a loss of—or search for—identity. This pattern of exile is not, of course, equally present in the theatres of the two countries. The past half century has witnessed waves of Spanish emigrés, first crossing the Pyrenees to seek refuge in France and then returning to their native land. There is no counterpart movement of the French into and out of Spain.

In France, following the Spanish Civil War, there was, quite literally, a Spanish-language exile theatre, established by the emigré community for the maintenance of their own culture and therefore marginal to the dominant currents of the French stage. Later other Spanish emigrés, like Martín Elizondo and Martínez Azaña, promoted Spanish theatre in France, but still aimed at a selected audience. Within mainstream French theatre, some Spanish authors were staged precisely because they were "exiles," either geographically displaced, like Alberti, or victims of "inner exile," like Sastre.

More characteristically, however, to the French imagination, Spain *was* different, just as the tourist slogan proclaimed. South of the Pyrenees was the Other: baroque, passionate, and violent. The early Lorca vogue in France, culminating in the 1960s, was built on that image, and Spanish plays that did not conform to the expectation did not readily meet with success. The continuing presence of Spanish theatre on the French stage in the past quarter century, as well as the recent major stagings of Lorca and Valle-Inclán, may be attributed, at least in part, to other "exiles": to Argentine-born directors, like García and Lavelli, who have strongly identified with their Spanish roots, or to Pasqual, who has left his native Spain to direct the Théâtre de l'Europe in France. And, to be sure, the one contemporary Spanish playwright who is fully integrated into the French stage is another voluntary exile, Arrabal.

Although there are French theatre professionals, like André Camp, who have actively promoted Spanish theatre in France without such Spanish roots, the leadership of Ibéral includes others with connections to the experience of exile: Casarès and Semprun-Maura, who became political exiles in their childhood; Martín Elizondo, a voluntary, economic exile; Valverde, who is the son of Spanish emigrés; Demarigny, who is French but lived for many years in South America. In the chapters on individual playwrights, not only Semprun-Maura but also the other two French-language authors may be considered under my flexible definition of "exiles." The Cuban-born Manet, as a political exile estranged from his native land, has apparently sought out the Spanish identity of his parents; his French version of a Spanish Golden Age comedy is overtly intended as a vindication of another displaced author, as well as a response to the French notion of *espagnolade*. The Algerian-born Roblès, like his friend Camus, has always openly proclaimed his Spanish heritage, perhaps because he has seen himself as Other with respect to the dominant French culture.

The presence of French theatre on the contemporary Spanish stage has responded to different motivations, although not necessarily unrelated to issues of exile and otherness. During the early postwar years, French plays were eagerly produced in mainstream Spanish theatres because of the cultural and box office value attached to anything imported from Paris. Both the French and the

Spanish perceived French culture as superior and Spanish culture as somehow inferior. The explanation of playwrights Buero-Vallejo and Rodríguez Méndez for the relative absence of Spanish plays on the French stage is merely the reverse side of the same cultural pattern that brought Parisian hits so readily to Madrid playhouses. The later polemics in Spain on authors like Ionesco and Sartre might be seen as debates between those who turned to France for aesthetic, philosophical, or political leadership and those who feared that very same influence. On either side, they were attributing to the French a potentially significant impact on Spanish society. It should be noted that the French from time to time have turned to Spain for inspiration—Vilar, in search of "popular" theatre, for example—but that traditionally the French have not perceived Spanish influence as specifically threatening to their own identity or the moral fiber of their nation.

Spain's growing acceptance as a Western European nation, no longer so widely perceived as Other, has coincided with the declining interest in French theatre on the Madrid stage. Nevertheless, returning "exiles" have helped to retain a cultural exchange. Nieva was back in Spain early enough to contribute his designs to several landmark productions of French works, and his own plays often reflect his deep personal knowledge of French literature and art; his dramatic treatment of Larra reveals his sympathies for another returning emigré. Since coming home to Barcelona, Flotats has brought French plays and even French theatre professionals to his government-subsidized playhouse; in 1989, his accomplishments at the Poliorama were officially recognized by his being awarded the Spanish National Theatre Prize.

Ties between France and northeastern Spain remain strong, no doubt in part because of the Catalan-speaking region's resistance to the influence of the dominant, Castilian-speaking society. Flotats indeed became immersed in French language and culture as a child because of his father's sense of inner exile. In Spain today, nationally, French is no longer the primary foreign language taught in the schools; the "prestige" language now, chosen on economic grounds, is English. The decline in the study of French in Spain no doubt explains why a group like Ibéral has perceived a need to promote contemporary French playwrights in Spain, not just Spanish playwrights in France. Without the concerted efforts of such official organisms as the Centro Dramático Nacional and *El Público*, there would be no "Koltès myth" south of the Pyrenees.[1]

In this concluding section, I have suggested a sociological perspective on the cultural exchange between the theatres of France and Spain. It is an approach to the recent past that I believe merits further study, as does the apparently changing relationship between the two stages over the past decade or two. Today, in comparison with the early post-war period, there is a greater Hispanic presence in France, a lessening French influence in Spain, and a breaking down of stereotypical images. Certainly the plays of Pedrero and Tomeo that have achieved some level of acceptance in France are far removed from Lorca or *espagnolade*. The 1990s promise to bring an end to the exclusion of Spanish plays from the Parisian stage and therefore invite continuing research on the subjects I have introduced in this book.

NOTES

3. SPANISH THEATRE ON THE CONTEMPORARY FRENCH STAGE

1. ATAC (Association Technique pour l'Action Culturelle) in September 1972 published a special issue of its monthly journal titled *25 Ans de décentralisation: Les Auteurs.* The information provided is consistent with that found in Willey. A related special issue of ATAC for September 1973 reviewed the quarter century of decentralization by productions.

2. The dissemination of Spain's theatre in France has been actively fostered by directors who, while not born in Spain themselves, are of Spanish descent. When Víctor García died, Eduardo Manet's tribute to him spoke directly of this shared aspect of their cultural heritage: an obsession with the Spanish "classics," especially Valle-Inclán. Once they reached Europe, the reality of Spain did not fit the image created for them by their nostalgic parents. Nevertheless, when the dream Spain had been demythologized, Manet affirmed that García and he were both left with another, indestructible reality: "the idealized vision of childhood" ("Victor Garcia: tentative de portrait" 149).

3. The cultural and linguistic relationship between Spain and Spanish America is more complex than I have indicated here. Spanish-language theatre texts do not always travel easily across the Atlantic, and there are cases in which Argentine plays have been "translated" for Madrid audiences. While some Latin Americans view Spanish culture negatively, rejecting the colonized status of their countries, Latin Americans living in Europe may have more ambiva-

lent attitudes. Manet, for example, both defends Ruiz de Alarcón's true identity as a Mexican—not a Spaniard—and, during his own second exile from Cuba, declares himself to be Spanish—not Cuban; in interviews he has repeatedly emphasized that his parents were born in Spain. In any event, Valle-Inclán's theatre has transcended any Spain vs. Spanish America conflicts and has long been an important influence on the Latin American stage.

4. The biographical note accompanying the text of Gómez-Arcos's *Diálogos de la herejía*, published in 1964, indicated that he was thirty-one years old at the time (*Primer Acto* 54: 27). The biographical note in the 1991 Spanish edition of *Interview de Mrs. Muerta Smith por sus fantasmas*, however, gives the birth year as 1939 (13).

5. With respect to the rivalry between Ibéral and Hispanité-Explorations, I am not in a position to judge Sadowska-Guillon's personal knowledge of Spanish theatre. I would observe, however, that, with the notable exception of the writers who are primarily novelists, the texts she has chosen generally coincide with those previously selected by Moisés Pérez-Coterillo for publication by *El Público* and, to a lesser extent, those appearing in Guillermo Heras's collection Nuevo Teatro Español, published by the National Center for New Tendencies of the Stage. I am also not in a position to determine why the theatre of Sergi Belbel has been promoted to the apparent exclusion of other young playwrights. Winner of the Marqués de Bradomín Prize for new dramatists in 1985, Belbel is a colleague and former student of Sanchis Sinisterra. There is possibly a certain amount of networking that takes place among Catalan theatre people, a group that includes Pasqual, and Belbel is also the translator of French plays being promoted in Spain.

4. FRENCH THEATRE ON THE CONTEMPORARY SPANISH STAGE

1. There is no identification by nationality in the index of either Francisco Alvaro's theatre annual or the one prepared

by *El Público.* Nor do the commentaries in *El espectador y la crítica* necessarily identify the nationality of the author. Classifications are my own, based on my recognition of French writers, and hence subject to error. It has been my intention to exclude French-language writers of other nationalities unless they are primarily identified with the French stage. I have included French stage adaptations of foreign works but not foreign plays based on French literature (e.g., in 1959 Jean Pierre Aumont's adaptation of an Irving Shaw novel but not Anita Loos's adaptation of Colette's *Gigi*).

2. Clearly the numbers of productions highlighted by Alvaro also shifted considerably between the two periods discussed here. Aside from a general malaise in the Madrid theatre, particularly in the late 1970s, the lower number of productions reflects other changes in the Spanish stage. By the 1970s, successful plays tended to have much longer runs in commercial theatres than they did in the 1950s, when a run of 200–300 performances was exceptional. Moreover the traditional pattern of two performances a night (at around 7 P.M. and 10:30 P.M.), every night, has virtually disappeared, thus extending successful productions in time and providing less space for new productions. The total explanation for the changes is complex and lies beyond the scope of the present study.

3. For 1960 Alvaro incorrectly places the Catalan playwright Jaime Salom under "foreign" rather than "Spanish." I have corrected that error in my data here.

4. I have compiled a computerized data base drawing from *El espectador y la crítica,* 1965–1985, and from *El Público's* first two theatre annuals for the years 1985–1986. The information in the former is limited to Madrid, Barcelona, and some tours. The latter attempts to include all provincial productions as well. The total entries for Molière is 20. The other authors are represented by between 14 (Ionesco) and 11 (Anouilh) productions each.

5. I am referring once again to my computerized data base, cited above.

6. Larra prizes were given by *Primer Acto* for 1962 and 1964. They established the format later adopted by Francisco Alvaro for his Espectador y la Crítica awards. By vote of newspaper and magazine theatre critics based in Madrid, winners were determined in a variety of categories: best Spanish play, best foreign play, best director, best actors, etc. Following Alvaro's death in 1987, *Primer Acto* announced that the Larra awards would be reinstituted (*Primer Acto* 220: 4).

7. In addition to a monthly (from 1990 to 1992, bimonthly) magazine, *El Público* published a monograph series (Cuadernos el Público); periodic directories of productions, theatre groups, etc. (Carteleras and Guías); the theatre annual (Anuario), and, most recently, a series of plays. The Anuario Teatral includes excerpts of criticism on important productions and focuses on the plays performed. The Cartelera variously refers to the time of publication or to a limited season (e.g., fall or spring), while the Guía, appearing in summer, is more extensive in its listings. The Guía and the Anuario are not synonymous, not only because they appear at different times. The Guía tends to list both plays that have recently been performed and all the productions that a particular company, amateur or professional, has available for performance. For example, individual entries specify contract terms and space requirements. At the time of this writing, the last Anuario in print was that for 1988.

8. Similarly when Copi died, also from AIDS, *Primer Acto* dedicated several articles to him and his work, with emphasis on the Barcelona production of *Una visita inoportuna* (No. 231, November–December 1989).

6. VINDICATING RUIZ DE ALARCÓN

1. Manet clarifies that he was born 19 June 1930 in Santiago de Cuba, although most sources state March 1927 in Havana. He explains that his father had not registered his birth and later falsified the date to facilitate the precocious

boy's early receipt of a high school diploma (Personal letter 1991).

2. Although Marius literally means "poor" in the economic sense, he may also be alluding to Jerzy Grotowski's concept of "poor theatre." Grotowski's internationally acclaimed version of Calderón's *El príncipe constante* reached the Théâtre des Nations in Paris in 1966 and had a significant impact on theatre practitioners there. At that time Manet was in Cuba, but he had already met Grotowski in Warsaw in 1963 and found the concept of "poor theatre" especially relevant for revolutionary Cuba (Mambrino 364). At a later point in the play, Grotowski's theories, like various other contemporary theatre movements, are mentioned directly in the dialogue and stage directions.

3. In his 1972 book on Alarcón, Walter Poesse establishes that the author's works were neither so classical nor so moralistic as they are generally labeled. Nevertheless, to the extent that these tendencies are present in *Las paredes oyen*, Manet has subverted them.

4. Manet's *Les Nonnes* calls for male actors as the nuns—not as men hiding out in a convent, like a recent Hollywood movie, but as true cross-gender acting. When the play was revived in New York in December 1989–January 1990, director William Hunt lost his initial choice for a lead actor because the man's new wife objected to her husband appearing in a female costume.

5. I realize that, once again, I am somewhat blurring here the distinction between "Spanish" and "Spanish American." (I use "Hispanic" to include both.) Certainly there are enough points of cultural conflict between Spain and her former colonies that exiles from Latin America do not necessarily feel at home in Spain. Nevertheless, I have talked to Latin Americans living in Europe, Manet included, who are very conscious of their Spanish roots and identify with them. While Manet carefully points out in his prologue that Ruiz de Alarcón was born in Mexico, his very

free version of *Las paredes oyen* highlights cultural aspects, like the bullfight, that are clearly of Spanish origin, although they may have subsequently been exported to the New World. On other occasions in his theatre, Manet has dealt directly with Spain, for example in plays relating to Velázquez's famous painting "Las Meninas" and in an as-yet-unstaged text on Santa Teresa and San Juan de la Cruz.

7. SCRIBE TWICE REMOVED

1. For a comparison of these two plays, see Hazel Cazorla's "La presencia de Larra en el teatro de Antonio Buero Vallejo y Francisco Nieva."

2. Page numbers are to my 1990 edition of the play.

9. CONCLUSION

1. While this book was in preparation, the Spanish Ministry of Culture discontinued its support of *El Públicio*. The last issue published was No. 93, November-December 1992.

WORKS CITED

Abel, Lionel. *Metatheatre: A New View of Dramatic Form.* New York: Hill and Wang, 1963.

Abellán, Joan. "Conversación con Lluís Pasqual: El Lliure/Genet/El Balcó." *Pipirijaina* 16 (September–October 1980): 59–68.

———. "Notas de lectura y montaje." *Primer Acto* 187 (November 1980–January 1981): 55–56.

———. "Imágenes de un espectador fiel." *El Teatre Lliure cumple diez años. Cuadernos El Público* 10 (January 1986): 49–69.

Adamov, Arthur. "Une pièce progressiste quand même." *Cahiers Renaud-Barrault* 43 (March 1963): 56–58.

Alberti, Rafael. *Le Repoussoir.* Trans. Robert Marrast. 2nd ed. Paris: L'Arche Editeur, 1984.

Alonso, José Luis. "En la muerte de Anouilh." *Primer Acto* 221 (1987): 4–9.

Alonso de Santos, José Luis. "Horrores cotidianos." *Primer Acto* 230 (September-October 1989): 64–65.

Alvaro, Francisco, ed. *El espectador y la crítica (El teatro en España, 1973–1985)* [theatre annual]. Vols. 1–28. Valladolid: Edición del autor, 1959–1970, 1978–1986; Madrid: Prensa Española, 1971–1977.

L'Arche Editeur. Catalogue. Paris, 1987.

Archet, Marlène. "Le Théâtre à Toulouse dans les milieux de l'émigration espagnole (1945–début des années 60)." Master's thesis, Université de Toulouse–Le Mirail, 1985.

———, and Frédéric Serralta. Personal interview. 3 May 1987.

Arrabal, Fernando. Personal interview. 14 May 1987.

———. Personal interview. 16 May 1992.

Aslan, Odette. *"Le Cimetière des voitures*: Un spectacle de Victor Garcia à partir de quatre pièces d'Arrabal." *Les Voies de la Création Théâtrale* 1 (1970): 309–340.

———. "Actors Versus Directors: An Overview of French Theater." *1968–1978: Theater in France—Ten Years of Research.* Ed. Josette Féral. *Sub-Stance* 18/19 (1977).

Astre, Georges-Albert. "Le Monde d'Emmanuel Roblès." *Folio* 15 (November 1983): 13–17.

———. *Emmanuel Roblès ou le risque de vivre*. Paris: Bernard Grasset, 1987.

ATAC Informations. Mensuel d'information de l'Association Technique pour l'action culturelle. *25 Ans de décentralisation: Les Auteurs*. Numéro spécial. September 1972.

———. *25 Ans de décentralisation: Les Spectacles*. Spécial numéro 2. September 1973.

L'Avant-Scène Théâtre. Valle-Inclan issue. 292 (July 1963).

———. Lorca issue. 452–453 (July 1970).

———. *L'Homme couché* (Semprun-Maura) issue. 474 (15 June 1971).

———. Picasso issue. 500 (August 1972).

———. *La Célestine* issue. 566 (June 1975).

———. *Lady Strass* (Manet) issue. 613 (1 July 1977).

———. *Le Bleu de l'eau-de-vie* (Semprun-Maura) issue. 703 (1 February 1982).

———. Contemporary Spanish theatre issue. 846 (15 March 1989).

———. Festival théâtral Ibéral issue. 878 (15 November 1990).

Benach, Joan Anton. "Palabras y música: Beckett pone la partitura de la danza." *El Público* 50 (November 1987): 23–25.

Bernat, Vicente. "*Noche de guerra* . . . en la Cité internationale." *Triunfo* 643. Reprinted in *Noche de guerra en el museo del Prado*, by Rafael Alberti. 3rd ed. Madrid: Editorial Cuadernos para el Diálogo, 1976.

Bertrand de Muñoz, Maryse. *La guerre civile espagnole et la littérature française*. Montreal: Didier, 1972.

Bourdet, Gildas. Interview with Julio A. Máñez. *El Público* 56 (May 1988): 13–14.

Bradby, David. *Modern French Drama, 1940–1980*. Cambridge: Cambridge University Press, 1984.

———. "Camus, Albert." In *The Cambridge Guide to World Theatre*. Ed. Martin Banham. Cambridge: Cambridge University Press, 1988.

Buero-Vallejo, Antonio. Personal interview. 23 April 1987.

Caillaud, Sylvie. Personal interview. 9 May 1987.

Camp, André. "Spectacles choisis." *L'Avant-Scène Théâtre* 663 (February 1980): 42.

———. "Les folies de Chaillot . . . et d'ailleurs." *L'Avant-Scène Théâtre* 693 (July 1981): 53–57.

———. "Théâtres d'Europe." *L'Avant-Scène Théâtre* 749 (1 May 1984): 48–50.

———. "A travers la France." *L'Avant-Scène Théâtre* 762 (15 January 1985): 40–41.

————. "Illusions comiques et dramatiques." *L'Avant-Scène Théâtre* 763 (1 February 1985): 49–51.

————. "Avignon 86." *L'Avant-Scène Théâtre* 795 (October 1986): 66.

————. Personal interview. 12 May 1987.

————. "La cinquième saison du Théâtre de l'Europe." *L'Avant-Scène Théâtre* 834 (July 1988): 45–47.

————. Personal interview. 29 May 1989.

Camp, Jean. "Ramon Maria del Valle-Inclan: Prince d'un art baroque et somptueux." *L'Avant-Scène Théâtre* 292 (15 July 1963): 8–9.

Caprices-Compagnie. Unpublished promotional booklet for *Wien 38*. 1986.

Carpenter, Charles A. *Modern Drama Scholarship and Criticism, 1966–1980: An International Bibliography*. Toronto, Buffalo, and London: University of Toronto Press, 1986.

Casarès, Maria. *Residente privilegiada*. Trans. Fabián García-Prieto Buendía and Enrique Sordo. Barcelona: Argos Vergara, 1981.

————. Telephone interview. 14 October 1987.

Cazorla, Hazel. "Avant-garde Spanish Playwrights in the 1970s." In *The Contemporary Spanish Theater: A Collection of Critical Essays*. Ed. Martha T. Halsey and Phyllis Zatlin. Lanham, MD, New York, and London: University Press of America, 1988.

————. "La presencia de Larra en el teatro de Antonio Buero Vallejo y Francisco Nieva." In *Resonancias románticas: Evocaciones del romanticismo hispánico*. Ed. John R. Rosenberg. Madrid: Ediciones José Porrúa Turanzas, 1988. Pp. 201–216.

Cioranescu, Alexandre. *Le Masque et le visage: Du baroque espagnol au classicisme français*. Geneva: Librairie Droz, 1983.

Copfermann, Emile. *Le Théâtre populaire pourquoi?* Paris: François Maspero, 1969.

de la Hoz, Enrique, ed. *Panorámica del teatro en España*. Madrid: Editora Nacional, 1973.

Demarigny, Claude. Personal interview. 3 June 1988.

Depierris, Jean-Louis. *Entretiens avec Emmanuel Roblès*. Paris: Aux Editions du Seuil, 1967.

Diosdado, Ana. *Los comuneros*. Madrid: Ediciones MK, 1974.

DiPuccio, Denise M. "*Juana del amor hermoso*: A Struggle for Identity." *Estreno* 13.1 (1987): 8–11.

Domenech, Ricardo. Review of *Divinas palabras*. *Primer Acto*, August 1964. Reprinted in *Valle-Inclán y su tiempo hoy*. Exposición: "Montajes de Valle-Inclán." Madrid: Ministerio de Cultura, 1986. Pp. 105–106.

————. "Aproximación al teatro del exilio. I: Un teatro en el exilio." *El exilio español de 1939.* 6 vols. Madrid: Taurus, 1976–1978. 4: 185–194.

Domergue, Lucienne, and Marie Laffranque. "L'Exil des libertaires espagnols: ruptures et fidelités." In *L'Espagne face aux problèmes de la modernité (Actes du Colloque International de Toulouse, 25–28 avril 1978).* Toulouse: France-Ibérie Recherche. Pp. 81–99.

Dort, Bernard. *Théâtre en jeu, 1970–1978.* Paris: Editions du Seuil, 1979.

————. Personal interview. 23 October 1986.

Dumas, Danielle. "Scènes que j'aime." *L'Avant-Scène Théâtre* 824 (15 February 1988): 53.

Durán i Domenge, Rafael. "La llegada de Koltès a España." *El Público* 62 (November 1988): 28–29.

Dux, Pierre. *La Comédie Française: Trois Siècles de Gloire.* Paris: Denoël, 1980.

Equipo Pipirijaina. *Tábano: Un zumbido que no cesa.* Madrid: Editorial Ayuso, 1975.

Espert, Nuria. Interview with Evelyne Ertel. *Travail Théâtral* 23 (April-June 1976): 35–42.

————. Interview with José Monleón. *Primer Acto* 196 (November–December 1982): 44–45.

Esslin, Martin. "Actors Acting Actors." *Modern Drama* 30.1 (1987): 71–79.

Fernández Insuela, Antonio. "Teatro realista español y teatro extranjero." *Archivum* 27–28 (1977–78): 141–179.

Fernández-Santos, Angel. "El escenario como infierno." *El País.* Edición International Semanal (21 April 1986): 21.

Foulkes, A. P. *Literature and Propaganda.* London and New York: Methuen, 1983.

Fredrick, Edna C. *The Plot and Its Construction in Eighteenth Century Criticism of French Comedy: A Study of Theory with Relation to the Practice of Beaumarchais.* 1934; reprint, New York: Burt Franklin, 1973.

Gallego, Andrés. Personal interview. 5 May 1987.

García Ruiz, Víctor [nephew of Víctor Ruiz Iriarte]. Personal interview. 20 May 1987.

Gatti, Armand. "La Passion selon les émigrés." *L'Avant-Scène Théâtre* 586 (1 May 1976): 4.

Gaudin, Lois Frances (Strong). *Bibliography of Franco-Spanish Literary Relations (Until the XIXth Century).* 1930; reprint, New York: Burt Franklin, 1973.

Genet, Jean. "Genet, 70: Sobre España, El Opus Dei, el socialismo, los judíos, los árabes, la libertad, la música de Mozart y unas cuantas cosas más." Interview with José Monleón. *Primer Acto* 187 (November 1980-January 1981): 49–54.

Gérome, Raymond. Preface to *Pré-Papa,* by Agustin Gomez-Arcos. *L'Avant-Scène Théâtre* 434 (1969): 37.

Godard, Colette. " 'Divines paroles' à Chaillot: La luxure, l'avarice et la mort." *Le Monde* (5 February 1976): 14.

Gómez-Arcos, Agustín. Personal interview. 19 October 1987.

———. *Interview de Mrs. Muerta Smith por sus fantasmas. El Público* Teatro 15. Madrid: Centro de Documentación Teatral, 1991.

Gorna-Urbanska, Katarzyna. "Viaje al teatro de Francisco Nieva." *Cuadernos El Público* 21 (February 1987): 21–61.

Guérin, Jeanyves. "Is There Something Rotten in the State of French Theater?" In *Myths and Realities of Contemporary French Theater: Comparative Views.* Ed. Patricia M. Hopkins and Wendell M. Aycock. Lubbock: Texas Tech Press, 1985.

Halsey, Martha T. "Juana la Loca in Three Dramas of Tamayo y Baus, Galdós, and Martín Recuerda." *Modern Language Studies* 9.1 (1978–79): 47–59.

———. *"El engañao* o el nuevo drama histórico de la posguerra." In *El engañao. Caballos desbocaos,* by José Martín Recuerda. Ed. Halsey and Angel Cobo. Madrid: Cátedra, 1981. Pp. 27–50.

———. "Introduction to the Historical Drama of Post-Civil War Spain." *Estreno* 14.1 (1988): 11–12.

Hamner, Robert D. *Derek Walcott.* Twayne's World Authors Series, 600. Boston: G. K. Hall, 1981.

Haro Tecglen, Eduardo. "Conocemos a Koltès." *El País.* Edición Internacional. Panorama Semanal (30 April 1990): 20.

———. "Rebelión contra Sartre." *El País.* Edición Internacional. Panorama Semanal (2 July 1990): 21.

———. "Lecturas de 'Calígula.' " *El País.* Edición Internacional. Panorama Semanal (3 September 1990): 20.

Heming, Barbara Jean. "The Spanish Theatre in Exile, 1939–1969." Dissertation, State University of New York at Stony Brook, 1975 (*DAI* 36: 2878A).

Hernández, José A. "El teatro de la crueldad en *Tórtolas, crepúsculo y . . . telón* de Francisco Nieva." *Estreno* 12.2 (1986): 72–74.

Hispanité-Explorations. Newsletter. 8 June 1992.

Holt, Marion P. *The Contemporary Spanish Theater (1949–1972).* Twayne's World Author Series, 336. Boston: G. K. Hall, 1975.

Hornby, Richard. *Drama, Metadrama, and Perception*. Lewisburg, PA: Bucknell University Press; London and Toronto: Associated University Presses, 1986.

Hunt, William. Personal interview. 11 March 1990.

Ibéral. Bulletins and programs. September 1988–November 1990.

Ilárraz, Felix. "Sartre y Sastre: ¿Dramaturgos existencialistas?" *Papers on French-Spanish, Luso-Brazilian, and Spanish-American Literary Relations*. Discussed at Conference 15, Modern Language Association Convention. Chicago, 27–30 December 1967. Ed. Martha O'Nan. Athens: Department of Modern Languages, Ohio University, n.d.

Knowles, Dorothy. "Ritual Theatre: Fernando Arrabal and the Latin-Americans." *Modern Language Review* 70.3 (1975): 526–538.

Koniecpolski, Jan. " 'Las criadas,' de Facio en la ciudad más fea de Polonia." *El Público* 24 (September 1985): 56–57.

La Bossière, Camille R. "Of Happiness in Emmanuel Roblès." *Folio* 15 (November 1983): 34–40.

Lafarga Maduell, Francisco. *El teatro francés en España desde 1700 hasta el romanticismo: Las traducciones—Ensayo bibliográfico*. Typescript. Recipient of scholarship for Estudios en España, Departamento de Literatura y Filología. Madrid: Fundación Juan March, 1980.

Laffranque, Marie. "La Savetière et l'enfant." *Thèâtre à Toulouse et ailleurs . . .* Dossier Lorca. 5 (1986): 21.

Lamartina-Lens, Iride. "Literary, Historical and Social Myths in Contemporary Spanish Theater: A Feminist Interpretation." Dissertation, Rutgers University, 1986.

Lavelli, Jorge. Interview with Vicente Molina Foix. *Primer Acto* 184 (April-May 1980): 68.

———. Telephone interview. 11 May 1987.

Lebel, Jean-Jacques. "Une ébauche géniale du théâtre total." *L'Avant-Scène Théâtre* 500 (August 1972): 10–11.

Lewis, Ward B. "Exile Drama: The Example of Argentina." In *Latin America and the Literature of Exile*. Ed. Hans-Bernhard Moeller. Heidelberg: Carl Winter Universitätsverlag, 1983.

Librairie Théâtrale. Catalogue des pièces des grands auteurs modernes. Paris: January 1987.

Lindenberger, Herbert. *Historical Drama: The Relation of Literature and Reality*. Chicago and London: University of Chicago Press, 1975.

Linsalata, Carmine Rocco, and Frank Sedwick, eds. *La forja de los sueños,* by Manuel Martínez Azaña. Boston: Houghton Mifflin, 1960.

Llorens, Vicente. "La emigración republicana de 1939." In *El exilio español de 1939.* 6 vols. Madrid: Taurus, 1976–1978. 1: 100–105.

Londré, Felicia Hardison. "Bringing Arrabal Home: The Theatre of Nuria Espert." American Theatre Association Convention. Toronto, 4–7 August 1985.

———. "Lorca Production in France: Abstraction or 'Espagnolade'?" Session on Cultural Interchange and the Contemporary Spanish and French Stages, Modern Language Association Convention. New Orleans, 29 December 1988.

Lorcey, Jacques. *La Comédie Française.* Paris: Fernand Nathan, 1980.

Lottman, Herbert R. *Albert Camus.* Garden City, NY: Doubleday, 1979.

Mambrino, Jean. "Entretien avec . . . Eduardo Manet." *Revue Etudes* (March 1985): 359–374.

Manet, Eduardo. *L'Autre Don Juan.* Le Manteau d'Arlequin. Paris: Gallimard, 1973.

———. "Victor Garcia: tentative de portrait." *L'Annuel du Théâtre.* Centre National des Lettres, Meudon (Saison 1982–83): 148–152.

———. *Un Balcon sur les Andes, Mendoza, en Argentine . . . , Ma'Déa.* Paris: Gallimard, 1985.

———. Personal interview. 19 October 1987.

———. Letter to the author. 3 March 1989.

———. Interview. Playbill for *Lady Strass.* Théâtre Royal du Parc, Brussels, 25 October–24 November 1990.

———. Letter to the author. 25 January 1991.

Martín Elizondo, José. *Juana creó la noche.* Unpublished play, 1960.

———. Interview with Angel Berenguer. *Pipirijaina-Textos* 15 (September–October 1980): 53–56.

———. Personal interview. 11 May 1987.

———. Personal interview. 12 October 1987.

———. Personal interview. 4 June 1988.

Martín Recuerda, José. *El engañao.* Published with *Caballos desbocaos.* Ed. Martha T. Halsey and Angel Cobo. Madrid: Cátedra, 1981.

Martinenche, Ernest. *La Comedia espagnole en France de Hardy à Racine.* 1900; reprint, Geneva: Slatkine Reprints, 1970.

———. *L'Espagne et le romantisme français.* Paris: Librairie Hachette, 1922.

Martínez Azaña, Manuel. Personal interview. 9 November 1987.

Martínez Mediero, Manuel. *Juana del amor hermoso.* Published with *Las bragas perdidas en el tendedero.* Madrid: Editorial Fundamentos, 1982.

Marula, Xavier. Review of *La Chemise,* by Lauro Olmo. *Le Monde* (12 November 1970): vii.

Méreuze, Didier. "Alfredo Arias dirige el C.D.N. de Aubervilliers." *El Público* 30 (March 1986): 50–51.

———. "El viaje de Vázquez Montalbán a los Alpes." *El Público* 69 (June 1989): 57.

Mignon, Paul-Louis. "Le théâtre de A jusqu'à Z. José Maria Flotats." *L'Avant-Scène Théâtre* 672 (15 June 1980): 5–6.

———. *Le théâtre au XXe siècle.* 2nd ed. Collection Folio/Essais. Paris: Gallimard, 1986.

Miller, Judith Graves. *Theater and Revolution in France Since 1968.* Lexington, KY: French Forum, Publishers, 1977.

Miller, Townsend. *The Castles and the Crown: Spain, 1451–1555.* New York: Coward-McCann, 1963.

Miralles, Alberto. *Nuevo teatro español: Una alternativa cultural social.* Madrid: Editorial Villalar, 1977.

Monleón, José, ed. *Larra: escritos sobre teatro.* Madrid: Editorial Cuadernos para el Diálogo (EDICUSA), 1976.

———. "Homenaje a un poeta del escenario." *Primer Acto* 196 (November–December 1982): 43.

———. "Cuando Beckett era un 'camelo.'" *Primer Acto* 206 (November–December 1984): 26–32.

Monod, Richard. "Dramaturgie pour un théâtre non institué." *Travail Théâtral* 18–19 (January–June 1975): 203–206.

Monory, Monique. "Les trois premières mises en scène de Victor Garcia en France." *Les Voies de la Création Théâtrale* 12 (1984): 105–131.

Narros, Miguel. Interview with Alfonso Armada. *Primer Acto* 206 (November–December 1984): 33–35.

Newberry, Wilma. "The New Spanish 'Tartuffe.'" *Hispania* 55.4 (1972): 922–928.

Nieva, Francisco. Introduction to *Sombra y quimera de Larra (Representación alucinada de "No más mostrador").* Madrid: Editorial Fundamentos, 1976.

———. "Esencia teatral del relato de Genet." *Pipirijaina* 7 (June 1978): 38–41.

———. "El espectáculo como técnica de persuasión en Brecht." *Primer Acto* 184 (April–May 1980): 29–37.

———. "Final de partida: La cosificación oficial de Genet." *El Público* 32 (May 1986): 3.

———. *Te quiero, zorra. Estreno* 15.2 (1989): 5–11.

————. *El combate de Opalos y Tasia. Sombra y quimera de Larra. La Magosta*. Ed. Phyllis Zatlin-Boring. Madrid: Alhambra-Longman, 1990.

Obregón, Osvaldo. "Apuntes sobre el teatro latinoamericano en Francia." *Cahiers du Monde Hispanique et Luso-Brésilien* 40 (1983): 17–45.

O'Connor, Garry. *French Theatre Today*. London: Pitman House, 1975.

Olmo, Lauro. Personal interview. 27 May 1987.

O'Nan, Martha. "Emmanuel Roblès: Spanish Themes in a French Writer." *Papers on Romance Literary Relations*. Ed. Olga Ragusa. New York: Department of Italian, Columbia University, 1978. Pp. 18–26.

————. "Emmanuel Roblès: His 'Spanish' Theater." Session on Cultural Interchange and the Contemporary Spanish and French Stages, Modern Language Association Convention. New Orleans, 29 December 1988.

Orenstein, Gloria. *The Theatre of the Marvelous: Surrealism and the Contemporary Stage*. New York: New York University Press, 1975.

Page, Tim. Review of *Juana, La Loca*, by Gian Carlo Menotti. *New York Times* (3 June 1984): 61.

El País. Edición Internacional. Panorama Semanal (2 January 1989): 23.

————. Edición Internacional. Panorama Semanal (19 March 1990): 18.

————. "Cuatro novelistas españoles se lanzan a la aventura escénica." Edición Internacional. Panorama Semanal (28 May 1990): 18.

Paris Théâtre 195 (April? 1963).

Pasqual, Lluís. Interview with Joan Abellán. *Pipirijaina* 16 (September–October 1980): 59–68.

Pérez Coterillo, Moisés. "Nuria Espert: 'Víctor García mereció la palabra genio.' " *El Público* 14 (November 1984): 9–11.

————. "Lorca en la Colina de Lavelli." *El Público* 52 (January 1988): 3–6.

————. "Alfredo Arias enciende todas las luces de Valle." *El Público* 54 (March 1988): 4–6.

————. "Aviñón-Barcelona. El último viaje de 'La Celestina.' " *El Público* 70–71 (July-August 1989): 6–10.

Pérez de Olaguer, Gonzalo. "Crónica de una historia polémica." *Els Joglars: veinticinco años y un día. Cuadernos El Público* 29 (December 1987): 25–35.

Pérez Galdós, Benito. *Santa Juana de Castilla. Cuentos y Teatro*, by Pérez Galdós. Madrid: Aguilar, 1971.

Pfandl, Ludwig. *Juana la Loca: Su vida, su tiempo, su culpa*. 1937. 10th ed., Madrid: Espasa-Calpe, 1977.

Pipirijaina: Revista de Teatro. Madrid. Vols. 1–25 (October 1976–April 1983).

Podol, Peter. "Spain: A Recurring Theme in the Theater of Fernando Arrabal." In *The Contemporary Spanish Theater: A Collection of Critical Essays*. Ed. Martha T. Halsey and Phyllis Zatlin. Lanham, MD, New York, and London: University Press of America, 1988.

———. "The Influence of France on the Dramaturgy of Fernando Arrabal." Session on Cultural Interchange and the Contemporary Spanish and French Stages, Modern Language Association Convention. New Orleans, 29 December 1988.

Poesse, Walter. *Juan Ruiz de Alarcón*. Twayne's World Authors Series, 231. New York: Twayne, 1972.

Primer Acto: Cuadernos de investigación teatral. Madrid. Segunda época. Vols. 182–237 (December 1979–January/February 1991).

El Público. Periódico mensual del Centro de Documentación Teatral. Madrid. Vols. 0–84 (Summer 1983–May/June 1991).

———. Guía Teatral de España. 1984–1989/90.

———. Anuario Teatral. 1985–1988.

———. *El teatre lliure cumple diez años*. Cuaderno 10. January 1986.

———. *El Théâtre du Soleil. Amanecer en otoño*. Cuaderno 16. September 1986.

———. *Arias, Lavelli, Quintana, Ruiz. Directores iberoamericanos en Europa*. Cuaderno 31. March 1988.

———. *Jean Genet: Camino de santidad*. Cuaderno 41. October 1989.

Revuelta, Vidal Benito. *San Juan de Dios*. Temas Españoles 395. Madrid: Publicaciones Españolas, 1959.

Riaza, Luis. Personal interview. 8 November 1987.

———. Personal interview. 26 May 1988.

Roblès, Emmanuel. *Théâtre: Montserrat. La Vérité est morte. Mer libre. Un Château en novembre*. Paris: Grasset, 1985.

———. *Théâtre: Plaidoyer pour un rebelle. L'Horloge. Les Yaquils. La Fenêtre. Ile déserte*. Paris: Grasset, 1987.

———. Personal interview. 12 and 21 October 1987.

Rodríguez-Gago, María Antonia. "Beckett y la capitulación humana." *El Público* 7 (April 1984): 26–27.

Rosales, Arturo F. "Spanish-Language Theatre and Early Mexi-

can Immigration." In *Hispanic Theatre in the United States*. Ed.
Nicolás Kanellos. Houston: Arte Público Press, 1984.

Ruiz de Alarcón, Juan. *Las paredes oyen*. In *Teatro*. Ed. Alfonso
Reyes. Clásicos Castellanos. Madrid: Espasa-Calpe, 1961.

Sadowska-Guillon, Irène. " 'Amado monstruo', de Javier Tomeo:
una epopeya de lo ordinario." *El Público* 65 (February 1989):
52–53.

———. "Bayona: Diez años de intercambio." *El Público* 82 (January–February 1991): 144–145.

———. "I Festival Iberal en París." *El Público* 82 (January-February 1991): 145.

———. Personal letter. 8 June 1992.

Sainz de Robles, Federico Carlos, ed. *Teatro español 1949/50–1964/65*. Madrid: Aguilar, 1951–1966.

San Bartolomé, Pierre-Jean de. Interview. *L'Avant-Scène Théâtre*
619 (15 November 1977): 37.

Sanchis Sinisterra, José. " 'Happy Days', una obra crucial." *Primer
Acto* 206 (November-December 1984): 36–41.

Sanz, Marc-Ange. Personal interview. 20 October 1987.

Saurel, Renée. "Valle-Inclán, hidalgo y libertario." *Primer Acto*,
1964. Reprinted in *Valle-Inclán y su tiempo hoy*. Exposición:
"Montajes de Valle-Inclán." Madrid: Ministerio de Cultura,
1986. Pp. 92–96.

Schmeling, Manfred. *Métathéâtre et intertexte: Aspects du théâtre
dans le théâtre*. Paris: Lettres Modernes, 1924.

Sellin, Eric. "The Algerian Roots of Emmanuel Roblès and Jean
Pélégri." Paper read at Modern Language Association Convention. New Orleans, 27 December 1988.

Semprun-Maura, Carlos. *Sur une plage de l'ouest*. *L'Avant-Scène
Théâtre* 191 (1959): 38–41.

———. *La Salle d'attente*. *L'Avant-Scène Théâtre* 388 (1967): 32–35.

———. *L'Homme couché*. *L'Avant-Scène Théâtre* 474 (1971): 1–23.

———. *Derrière la nuit, la nuit*. Unpublished typescript. 25 May
1972. France-Culture. R-19456.

———. *Personne, ici*. Unpublished typescript. 1 February 1974.
France-Culture. R-20836.

———. *Magnifique la luxure*. Unpublished typescript. 8 July 1981.
France-Culture. R-23953.

———. *Le Bleu de l'eau-de-vie*. *L'Avant-Scène Théâtre* 703 (1982):
1–21.

———. *Nuits ouvertes comme des lits*. Unpublished typescript. 31
March 1983. France-Culture. R-24592.

———. *C'étaient des tilleuls, je me souviens*. Unpublished typescript. 28 November 1985. France-Culture. R-25523.

———. *Ma chanson la plus triste est espagnole*. Unpublished typescript. 20 May 1987. France-Culture. R-26138.

———. Personal interview. 20 October 1987.

———. Personal letter. 7 January 1988.

———. Personal interview. 31 May 1988.

———. Personal letter. 25 March 1990.

Signes, Emil. "The Theatre of Francisco Nieva." Dissertation, Rutgers University, 1982.

Sociedad General de Autores de España. Unpublished data on productions of Spanish plays in France made available by Francisco Galindo Villoria, Coordinador de Derechos Dramáticos. May 1988.

Soulier, Daniel. "Homenaje a la cultura mediterránea." Interview with Fernando Bejarano. *Diario 16* (30 October 1987): Guía: v.

———. "Reflexiones sobre el primer mes de ensayo." Playbill for *Los enredos de Scapin* by Molière. Teatro Español, 30 October 1987. N.p.

Stembert, Rodolphe. "La recepción del teatro de Valle-Inclán en Francia y en Bélgica." *Ramón del Valle-Inclán (1866–1936)*. Akten des Bamberger Colloquiums vom 6.-8. November 1986. Ed. Harald Wentzlaff-Eggebert. Tübingen: Max Niemeyer Verlag, 1988. Pp. 271–280.

Sullivan, Henry W. *Calderón in the German Lands and the Low Countries: His Reception and Influence, 1654–1980*. Cambridge: Cambridge University Press, 1983.

Tamayo y Baus, Manuel. *La locura de amor*. Published with *Un drama nuevo*. 3rd ed. Madrid: Espasa-Calpe, 1970.

Temkine, Raymonde. *Mettre en scène au présent*. 2 vols. Lausanne: Editions l'Age d'Homme, 1977, 1979.

Théâtre à Toulouse et ailleurs . . . Dossier Lorca. 5 (October/November/December 1986).

Théâtre Acteurs. "Anniversaire—Il y a vingt ans: La Bataille des Paravents." 36 (May 1986): inside cover.

Théâtre en Europe 2 (1984).

Thompson, John A. *Alexandre Dumas Père and Spanish Romantic Drama*. Baton Rouge: Louisiana State University Press, 1938.

Torre Giménez, Estrella de la. "Michel de Ghelderode: ¿Un flamenco de España o un español de Flandes?" *Gades* 2 (1979): 227–238.

Torres Monreal, Francisco. "El teatro español en Francia (1935-

1973): Análisis de la penetración y de sus mediaciones." 2 vols. Dissertation, Universidad de Murcia, 1974.

———. *El teatro español en Francia (1935–1973): Análisis de la penetración y de sus mediaciones.* Madrid: Fundación Juan March, 1976.

———. " 'La Célestine', de J. Gillibert (Adaptación teatral francesa de la obra de Rojas)." *Homenaje al prof. Muñoz Cortés.* Murcia: Universidad de Murcia, 1976. Pp. 765–776.

Toso Rodinis, Giuliana. "L'*Ailleurs* dans le théâtre d'Emmanuel Roblès." *Folio* 15 (November 1983): 57–70.

Trancón, Santiago. "Javier Tomeo o el descubrimiento de teatro." *Primer Acto* 230 (September-October 1989): 60–63.

Valiente, Pedro. "Sartre-Facio: A puerta cerrada—El infierno son los otros." *El Público* 74 (November 1989): 28–30.

Vilar, Jean. *Le Théâtre service public et autres textes.* Ed. Armand Delcampe. Paris: Gallimard, 1975.

Les Voies de la Création Théâtrale. Vol. 1. Paris: Editions du Centre National de la Recherche Scientifique, 1970.

Walcott, Derek. *The Joker of Seville and O Babylon!: Two Plays.* New York: Farrar, Straus and Giroux, 1978.

White, Kenneth S. *Les Centres Dramatiques Nationaux de Province 1945–1965.* Berne: Peter Lang, 1979.

Willey, Mireille. *"Théâtres populaires" d'aujourd'hui en France et en Angleterre (1960–1975): Etude comparative.* Paris: Didier-Erudition, 1979.

Zatlin-Boring, Phyllis. "Traces of Giraudoux in the Contemporary Spanish Theatre." *Romance Notes* 11.1 (1969): 8–11.

———. "El teatro de Antonio Gala." In *Noviembre y un poco de yerba. Petra Regalada,* by Antonio Gala. Madrid: Cátedra, 1981.

———. "Martínez Mediero, Gala, and the Demythification of Spanish History." *Modern Language Studies* 16.4 (1986): 3–8.

APPENDIX A

PLAY TITLES IN CATALAN

balcó, El (Genet) — The Balcony

Combat de nègre i de gossos (Koltès) — Struggle of the Dogs and the Black

Fulgor i mort de Joaquín Murieta (Neruda) — The Glory and Death of Joaquín Murieta

intercanvi, L' (Claudel) — The Exchange

misantrop, El (Molière) — The Misanthrope

noces de Figaro, Les (Beaumarchais) — The Marriage of Figaro

Oh! els bones dies (Beckett) — Happy Days

Per un si, per un no (Sarraute) — For the Least Little Thing

Talem (Belbel) — The Wedding Bed

tango de Don Joan, El (Savary & Monzó) — Don Juan's Tango

Tos assajant Don Joan (Jouvet) — Everyone Wants to Play Don Juan

venin du théâtre, Le (Sirera) — The Audition

PLAY TITLES IN FRENCH

Adieux au comptoir, Les (Scribe) — Goodbye to the Cashier's Desk
Aigle a deux têtes, L' (Cocteau) — The Two-Headed Eagle
Alcade de Zalaméa, L' (Calderón) — The Mayor of Zalamea
Alouette, L' (Anouilh) — The Lark
Amour de Don Perlimpin (García Lorca) — Love of Don Perlimpin with Belisa in the Garden
Appel de Lauren, L' (Pedrero) — Lauren's Call
Architecte et l'empereur d'Assyrie, L' (Arrabal) — The Architect and the Emperor of Assyria
Ardente obscurité, La (Buero-Vallejo) — In the Burning Darkness
Autre Don Juan, L' (Manet) — The Other Don Juan
Bal des ardents, Le (Nieva) — The Dance of the Passionate
Balcon, Le (Genet) — The Balcony
Balcon sur les Andes, Un (Manet) — A Balcony over the Andes
Barque sans pêcheur, La (Casona) — The Boat Without a Fisherman
Bestiaires, Les (Montherlant) — Gladiators
Bleu de l'eau-de-vie, Le (Semprun-Maura) — Brandy Blues
Bonnes, Les (Genet) — The Maids
Bréviaire d'amour d'un haltérophile (Arrabal) — The Body Builder's Book of Love
C'étaient des tilleuls, je me souviens (Semprun-Maura) — I Remember the Linden Trees
Cantatrice chauve, La (Ionesco) — The Bald Soprano
Cardinal d'Espagne (Montherlant) — The Cardinal of Spain
Caverne de Salamanque, La (Cervantes) — The Cave of Salamanca

Célestine, La (Rojas) — The Spanish Bawd

Cène du quatrième monde, La (Martín Elizondo) — The Fourth World's Last Supper

Château en novembre, Un (Roblès) — A Castle in November

Chemise, La (Olmo) — The Shirt

Chevalier d'Olmedo, Le (Lope de Vega) — The Knight from Olmedo

Christophe Colomb (Claudel) — Christopher Columbus

Chroniques romaines (Sastre) — Roman Cronicles

Cimetière des voitures, Le (Arrabal) — The Automobile Graveyard

Cocu, battu, content (Casona) — Farce of the Trashed Cuckold

Colonne Durruti, La (Gatti) — The Durruti Column

Combat de nègre et de chiens (Koltès) — Struggle of the Dogs and the Black

Comédie (Beckett) — Comedy

Coq volait bas, Le (Salom) — The Cock's Short Flight

Cornes de Don Sapristi, Les (Valle-Inclán) — Don Friolera, the Cuckold

Dame aux Camelias, La (Dumas, *fils*) — The Lady of the Camellias

Dame de l'aube, La (Casona) — The Lady of the Dawn

Dans la solitude des champs de coton (Koltès) — In the Loneliness of the Cotton Fields

Défunt, Le (Obaldia) — The Dead Man

Dernier rond (Cabal) — Big Match Tonight!

Dernières jours de solitude de Robinson Crusoé, Les (Savary) — Robinson Crusoe's Last Days of Loneliness

Derriére la nuit, la nuit (Semprun-Maura) — Beyond the Night, More Night

Désire attrapé para la queue (Picasso) — Desire Caught by the Tail

Deux bourreaux, Les (Arrabal) — The Executioners

Devotion à la croix, La (Calderón) — Devotion to the Cross

Divines paroles (Valle-Inclán) — Divine Words

Don Juan ou Les amantes chimériques (Ghelderode) — Don Juan; or, The Fanciful Lovers

Du vent dans les branches de Sassafras (Obaldia) — Wind in the Sassafras Branches

Echange, L' (Claudel) — The Exchange

Ecrit sur le sable (Buero-Vallejo) — Words in the Sand

Elle est là (Sarraute)	She's There
En attendant Godot (Beckett)	Waiting for Godot
Entrainement du champion avant la course, L' (Deutch)	The Champion's Training Before the Race
Escouade vers la mort (Sastre)	Condemned Squad
Et si l'on aboyait? (Gómez-Arcos)	What If They Barked?
Etat de siège, L' (Camus)	State of Siege
Fable du secret bien gardé, La (Casona)	Little Fable of the Well-Kept Secret
Farce enfantine de la tête du dragon (Valle-Inclán)	The Dragon's Head
Femmes Savantes, Les (Molière)	The Learned Ladies
Fin de Partie (Beckett)	Endgame
Flemme, La (Talesnik)	Laziness
Fleur de cactus (Barillet & Grédy)	Cactus Flower
Folle de Chaillot, La (Giraudoux)	The Madwoman of Chaillot
Fourberies de Scapin, Les (Molière)	The Tricks of Scapin
Guillaume Tell a le regarde triste (Sastre)	Sad Are the Eyes of William Tell
Haute surveillance (Genet)	Deathwatch
Histoire d'un soldat (Savary)	A Soldier's Story
Homme couché, L' (Semprun-Maura)	The Man Who Wouldn't Get Out of Bed
Horloge, L' (Roblès)	The Clock
Huis-clos (Sartre)	No Exit
Illusion comique, L' (Corneille)	The Theatrical Illusion
Illustre théâtre de Eldorado, L' (Sanchis Sinisterra)	The Illustrious Theatre of Eldorado
Images d'une mise à mort (Martín Elizondo)	Images of an Execution
Inés de Portugal (Casona)	The Crown of Love and Death
Intermèdes (Cervantes)	Interludes
Intermezzo (Giraudoux)	The Enchanted
Interview de Mrs Morte Smith par ses fantômes (Gómez-Arcos)	Interview of Mrs. Morte Smith by Her Ghosts
Je meurs donc j'existe (Díaz)	I Die, Therefore, I Am
Justes, Les (Camus)	The Just Assassins
Lien de sang (Valle-Inclán)	The Blood Pact
Lit nuptial (Belbel)	The Wedding Bed

Lope de Aguirre, le traître (Sanchis Sinisterra) — Lope de Aguirre, the Traitor

Lumières de Bohême (Valle-Inclán) — Bohemian Lights

M.S.V. ou le sang et la cendre (Sastre) — Blood and Ash

Ma chanson la plus triste est espagnole (Semprun-Maura) — My Saddest Song Is Spanish

Magnifique la luxure (Semprun-Maura) — Magnificent Passion

Mains sales, Les (Sartre) — Dirty Hands

Maison de Bernarda, La (García Lorca) — The House of Bernarda Alba

Maison de Bernarda Alba, La (García Lorca); previous title, *La Maison de Bernarda* — The House of Bernarda Alba

Maître, Le (Ionesco) — The Leader

Majordome myope, Le (Tomeo) — The Nearsighted Butler

Malentendu, Le (Camus) — Cross-Purpose

Mariage de Figaro, Le (Beaumarchais) — The Marriage of Figaro

Mathilde ou Les morts (Aub) — Mathilde; or, The Dead

Médecin malgré lui, Le (Molière) — The Doctor in Spite of Himself

Mendoza, en Argentine . . . (Manet) — Mendoza, in Argentina . . .

Menteur, Le (Corneille) — The Liar

Mer libre (Roblès) — Open Sea

Monstre aimé (Tomeo) — Beloved Monster

Mouches, Les (Sartre) — The Flies

Murs ont des oreilles, Les (Ruiz de Alarcón) — The Walls Have Ears

Nègres, Les (Genet) — The Blacks

Noces de sang (García Lorca) — Blood Wedding

Nonnes, Les (Manet) — The Nuns

Notre Natache (Casona) — Our Natacha

Nouveau locataire, Le (Ionesco) — The New Tenant

Nuit de guerre au musée du Prado (Alberti) — Night of War at the Prado Museum

Nuit de Mme Lucien, La (Copi) — Madame Lucien's Night

Nuit chez vous, Madame, Une (Letraz) — A Night at Your Place, Madame

Nuit d'insomnie (Cabal) — Get Thee Behind Me!

Nuits ouvertes comme des lits (Semprun-Maura) — The Night Beckons Like an Open Bed

Oh, les beaux jours (Beckett) — Happy Days

Paravents, Les (Genet) — The Screens

Partage (Mesalles) — Division

Passion du Général Franco par les émigrés eux-mêmes (Gatti) — The Passion of General Franco by the Emigrés Themselves

Personne, ici (Semprun-Maura) — No One Is Here

Petit retable de Don Cristobal, Le (García Lorca) — The Puppet Play of Don Cristóbal

Pique-Nique en campagne (Arrabal) — Picnic on the Battlefield

Plaidover pour un rebelle (Roblès) — Case for a Rebel

Poison du théâtre (Sirera) — The Audition

Poissons rouges, Les (Anouilh) — The Goldfish

Pour la Grèce (Martín Elizondo) — For Greece

Pour un oui, pour un non (Sarraute) — For the Least Little Thing

Pré-Papa (Gómez-Arcos) — Expectant Father

Prince constant, Le (Calderón) — The Constant Prince

Public, Le (García Lorca) — The Audience

Putain de ta mère! (Alegre Cudos) — Your Mother!

Putain respectueuse, La (Sartre) — The Respectful Prostitute

Quatres petites filles (Picasso) — The Four Little Girls

Reine morte, La (Montherlant) — Queen After Death

Repoussoir, Le (Alberti) — The Odd One

Rétable des merveilles, Le (Cervantes) — The Wonder Show

Révolte aux Asturies (Camus) — Rebellion in Asturias

Roi se meurt, Le (Ionesco) — Exit the King

Salle d'attente, La (Semprun-Maura) — The Waiting Room

Sarpeleau, Le (Bourdet) — Saperling

Sauvage, La (Anouilh) — The Restless Heart

Savetière prodigieuse, La (García Lorca) — The Shoemaker's Prodigious Wife

Schisme d'Angleterre, Le (Calderón) — The English Schism

Sentinelle vigilante, La (Cervantes) — The Hawk-Eyed Sentinel

Sept cités de Cibola (Ferrero) — The Seven Cities of Cíbola

Sigismond (ou l'ascension des trois petites cochons) (Martín Elizondo) — Segismundo; or, the Ascension of the Three Little Pigs

Soulier de satin, Le (Claudel) — The Satin Slipper

Soupçonneux magnifique, Le (Aub) — The Prodigious Doubter

Soupière, La (Lamoreux) — The Soup Bowl

Sur une plage de l'ouest (Semprun-Maura) — On a Western Beach

Tour de Babel, La (Arrabal) — The Tower of Babel

Traversée de l'empire (Arrabal) — Crossing the Empire

Trèfle fleuri, Le (Alberti) — The Flowering Clover

Treteau de marionettes (Valle-Inclán) — Theatre for Marionettes

Troix chapeaux claque (Mihura) — Three Top Hats

Usage de la parole, L' (Sarraute) — The Power of Speech

Venin de théâtre, Le (Sirera); previous translation, *Poison du théâtre* — The Audition

Vérité est morte, La (Roblès) — Truth Is Dead

Vie est un songe, La (Calderón) — Life Is a Dream

Vieillard jaloux, Le (Cervantes) — The Jealous Old Husband

Visite inopportune, Une (Copi) — An Unwelcome Visit

Wien 38 (Aub) — Vienna 1938

APPENDIX C

PLAY TITLES IN SPANISH

¡Abajo las armas! (Gómez de Miguel & Borrás) — Lay Down Your Arms!

adefesio, El (Alberti) — The Odd One

Aquila de Blasón (Valle-Inclán) — The Emblazoned Eagle

águila de dos cabezas, El (Cocteau) — The Two-Headed Eagle

alondra, La (Anouilh) — The Lark

Amado monstruo (Tomeo) — Beloved Monster

A media luz los tres (Mihura) — Three with the Lights Turned Down

Andalucía Amarga (Cuadra de Sevilla) — Bitter Andalusia

andaluz en Toulouse, Un (Morales Guzmán) — An Andalusian in Toulouse

Anillos para una dama (Gala) — Rings for a Lady

Antígona entre muros (Martín Elizondo) — Antigone Behind Walls

A puerta cerrada (Sartre) — No Exit

árboles mueren de pie, Los (Casona) — Trees Die Standing

Ardele o la Margarita (Anouilh) — Cry of the Peacock

Así que pasen cinco años (García Lorca) — Once Five Years Pass

¡Ay, Carmela! (Sanchis Sinisterra) — Oh, Carmela!

baile de los ardientes, El (Nieva) — The Dance of the Passionate

baños de Argel, Los (Cervantes-Nieva) — The Baths of Algiers

barca sin pescador, La (Casona) — The Boat Without a Fisherman

baúl de disfraces, El (Salom) — The Trunk of Disguises

Becket o el honor de Dios (Anouilh) — Becket; or, The Honor of God

Bodas de sangre (García Lorca) — Blood Wedding

Burlador de Sevilla, El (Tirso de Molina) — The Trickster of Seville

camisa, La (Olmo) — The Shirt

cantante calva, La (Ionesco) — The Bald Soprano

Cara de plata (Valle-Inclán) — Silver Face

casa de Bernarda Alba, La (García Lorca) — The House of Bernarda Alba

Castañuela 70 (Tábano) — Castanets of 1970

Celestina, La (Rojas) — The Spanish Bawd

Combate de negro y de perros (Koltès) — Struggle of the Dogs and the Black

Comedia sin titulo (García Lorca) — Play Without a Title

Comedias bárbaras (Valle-Inclán) — Barbaric Comedies

Condecoración (Olmo) — The Medal

Cornudo, apaleado y contento (Casona) — Farce of the Trashed Cuckold

coronel . . . ?, El (Bricaire & Lasaygues) — The Colonel . . . ?

corto vuelo del gallo, El (Salom) — The Cock's Short Flight

criadas, Las (Genet) — The Maids

cuernos de Don Friolera, Los (Valle-Inclán) — Don Friolera, the Cuckold

dama del Alba, La (Casona) — The Lady of Dawn

decente, La (Mihura) — The Proper Woman

detonación, La (Buero-Vallejo) — The Shot

Diálogos de la herejía (Gómez-Arcos) — Dialogues of Heresy

difunto, El (Obaldia) — The Dead Man

Divinas palabras (Valle-Inclán) — Divine Words

Doña Rosita la soltera (García Lorca) — Doña Rosita the Spinster

dos verdugos, Los (Arrabal) — The Executioners

drama nuevo, Un (Tamayo y Baus) — A New Drama

En la ardiente oscuridad (Buero-Vallejo) — In the Burning Darkness

En la soledad de los campos de algodón (Koltès) — In the Loneliness of the Cotton Fields *engañao, El* (Martín Recuerda) — The Deceived One

enredos de Scapin, Los (Molière) — The Tricks of Scapin

Enséñame . . . tu piscina (Letraz); previous title: *Las mujeres nos asustan* — Show Me . . . Your Swimming Pool

Entre las ramas de la arboleda perdida (Alberti) — Amid the Branches of the Lost Woods

Entremeses (Cervantes) — Interludes

Escuadra hacia la muerte (Sastre) — Condemned Squad

Esperando a Godot (Beckett) — Waiting for Godot

¡Esta noche, gran velada! (Cabal) — Big Match Tonight!

Estado de sitio (Camus) — State of Siege

fablilla del secreto bien guardado, La (Casona) — Little Fable of the Well-Kept Secret

Farsa infantil de la cabeza del dragón (Valle-Inclán) — The Dragon's Head

fiaca, La (Talesnik) — Laziness

Final de partida (Beckett) — Endgame

Flor de cactus (Grédy & Barillet) — Cactus Flower

Flor de otoño (Rodríguez Méndez) — Autumn Flower

Flor de santidad (Valle-Inclán) — Saintly Flower

forja de los sueños, La (Martínez Azaña) — The Forge of Dreams

galas del difunto, Las (Valle-Inclán) — The Dead Man's Finery

gran visir, El (Obaldia) — The Grand Vizier

Herramientas (Cuadra de Sevilla) — Tools

Historia de una escalera (Buero-Vallejo) — Story of a Stairway

Historia de un idiota contada por él mismo (de Arzúa) — The Story of an Idiot Told by Himself

hoguera al amanecer, Una (Salom) — Bonfire at Dawn

hora sin televisión, Una (Salom) — An Hour Without Television

intereses creados, Los (Benavente) — The Bonds of Interest

Juana del amor hermoso (Martínez Mediero) — Juana of the Beautiful Love

Juana creó la noche (Martín Elizondo)	Juana Created the Night
Jueces en la noche (Buero-Vallejo)	Judges in the Night
labrador de más aire, El (Hernández)	The Peasant with the Most Appeal
lección, La (Ionesco)	The Lesson
Letra y Música (Beckett)	Words and Music
Ligazón (Valle-Inclán)	The Blood Pact
llamada de Lauren, La (Pedrero)	Lauren's Call
loca de Chaillot, La (Giraudoux)	The Madwoman of Chaillot
locura de amor, La (Tamayo y Baus)	The Madness of Love
Lope de Aguirre, traidor (Sanchis Sinisterra)	Lope de Aguirre, the Traitor
Luces de bohemia (Valle-Inclán)	Bohemian Lights
madre que te parió!, ¡La (Alegre Cudos)	Your Mother!
maestro, El (Ionesco)	The Leader
maleficio de la mariposa, El (García Lorca)	The Butterfly's Evil Spell
malentendido, El (Camus)	Cross-Purpose
mancebo que se casó con mujer brava, El (Casona)	Interlude of the Young Man Who Married the Shrew
manos sucias, Las (Sartre)	Dirty Hands
marquesa Rosalinda, La (Valle-Inclán)	Lady Rosalind
Matilde o Los muertos (Aub)	Mathilde; or, The Dead
Milagro (Olmo)	Miracle
molinera de Arcos, La (Casona)	The Miller's Wife of Arcos
monjas, Las (Manet)	The Nuns
moscas, Las (Sartre)	The Flies
mujeres sabias, Las (Molière)	The Learned Ladies
muralla, La (Calvo-Sotelo)	The Wall
Ninette y un señor de Murcia (Mihura)	Ninette and a Gentleman from Murcia
No más mostrador (Larra)	A Shopclerk No More
noche en su casa Señora, Una (Letraz)	A Night at Your Place, Madame
Noche de guerra en el museo del Prado (Alberti)	Night of War at the Prado Museum
noche de los asesinos, La (Triana)	The Night of the Assassins
Nuestra Natacha (Casona)	Our Natacha

nuevo inquilino, El (Ionesco) — The New Tenant
Oficio de tinieblas (Cela) — Tenebrae
orquesta de señoritas, Una (Anouilh) — The Orchestra
otro Paulo y el minotauro, El (Martín Elizondo) — Another Paulo and the Minotaur
Oye, patria, mi aflicción (Arrabal) — The Tower of Babel
pájara pinta, La (Alberti) — The Game of Forfeits
Palabras en la arena (Buero-Vallejo) — Words in the Sand
paredes oyen, Las (Ruiz de Alarcón) — The Walls Have Ears
peces rojos, Los (Anouilh) — The Goldfish
pianista, El (Vázquez Montalbán) — The Pianist
piel del limón, La (Salom) — Bitter Lemon
pobrecito embustero, El (Ruiz Iriarte) — The Poor Little Liar
Poeta en Nueva York (García Lorca) — The Poet in New York
Primer amor (Beckett) — First Love
príncipe constante, El (Calderón) — The Constant Prince
público, El (García Lorca) — The Audience
Que en España empieza a amanecer (Avecilla) — In Spain the Dawn Is Breaking
¡Qué hermosos días! (Beckett); previous title: *Días Felices* — Happy Days
Quejío (Cuadra de Sevilla) — Laments
respetuosa, La . . . (Sartre) — The Respectful Prostitute
retablillo de don Cristóbal, El (García Lorca) — The Puppet Play of Don Cristóbal
retablo de la avaricia, la lujuria y la muerte, El (Valle-Inclán) — The Theatre of Avarice, Lechery, and Death
retablo de las maravillas, El (Cervantes) — The Wonder Show
retablo de la flautista, El (Teixidor) — The Legend of the Piper
Retrato de dama con perrito (Riaza) — Portrait of a Lady with Lapdog
Revolución del trapo (Riaza) — Rag Doll Revolution
rey de Sodoma, El (Arrabal) — The King of Sodom

rey se muere, El (Ionesco)	Exit the King
Rinoceronte (Ionesco)	Rhinoceros
Romance de Lobos (Valle-Inclán)	Ballad of Wolves
rosa de papel, La (Valle-Inclán)	The Paper Rose
salvaje, La (Anouilh)	The Restless Heart
saperlón, El (Bourdet)	Saperling
secuestrados de Altona, Los (Sartre)	The Condemned of Altona
señora presidenta, La (Bricaire)	Madame President
Sombra y quimera de Larra (Nieva)	Larra's Shadow and Chimera
sonata de los espectros, La (Strindberg)	The Ghost Sonata
soñador para un pueblo, El (Buero-Vallejo)	A Dreamer for a People
sopera, La (Lamoreux)	The Soup Bowl
sueño de la razón, El (Buero-Vallejo)	The Sleep of Reason
Tablado de marionetas (Valle-Inclán)	Theatre for Marionettes
Te quiero, zorra (Nieva)	Foxy, I Love You
Tierra baja (Guimerà)	The Low Land
Tio Vania (Chekhov)	Uncle Vanya
Tirano Banderas (Valle-Inclán)	The Tyrant
títeres de Cachiporra, Los (García Lorca)	The Billy-Club Puppets
Tórtolas, crepúsculo y . . . telón: Variaciones sobre el teatro (Nieva)	Turtledoves, Twilight and . . . Curtain: Variations on Theatre
tragaluz, El (Buero-Vallejo)	The Basement Window
trébol florido, El (Alberti)	The Flowering Clover
Tres sombreros de copa (Mihura)	Three Top Hats
últimos días de soledad de Robinsón Crusoe, Los (Savary)	Robinson Crusoe's Last Days of Loneliness
Vade retro! (Cabal)	Get Thee Behind Me!
vendaval, El (García Lora)	The Big Wind
vida es sueño, La (Calderón)	Life Is a Dream
Viento en las ramas del sasafrás (Obaldia)	Wind in the Sassafras Branches
Virtuosos de Fontainebleau, Los (Els Joglars)	The Musicians from Fontainebleau

visita inoportuna, Una (Copi)	An Unwelcome Visit
Yo tengo un tío en América (Els Joglars)	I Have an Uncle in America
zapatera prodigiosa, La (García Lorca)	The Shoemaker's Prodigious Wife
zapato de raso, El (Claudel)	The Satin Slipper

ABOUT THE AUTHOR

PHYLLIS ZATLIN (B.A., Rollins College; M.A. and Ph. D., University of Florida) is Professor of Spanish and coordinator of translator training in the Department of Spanish and Portuguese of Rutgers, The State University of New Jersey (New Brunswick). She is a specialist in contemporary Spanish theatre, with a strong emphasis on cultural exchange between the Spanish, French, and Latin American stages. Among her many publications are monographs dedicated to Spanish playwrights Víctor Ruiz Iriarte and Jaime Salom and editions published in Spain of plays by Salom, Ruiz Iriarte, Antonio Gala, and Francisco Nieva. With Martha T. Halsey, she is coeditor of *The Contemporary Spanish Theater: A Collection of Critical Essays*. She also serves as associate editor of *Estreno*, the American scholarly journal dedicated to contemporary Spanish theatre. Her articles on theatre have appeared in such journals as *Modern Drama, Modern Language Studies, Latin American Theatre Review, España Contemporánea, Western European Stages, Theatre Journal, Women and Performance,* and *TDR: The Drama Review*. Her play translations include *Bonfire at Dawn*, by Jaime Salom; *Lady Strass*, by Eduardo Manet; *Going Down to Marrakesh*, by J. L. Alonso de Santos; *The Elephant Graveyard*, by Jean-Paul Daumas; and *El color de agosto* and other short plays, by Paloma Pedrero.